TELEPEN

6 00 178309 5

UNIVERSITY OF NOTTINGHAM

WITHDRAWN

FROM THE LIBRARY

Students and External Readers	Staff & Research Students
DATE DUE FOR RETURN	**DATE OF ISSUE**
10.MAR76 0 0 0 8	-2. MAR 1967
	-4.MAR77 0 0 0 0 0 0

...orrow remains your responsibility
...loan slip is cancelled

SIDNEY BALL.

From the etching by S. Anderson, 1913.

SIDNEY BALL

MEMORIES & IMPRESSIONS OF 'AN IDEAL DON'

ARRANGED BY OONA HOWARD BALL

'An unexamined life is not worth living'
PLATO, *Apol.* 38A

'I like nothing but the truth'

Euthyphro, 14E

OXFORD
BASIL BLACKWELL, BROAD STREET
M·CM·XXIII

X-76-459685-2.

Printed in Great Britain

My warm thanks are due to all those who have helped, in various ways, towards the making or producing of this book, and particularly to Miss Daisy Hawkes for her generous aid.

O.H.B.

DUBLIN, 23 May, 1923.

TO

M. ALBERT KAHN

WITH GRATEFUL THANKS FROM

SIDNEY, OONA HOWARD AND OONA MARY BALL

CONTENTS

ILLUSTRATIONS

SIDNEY BALL

PREPARATION

' Every night and every morn
Some to misery are born;
Every morn and every night
Some are born to sweet delight;
Some are born to sweet delight;
Some are born to endless night.
Joy and woe are woven fine,
A clothing for the soul divine :
Under every grief and pine
Runs a joy with silken twine.
It is right it should be so :
Man was made for joy and woe;
And when this we rightly know
Safely through the world we go.'

BLAKE (from Proverbs in ' Ideas of Good and Evil ').

SIDNEY BALL was the son of Edwin Ball, of Pershore, and of Mary Ann Ffoulkes, daughter of Owen Ffoulkes, of Chester. The parents of each of them were dead. There were seven children of their marriage : first three boys, then three girls, then a boy. Sidney was the second child, born at Pershore, April 20th, 1857.

There was room in Pershore for a capable lawyer, and Edwin Ball was equal to the opportunity. His energy and sagacity were of great avail to his firm, but he himself had hardly reaped their first fruits when he died. Not only was he able and successful in his own affairs, but (in the words of a sermon preached in the Abbey Church soon after his death) ' for years the most prominent man in the place, in all public matters, who could always be relied on at whatever cost of time and trouble, and whatever cost of popularity, to take the lead in any movement which he believed to be for the good of the town.' As a warden of the Church of Holy Cross, the beautiful relic of the great Church of the Abbey, he took an ample share in the effort which led to its restoration by Sir Gilbert Scott in 1863—65; a memorable episode in the history of the place. The two stained windows in the south aisle of this church represent, in successive panels, the chief scenes in its history, and last of all the inaugural service after the restoration, conducted by Bishop Phillpotts of Worcester and by Arthur Stanley, the Dean and Chapter of Westminster being the patrons of the living. In this panel Edwin Ball, to whose memory the windows were erected, appears in his character of church-warden, and the portrait, according to those who knew him, is a faithful likeness.

His widow, whom he left in charge of the young family with none too copious means, was in much of her character his very opposite. If Sidney drew from his father the genial current of his soul, his intellectual disposition came to him in large measure from the other side. Mrs. Ball had a mind of no ordinary vigour, with keen tastes in literature, and an incisive judgment in the things of character and of life. With a far deeper sense of the value of education than most mothers had then or have now, she set herself to provide her children with the best possible, not only by sending them to first-rate schools, but by doing her own utmost to develop their abilities, and by feeding them on good literature. To anyone who reads the reminiscences of her, and knew her scholar son, it will

MARY ANN BALL,

To face p. 3.

seem that the main qualities of her mind were all received into his, and there combined and modified with others. She was eminently critical, a reasoner and a realist. Far from poor in sympathies, and herself so constituted as to appear at times and to some observers 'romantic' and 'dreamy,' she leaned at heart to those writers in whose pages logic and sentiment are met together and to the great observers. Among the novelists she preferred Jane Austen, and one of her favourite poets was Crabbe. She was a confirmed reader of sermons, with Newman for one choice, and Robertson of Brighton for another, and her Churchmanship was 'broad.' In family or social intercourse this critical strain came out in a rather rigorous common sense, very remedial to affectation or sentimentality, or to the vagaries of highly-strung natures. Humour she had also : not unfailing and radiant like her son's, but glinting now and then, as it did, for instance, in her droll stories excellently told. For under her reserve and her shrewdness she was kind. She ruled her children strictly, compelling them, whether with or against the grain, to be active, tidy, punctual, and using on their dress, their habits and their acquaintances a delicate sensibility to all that is vulgar or false. But her rigour was temperate, well considered, never depressing, and tasted of the love in which it grew. To Sidney Ball she was not only the mother who had done her duty to him more than well and the genius of a happy childhood, but down to her death in 1899, his constant counsellor.

The Balls lived in Bridge Street, Pershore, in what is now known as Perrott House, a tall red structure fronting immediately on the road. It was built in the sixties of the eighteenth century by one of the brothers

Adam, for the use of 'Judge' Perrott, a Baron of the Exchequer, who retired to this town rewarded for his public merits (whatever they had been) with the right of levying a toll on all goods carried to it by water. A solid and refined prosperity is the 'note' of the house, with its tall rooms decorated with plaster mouldings, its handsome staircase, and its deep well from floor to roof. Behind it is a long tree-shaded garden ending at the river's bank, and looking over the water on to green fields. And here in the Ball's time, to seal up the sum of pleasantness, was a family boat. It was mainly in that boat up and down the Avon that Sidney Ball began to grow into the love of nature and the open air which was a part of him and kept him young. He developed quickly in his own way, and the boy was father of the man—joyous, courteous, affectionate, a deviser of pleasure for others, a lover of his kind; and, last and chiefest, a student with vivid senses to mate with thought. Before his father's death in 1867, he was sent for two years to a preparatory school kept by a Miss Manchee at Weston-super-Mare; and in 1868 entered Stamford House School at Cheltenham under the Rev. William Wilberforce Gedge, where he remained three years, his mother having moved the home from Pershore into Cheltenham. When in 1871 Mr. Gedge shifted to Malvern, and set up what is now known as Wells House School, Sidney Ball accompanied him.

'He was distinguished,' writes his sister, Mrs. G. C. Hughes, 'by his gentle, thoughtful ways, and was the calm element in a rather turbulent and excitable family. The governesses and nurses, who were often rather worn out with their task, looked upon him on this account as a precious standby, and, if ever he joined in the mischief, rebuked him with special severity on the ground that his naughtiness was put on; a remark which used to pain him, and to which he would reply : " I don't see why I shouldn't be naughty like other boys." '

Occasionally his later accent comes out very quaintly in some incident of boyhood. 'Oh,' he exclaimed when, not yet in his teens, he lost his heart to a tiny partner at a dance, 'what eyes she has, and moreover she can converse.' If there is any difference between the earlier self and the later in fundamental things, it lies in a severity of gladness and gentleness which afterwards was not undimmed. But all the accounts testify to the plenteousness of that gift of pure charity which did not shrink with time. When his youngest brother left home for Lancing for the first time, Sidney rode with him in a hansom to the station, and unable to bear the trouble in his face, suddenly took off his watch and chain, and pressed them into his brother's hand, if only that ointment might mollify his sores.

The child in him was indeed father of the man that was to be. Mrs. Manchee writes of him to his mother, November, 1867 :

' An exceedingly nervous, sensitive child, the progress he has made in Latin is really astounding; he is a boy to do one credit and to teach whom is a pleasure. He is a very great favourite with all his schoolfellows. I have never seen him out of temper.'

The affectionate care of a sister had preserved his earliest literary effort. A tiny book some three inches square, 'Harry Newton, or Good for Evil,' by Sidney Ball, author and publisher.

' My dear children,' it begins, ' I am going to tell you a little tale, which I hope will amuse you.' It ends thus : 'Soon afterwards he went to Oxford, where he distinguished himself. He is now a missionary in India, his colleague is his old enemy Thomas, who loves him as a brother. Goodbye. The end.'

His letters must have been a delight to receive. It is pleasant to remember that some forty-five years later he was to see most of the sights which he describes so vividly in a letter of November, 1865.

'We went to a panorama on Wednesday last; it was so pretty, and we saw the Rocky Mountains in North America and the natives of Africa in canoes, and a hippopotamus nearly upsetting a canoe and one of the natives fell out of it, and some bulls tossing up a native; there were the Victoria Falls, in Africa, and the Chinese and Japanese looked so funny; and the Chinese cave, and there was a steamer rocked about in the sea and there were the people of Siberia riding in sledges over the snow; and there was the Cave of Elephanta and the Falls of Niagara, and a great deal more which I cannot mention. Goodbye, I can say no more.'

In December, 1866, he writes :

' My dearest Mama,
    ' I am very sorry to hear that you are so very ill, but I hope we shall all meet together when the holidays come; or else, if it is God's will to take you from this earthly home to that heavenly home above, we must submit to him, and I hope we may all meet together at the last day in heaven. What does Mr. Davis say is the matter with you? I have just written to Edwin. We went to Mr. Quarrell's yesterday. I am sorry I have not got much to say, so I must send my best love to you my dearest Mama. I read my Bible every day and learn a verse out of the text-book I have, and the text for to-day is, "The Lamb which is in the midst of the throne shall feed them, and shall lead them into

living fountains of waters : and God shall wipe away all tears from their eyes." Goodbye, dearest Mama. 'Your most affectionate Son.'

Perhaps it was after receiving this letter that his mother began to see in her second son a future Archbishop of Canterbury.

It so chanced that a chosen counsellor of the Ball family, Canon Frederick Wickenden, was an intimate friend of Edward White Benson, the first Headmaster of Wellington College. By his arrangement, Mrs. Ball took Sidney to Mumbles in the summer holidays of 1868, and there saw Benson, who was always watchful for any talent to be baited with a scholarship; the result being that the boy was sealed for Wellington. He tried for a scholarship in 1870 and won; he was placed in the Orange dormitory and the Upper Fifth. Thenceforth his career was phenomenal. He rose at once to the top of his Form; passed in the autumn of 1871 into the Sixth; and coming out first in the midsummer examination of 1873, was appointed at the age of sixteen to be Head of the School. At the same time Benson relinquished the mastership, and was succeeded in the following term by E. C. Wickham, whose first two years in office were the period of Ball's captaincy.

The rich and rapid development of his intellectual powers is the chiefest mark of Sidney Ball's boyhood. In the classics he was what is usually called a good scholar; but his extraordinary promise was in his power of interpreting and expressing. 'I may certainly say,' writes Dr. G. C. Allen, 'that my own enthusiasm for the classics dated from my acquaintance with him, and from the admiration I felt—as we all did —for his scholarship and for the ease with which he tackled fences in translation at which most of us would be hopelessly pounded.' 'He was certainly the ablest of Wellingtonians, except Verrall,' writes another. 'I remember he was given as a punishment to translate the Gorgo and Praxinoe Idyll of Theocritus, and did it so well (albeit with some help from Calverley) that Benson read it out to the Sixth with immense gusto.' 'The cleverest schoolboy I have ever known,' said T. H. Grose of him, after examining the school. But this was not all. By the time he left for Oxford there was a remarkable maturity in the texture of his language and the style of his thought. He wrote, it is true, as the way of youth is, with laboured brilliance, loading every rift with culture, and with some unconscious parody of the academic vein. We read in the annals of the Debating Society that on one occasion 'S. Ball thought that the last speaker had treated the word "civilisation" in a far too cursory way, and entered upon a very lengthy discussion of the meaning of the word, giving among others Guizot's definition of it, and rejecting interpretations by many other writers.' And on the next speaker complaining that he 'did not see the drift' of the speech, and thought the arguments inconclusive, 'S. Ball admitted this, saying that they were very fanciful, some being thrown in as suggestions,' so that the House was greatly amused. But if his crtiics were so far not unfair, it only needs a glance at the essays written by him from time to time in *The Wellingtonian* to discover under the mannerism a real distinction and an indubitable power. He must have read devotedly both in and out of school. Benson had a habit of proposing to his pupils every now and then some big book in history or divinity as a subject of examination and a wedge to open their minds, and none of his ways and means was more dreaded. To Ball these were welcome tasks, if only as 'something craggy to try his teeth on.'

'Benson,' writes an old Wellingtonian, 'either lent him or advised him to read Westcott's *Introduction to the Study of the Gospels* when he was fifteen, I should think, and was much delighted by S.B. telling him that he found it necessary to read each sentence over twice.'

In Wickham's time, as the terminal reports show, his work in school was less steady and made less way than before; he became frankly indifferent to the mathematics and deviated into studies of his own, with some detriment to those of the routine. In particular he read much in the English poets and in literary criticism, and culled with a characteristic modernity from the monthly reviews. Moreover, Wickham's teaching was in some ways more enterprising than his predecessors, though possibly less brilliant, and brought in subjects not often attempted by boys at school. There was, especially, for instance, an introduction to metaphysics in a course of lectures on the first two or three of the Thirty-nine Articles. Mr. J. L. Bevir, one of Ball's closest school friends, can still remember how those lectures appealed to him and exercised his thoughts.

'Through all his school days,' he writes, 'he was a seeker after truth. He would never accept the conventional views of life, but always wanted to get deeper. I can think of many occasions when we discussed, as boys will, all things in heaven and earth, and there was always at the back of his mind a suspicion that there might be something more satisfying, whether with regard to the accepted form of religion or the condition of the world as he saw it around him.'

In his last two years he was several times first, or nearly first, in the steeplechases, and the mile race of the sports of '75, which he lost by one or two yards, was a famous contest of three runners neck and neck for most of the way. He was a stirring member of the school societies, spoke often in debates with a nervous manner but a good flow of words, and played with great zest the forlorn rôle of red reformer, with sweeping schemes to remodel the self-government of the school, or motions against the monarchy, launched and lost in clamorous storms. At the end of his time he had discovered his talent for acting in a rendering of his henceforth favourite part of *Hardcastle* in ' She Stoops to Conquer,' and was busy with the project of a Dramatic Club Society. There is an account in *The Wellingtonian* of a lecture on Phrenology which he gave to the Natural History Society, ' eliciting much laughter with a description of himself written by a phrenologist.'

' Messrs. Pope and Laing kindly allowed him to make use of their heads for illustration, to the infinite amusement of the audience, and subsequently the lecturer engaged in a successful and amusing passage of arms with incredulous members.'

' I first met him,' writes Mr. Bevir, ' in September, 1869. There were some twelve of us candidates for a scholarship put up in the Sanatorium. He was a small boy in knickerbockers, somewhat smaller than the rest of us. He was not elected that year, and came up the following September to compete. I had then been at Wellington a year, and was somewhat surprised by one of the candidates coming up and presenting me with a shilling. It was Ball. I had apparently paid for his share of a vehicle to the station the previous year, a fact which I had quite forgotten.'

AT WELLINGTON.

SIDNEY BALL.

AT MRS. MANCHEE'S SCHOOL.

'A born scholar,' writes another contemporary, 'patient, gentle, refined, unselfish, and always ready to help other boys.'

In May, 1874, in conjunction with Mr. Bevir, he started an independent journal entitled *The Rocket,* with the motto, *Sic itur ad astra.* It was to eschew cricket and football, and deal with literary and political questions, its political sympathies being Radical. It should be for 'those members of the school who have opinions of their own,' and the editors 'would not be scared by the scathing sarcasms of higher tribunals.' One number was published, and the undertaking was suppressed by the authorities, for what reason I do not know. An article on the recent defeat of the Gladstonian Government, entitled Ὁι Νῦν is of no little interest. The first cause of the Liberal overthrow, he argues, has unquestionably been *beer.* Liberalism is always harrassing vested interests, and must do so, 'being essentially energetic and active'; so that 'a group of inconsistent and partial disapprobations make up its aggregate unpopularity.' On what other ground could working men support the Conservatives but a dislike of being incommoded by change? The Conservative working man is a phrase, 'which, to say the least of it, is an ironical oxymoron, a jacket and apron stitched on a pole, and made to do duty as a scarecrow for pusillanimous Liberals.' The labourer in his right mind must recognise the Liberal as his best friend, whose reforming hand will spare nothing that needs its touch, not even the Church.

'They (the Liberals) look upon the Church as an institution existing for the State at large, and not for an exclusive clique, and consider disendowment merely as a transfer of public funds from one purpose

to another.'   In fact ' we are now beginning to realise
the forecast of Mr. Mill, and are being hurried on by
the irresistible tendency of the times to an equality of
conditions. We are beginning to conceive that the progress of democracy is a law of Nature.' That law it is
that will heal us of the commercial spirit, which we
must oppose, not by vain attempts to revive the past,
but ' by setting up counter-balancing modes of thought
and principles of action.' Many ' will set us down as
a degenerate species of the Shelley school.

'And at the name of Shelley we think of one who
united in himself the mightiest tendencies of our time
—its democratic, its sceptical, its pantheistic, and its
socialistic spirit; and thus he has become the watch-
word of those who aim at reconstructing society in its
forms, in its principles, and in its beliefs, and who regard the past as an unmitigated failure. And the idol
was worthy of the homage; for when the passions and
theories which supplied Shelley with his subject-
matter have become merged in practical reality, there
will still remain a song such as mortal man never sang
before of inarticulate rapture and of freezing pain, of a
blinding light of truth and a dazzling weight of glory
translated into English speech as coloured as a painted
window, as suggestive, as penetrating, as intense as
music.'

There is a very characteristic letter of about this
time to his uncle at Birlingham, near Pershore :

' Dear Uncle,

' I thought I could not let Edwin's letter go without
enclosing a note to thank you for our pleasant rides,
and still more so for your kind counsel and encouragement. The interest which both of you take in our welfare, and the pleasure with which you hear of all our
little successes will always operate as keen incentives
to fresh exertions on our own part to meet your good
wishes and prove ourselves not unworthy of your kind

interest. I wish you had stayed one minute longer at the station, for I could have introduced you to one of my masters—he is identical with the one who so nearly made me ill with fruit and wedding-cake one Sunday afternoon. He was perfectly charmed with my 'good looks,' and assured me I had made the most of my time and only hoped I should not lose my healthy colour before I returned to Wellington. You must have seen him, I think, because he met you as you went away; he is tall, pale and rather prepossessing, in a long buttoned-up coat.'

So completely did Sidney Ball become identified with St. John's College that it was sometimes difficult for those who knew him later to think of him as an Oriel man.

'He came to Oriel,' writes Mr. F. H. Hall in the *Oriel Record* of September, 1918, 'as a scholar from Wellington in 1875. He was distinguished by his many-sided activity. He won the Freshmen's Mile in the University Sports, and he was a clever amateur actor. When, to celebrate Mr. Butler's marriage, his play, 'Charles I,' was performed in the Hall, Mr. Ball was unanimously selected for the part of the *King*. His friends in College were not chosen from any one class, but included men of the most diverse tastes and capacities.'

Some of these friends have been good enough to help us in the task of trying to reconstruct for ourselves the Sidney Ball of those early days. Sir Robert Chalmers[1] writes :

'I remember him quite well at Oxford when, in October, 1877, I went into residence at Oriel and sat at the same Scholars' table with him. He was two years my senior and, having taken his First in Classical Moderations in the summer, was reading for Greats

[1] Governor of Ceylon, 1913—1916.

under Cook Wilson. At this time (October, 1877) Sidney Ball was the outstanding undergraduate of the College. Though he did not row or play cricket, he used to win the College mile at the sports and had, I remember, a graceful style of running, combined with judgment and resolution when making his effort. Socially, he was a brilliant conversationalist (he and the late Sir Cecil Spring-Rice, of Balliol, remain in my memory as the two best talkers of my day), but a somewhat mordant wit did not endear him to all. He was in the Wine Club, was a great whist player, spoke rather interestingly than well in debate (but always with conviction and a certain nervousness of gesture with joined finger-tips) and, generally, lived the life neither of a recluse nor an ascetic. Philosophy had already, in 1877, marked him as her own, and, as the terms wore on and he became a fourth-year man, he lived (according to report) for nothing else. I remember well the bitter disappointment of the College that Sidney Ball missed his First in Greats. I saw little or nothing of him after 1878, when I moved out of College, but got next into touch with him when he wrote to me in London to go to Arnold Toynbee's lectures against Socialism. Others than I will be able to trace the evolution of the Liberal Undergraduate into the Socialist Don. When I was in Ceylon and was making acquaintance with the younger civilians there, I remember well how one of these (a John's man to whom I had mentioned Ball's name) was eloquent in tribute to his old tutor and to the formative influence for which the pupil expressed his abiding and growing gratitude. Happy is the teacher who earns such.

Mr. Walter Clode[2] gives a very vivid impression of Sidney Ball as he remembers him :

'Although there was a great deal in Sidney Ball, he was rather an " influence " than a " personality." When

[2] K. C. Master, Merchant Taylors Company, 1904.

Ball and I joined Oriel there was little machinery in the way of debating or essay clubs for making his influence felt; he was a bit of a runner (quarter-mile his distance, I think), but did not row or play cricket, so that one's opportunities of meeting him were limited.

'He was about medium height, slightly built, pale, nervous, had rather prominent blue (I think) eyes, short-sighted, which, after the fashion of the day, he mitigated with a single eyeglass, and for reading, spectacles: a thoughtful, absent, abstracted air, good square head, regular profile, thick brown wavy hair (rather disordered), parted in the middle, but with an obstinate knack of coming down over his forehead, so that pushing it back with the thumb and forefinger of the right hand was rather a characteristic gesture when talking. He had "a down look": the whole impression being that of a man of thought rather than a man of action. He had cheerful, open manners, with now and then a touch of irony.

'Coming from the more highly organised establishment of Wellington College, I think he found us a little backward and raw; but he entered into our life heartily and touched it at all points: he was nothing of a recluse or prig, could sing a comic song, and, when we organised a small dramatic club, joined it and performed with us at Stourbridge (Worcester) and Chatham, and as *Fluker* in Byron's "£100,000" made quite a hit. I mention these details to show how accessible he was, how human and "non-donnish." His curiosity also led him to subject himself to Madame Card's hypnotic influence at the old Vic Theatre, where, at her "suggestion," he delivered a most eloquent speech on temperance.

'On the other hand, he founded or revivified the Debating Club: and certainly by coming in and out amongst us did what he could for us by giving a thoughtful turn to chance conversation. Our horizon was then rather limited, and went little beyond the results of impending examinations; but Ball saw beyond this and was, I think, rather impatient of "scholarship" and "philosophy," and wanted to be at work, translating theory into beneficent action. "Estote factores verbi et non auditores tantum fallentes vos metipsos" would, I think, have been his text if he had preached; but he never did, only suggested. He was interested in social movements in connexion with the University, and it was from him that I first heard the name of Toynbee.

'In conversation he was hesitating and suggestive rather than dogmatic. My impression is that he was feeling his way: that there was a very serious leaven of thought and questioning silently working: if I heard from another that he had at this time dedicated himself to the objects to which he afterwards devoted himself I should not be surprised. I think that he had started on the great quest, whilst we were labelling our luggage.

'We had a great affection for him which we never lost: he was so transparently honest and sincere: in the next ten years we shall probably come abreast of his ideas.'

We have the first mention here of many traits which distinguished the Sidney Ball of later days. His own acting was for many years a great relaxation and pleasure to him, and he never ceased to delight in going to a good play. There is a letter to his mother written during his Oriel days in which he defends the art as one not unworthy of a man who was 'in for Mods.':

'I don't know why you should be so much exercised about my acting. I am only to re-act a character. I said that I would take no new part until Mods. was over, and if I am to take no recreation I shall run to seed pretty soon. Nor is — my greatest friend, as we have few interests in common. My chief friends are

SIDNEY BALL AS DR. MANETTE.

To face p. 17.

ones who would have been quite worthy of Mr. Gladstone in his undergraduate days : they are all fellows who might distinguish themselves in the world had they a fair chance. As for acting being on a low footing, it is very useful in many ways, and Dr. Benson certainly thought it an important item of education. A great man is composed of other elements than mere book-grubbing, and if you think my objects of ambition are exhausted you are leaping to conclusions for which there is no foundation.' This letter ends on a less lofty note : ' I've left a waistcoat.'

The present Provost of Oriel—Rev. L. R. Phelps—alludes very charmingly, in 1918, to those long past dramatic triumphs and finds a fresh justification for the spending of time in such a manner, which would be very pleasant to the writer of the justifying letter just quoted.

' In a small society like ours at Oxford it cannot but be that individuals count for a great deal, and in every generation there are those of whom we think as bringing some gift specially needed by the time, or peculiarly suited to its spirit. There have always been among us *e.g.* men to whom we looked to keep up the standard of conduct and of service, for fresh and live ideals, an extended and raised horizon. Now he was just one of these men, and if I were asked to sum up in a word the contribution which he made to his generation, it would be devotion. He was devoted to his friends, he was given whole-heartedly to causes and he never was false or cold to either. Just as in teaching, he not merely handed on the torch, he fed the flame; so for all of us he was a reproach and an encouragement in his " true-heartedness "—(to speak as the Psalmist)—for the true-hearted, as I take it, have the qualities of reality, of loyalty and of courage, and all were his. But more than this. It may be said of him, as has been said of another (Scott Holland), that he kept his interest and his zeal fresh, and this was one reason why he attracted young people so powerfully. He did not dwell on the achievements of a past generation, or of a passing, but he could feel as warmly for their ideals as they did. No one knew better than he that no generation is content to adopt and work out the ideals it inherits, and most of us, as time goes on, lose our power of sympathy with those who are coming after. This was just what he never did, and so young men could always feel that he united experience and sympathy—a rare union; that he brought wisdom and a keen interest into the discussion of growing problems and they repaid his loyalty with interest! It has been given to very few in modern Oxford to occupy this position.'

' Let me quote one scene which I always remember. I was asked to dine one year with the Merchant Taylors; one St. Barnabas Day when Clode was master, and it so happened that the President was ill and your husband represented the College. I had to propose the Master's health, and was moved to say that the last time I saw him and Ball together was on the stage of the Rochester Theatre, acting in "Whitebait at Greenwich." How long ago that was I do not like to think, but I have often thought how the power of self-effacement which makes an actor is the secret of so much successful good work in the world. Here again he had that quality; he could enter into the minds and feelings of others, and interpret them to themselves— in a word, he had a finely sympathetic imagination, the best equipment with which a teacher or a philanthropist can start life, and he used it for the good of others, securing indirectly his own high happiness.'

His acting must have been a very life-like and vivid thing.

' I remember very distinctly,' says the Rev. Hubert Sands, ' his taking the part of *King Charles Ist* when

Mr. Butler's play was given in Oriel College Hall, as I also took a minor part, *Hugh Peters*; Ball's rendering was very good. It is so fresh in my memory, it might have happened the other day. I am sorry I have no sayings of his or incidents stored in my memory, but only the vivid impression of a very brilliant, likeable, and influential personality, with eyes and manner suggestive of strong feelings and real genius.'

Our old friend Mr. G. H. Cobb writes :

'When I first remember Sidney Ball he was a scholar of the College, senior to me by a year or so. To a raw Freshman, lately come from a provincial school, a scholar of Oriel, recently Head (I believe) of Wellington, was, from that point of view only, an object of interest not unmixed with awe; but when I came to be admitted, as I afterwards was, to some degree of intimacy, I found that the man himself inspired interest and respect. He always seemed to take for granted the intrinsic importance and dignity of learning, such learning as the University laid itself out to supply—a frame of mind by no means universal among clever undergraduates. He was a keen student himself, and always followed up his work with thoroughness and apparently with little effort, whether it involved the study of *variæ lectiones* in Sophoclean choruses for Moderations, or later was concerned with more serious pursuit of Truth implied in philosophical reading for Greats. But though a leader in the intellectual life of the College, he did not display any signs of annoyance or "superiority," nor did he encourage the formation of any intellectual clique to the exclusion of less gifted contemporaries. There was nothing about him remotely suggestive of a prig.

'Oriel in those days was a thoroughly respectable College, which did well in the Schools, though it was not otherwise particularly distinguished, certainly not so athletically, for it was very low down on the river

and did not shine in cricket. Socially, although we
boasted the possession of no aristocrats, the level was
high. It was for the most part on good terms with the
Dons, among whom the present popular Provost was
Junior Fellow. Ball was, as might be expected, on
terms of friendship with most of them, especially with
the late Professor Wilson, who then had the chief
direction of Greats work in the College. But though
Oriel was a friendly College there were inevitably, of
course, distinctions produced by seniority or command
of money. The socially élite were represented by the
" Wine Club," an institution which even then was not
quite of such a bacchanalian character as its name
might seem to imply. Of this club Ball was a member; a fact which would mark his connexion with the
socially elect. He was also an ardent whist player,
though I think it was only the social and intellectual
aspect of the game which attracted him.

' He was in those days devoted to the theatre, not
only as a spectator (in which character he was wont to
describe himself as a " hot pitite " in vacation time), but
also as a performer in amateur theatricals, in which I
have seen him play " character " parts, especially those
of old men, excellently. In connexion with this side of
him I may mention that he was a great supporter of
the College Shakespeare Club, which met periodically
to read the plays (not always, I fear, in an over-serious
spirit), and the founder and inspirer of an Amateur
Dramatic Society, called, after his Christian name, the
St. Denys Club, of which I was a humble member.
On one memorable occasion we gave a performance
(for one night only) in the theatre at Rochester. The
Club was assisted by real live actresses in the female
parts and was attended by a decayed actor as stage
manager and general director. By all this it will be
seen how ready Ball was for any fun that might be
going. He was also occasionally not averse from what
I may by oxymoron call harmless mischief. I have a

distinct recollection of unauthorised midnight athletic
sports held on the sacred turf of the inner quad, with
towel horses for "hurdles" and other fantastic accom-
paniments, in which he bore a part, and which were
only broken up upon the appearance of Vice-Provost
Monro clad in academicals and uttering horror-
stricken, if somewhat bashful, expostulation.

'An anecdote which I have often heard him tell
against himself may further illustrate this lighter side
of him. Dear old A. G. Butler had lately taken up his
abode as Dean in part of the Provost's house, bringing
his newly-married wife with him. I think it must have
been the latter who was troubled by the unadorned
simplicity of the front quad. There were then, I think,
no flower beds, certainly no ampelopsis to mitigate the
severity of the bare stone. Accordingly, an innovation
was made in the shape of two stumps of tree trunks
which were planted just outside the entrance gate,
surmounted by tubs of geraniums. Your undergraduate is nothing if not conservative in such matters,
and some daring spirits in the dead of night tore up
the offending objects and hurled them out of an upper
staircase window into Oriel Street. A good deal of
noise accompanied the reformers' efforts, and the
Dean's housemaid complained next day that, opening
her window and looking out to discover the cause, she
was nearly decapitated by some heavy falling body.
That morning, therefore, the good Dean summoned
Ball and certain other leading members of the College
to discuss the outrage and the possibility of discovering the perpetrators, when Ball had to confess that he
himself had been one of them. The story is trivial,
but may serve to show how Ball was in touch not only
with the powers that were, but also with the more mis-
chievous element of the College.'

Mr. Cobb's story of the Dean's flower-pots is sup-
plemented very pleasantly by Mrs. Arthur Butler's
words in a letter of May, 1918.

'I have thought often of late of my first knowledge of your husband. He was, literally, the first undergraduate my husband asked in to meet me when I came to Oxford—he and Mr. Craufurd—and I well remember how puzzled I was at first by the constant shouts in Oriel quad for 'Ball,' till I learned how entirely he was the leading spirit in the College. And he, with Bishop Hamilton Baynes, came with us to Malvern on a pleasant little kind of reading party. I saw a good deal of him in those early days, which were full of promise to be so finely fulfilled!'

Sidney had a real and lasting devotion for Mr. Butler. How he delighted to tell the story of the advice which Mr. Butler gave to Cecil Rhodes as to methods of work, and the reply, 'You leave me alone, Mr. Dean, and *I'll worry through.*' The beautiful little memorial notice of Mr. Butler in the *Oriel Record* of February, 1909, is by S.B., and almost all of it might be a memorial notice of himself, so well had he absorbed the spirit of his old tutor. 'I do not think,' he writes, 'that there were any of us who were not, in some degree, the better for having come into contact with a nature at once so kindly and so bracing.'

Sidney Ball was a very human person, and he had to bear the defects of his qualities. His eager, inquiring spirit began early to be too strong for his highly-strung, sensitive nerves. The final strain of 'Greats' was too much for him.

Mr. F. H. Hall writes :

'He was probably thoroughly over-worked and, being of a nervous-sensitive temperament, was not in a condition to stand the strain of his examination. When the Aristotle paper was set he went out without showing up a paper—intending to "scratch." One of the examiners, who had been struck by his work in some of the other papers, communicated with his College authorities and suggested that he should be induced to continue the examination. This he did, but he had missed one of the most important papers. The examiners were prepared to give him every oppor tunity of making up for this in Vivâ Voce, but it was believed at the time that the examiner (Prof. Fowler) who took his Vivâ Voce in Philosophy, out of mistaken kindness, confined himself to asking him very simple, elementary questions such as would be put to a candidate for a pass, instead of asking him about Aristotle's philosophical system as a whole. A good Honours Man does not get up his " Ethics " in the way a Passman does, and probably Mr. Ball was not altogether at home in the minute details of the " Ethics." At any rate, his Vivâ Voce did not save his " First."

His friends stood by him and gave what consolation was possible. Mr. Butler wrote :

' I shall always remember 1879 as the year in which we had two First Class men, one of whom slipped, from a little over-anxiety, and so partly failed when within sight of the goal. Well, it is a great disappointment, I fear : and you may be sure of this, that we all feel greatly for you. No man more deserved success, or would have more surely won it, but for—health That little word health, or its correlative, nerves or temperament, explains more than half the failures in life. The successful men are the men of strong nerves and restful temperament : or else they are the men of calm judgment and seasoned powers, who measure their strength against their work with perfect accuracy, and never exert themselves one minute more than they are well up to. The more artistic, eager temperaments are constantly overdoing it, and constantly breaking down. And so the great thing in life is to take one's measure correctly, and if the temptation is to overdo working, then to get to some steady, regular, well-defined work in life which cannot easily be overdone. Excuse me thus sermonising or philosophising to you! You can doubtless say all this to yourself much better than I can say it for you. And I sit down to write to you, not with a view of sermonising, but of expressing my true and deep-felt sympathy. But you will remember I am one of those who have broken down, and have seen all the hopes with which I began life blighted : and I would do anything to prevent others from encountering the same misfortune. You, however, have not broken down, only, as I said, slipped or tripped in the race, and so failed of getting First Class Honours at the goal. But you are substantially strong and sound : you have a future before you full of hope and promise, and I will venture on a prophecy that from this time forward you will never come near to a breakdown again. You have the knowledge, you have the powers of a First Class man—and you will on occasion show it—you have everything but the honour and the name.'

True to what he was to be all his life, Sidney Ball pulled himself together when once the strain of Greats was over, and wrote cheerfully to his mother from Dorking, where he went to stay with his friend Clement Powell, before his vivâ.

'I feel rather tired, which is to be expected. The disappointment is rather severe, but I got too anxious about the result and depressed by my bad luck. If the papers had been in the reverse order I should have been quite safe. It is possible I may be given another paper, but I rather hope not. I have got a deal of good out of reading for Greats, which I must comfort myself with. Wilson has been very good about it and very sanguine. He tells me never to mind the result, but to read quietly for a Fellowship and the Craven, but not to make a point of the latter. If there isn't one at Oriel, I shall try at Magdalen. I am likely to do a great deal better in a Fellowship exam. than anything else, and I shouldn't be bothered by any anxiety, and, what is more, I shall not be inhaling the floods of Oxford. I have had a good deal more sympathy than I deserve for my breakdown, as I worked not wisely but too well. But still, I might have pulled through if it hadn't been for general ill-luck and sleeplessness. I hope you won't think any more about it, as its not worth it. I have arranged about rooms for the girls; they will be able to hear me vivâ'd, as I am in on Commem : Monday.

He began early to be known as an excellent speaker. He himself mentions, in a letter to his mother describing the wedding of Miss Craufurd—the sister of his Oriel friend, W. D. Craufurd—and Mr. Wordsworth :

'My speech has created quite a sensation and has made me quite uncomfortable. Lord Lyttleton assured me that he had heard many speeches, but nothing so perfect—it was a work of art and I don't know what. The fuss about it has been quite absurd, and I do hope the threat of its being published hasn't been carried out.'

A passage in the same letter reminds one of what was to be so marked a trait with him—his love of beauty as expressed in women's clothes.

'Lucy C. looked very pretty, and so did the other dresses, but the prettiest of all were the younger G—'s, light blue with white round the neck, perfectly exquisite. Mrs. Streeten, in peacock blue and peacock blue feather trimmings, and Mrs. Atkinson in a beautiful old-gold dress, were also much worth looking at.'

Three of the former friends at Oriel mention and lay stress upon their recollections of Sidney's visits to a mesmerist and to the extraordinary effect that she had upon him. Canon Woodruffe says :

'I think Ball must have been almost a " Freshman "

when the mesmerist, Madam Carde, visited Oxford in
1876. He was one of the first to submit himself to the
medium, whose influence over him was extraordinary.
I remember best his making a remarkably good temperance speech when under hypnotic influences. He
attended the séances on several other occasions and
was made to do such extraordinary things that, I believe, the College Authorities had at last to interfere,
and he went no more.'

Mr. Mortimer Rooke has
' a vivid memory of Madam Carde at the Vic : mes-
merising Sidney Ball and several others, including
Archdeacon John Sinclair, and making them think that
they were Christy Minstrels and that they were black-
ing their faces, which Sidney did very vigorously, and
they then gave an entertainment, although I think singing was not particularly in his line or banjo either.
After that he was given a sham baby to nurse, and was
quite good at the art ; and when brought to, chucked
the baby down the stage with much disgust.'

Mr. Rooke, too, gives us an early instance of that
abundant hospitality, the exercise of which was to be
one of the great features and the great delights of
Sidney Ball's life.

' I remember, when my father was staying with me
in College, that he entertained my father to a regular
old-fashioned breakfast, which my father much appreciated.'

During his last Long Vacation as an undergraduate
in the summer of 1878, Sidney paid his first visit to
Sark. He and the lovely island took to one another
at once.

' Our domestic life,' he writes to his mother, ' if a
monotonous one, might deservedly excite envy—a refined edition of Mrs. Leigh's, without the stimulus of
bread and milk—mullet and lobster may be honour-

ably mentioned in Miss Robin's provision. I am
generally up by six, read an hour or two in my bed-
room, then call the others for a morning bathe, which
is generally taken in the harbour; the rest of the morning I read; in the afternoon we search after beauty
and bathing places, both of which seem almost pro-
digal in such a small island; after dinner I read till
about eleven, at which hour we retire—or attend the
moon's levée on the Coupée—a recreation which must
convey very little meaning to you or even cause for
congratulation.'

In a letter to his sister Ethel (Mrs. Nance), he describes his prowess as a good sailor and a bold diver,
traits for which he was afterwards to be well-known
to many generations of St. John's men.

'Mr.— refuses to start in the present state of the
weather, but, in spite of having been tossed about in
a cutter for six hours between Guernsey and Sark (on
which occasion I quite won my spurs as a sailor), I am
not so far demoralised, on the occasion referred to. I
had been over to Guernsey with Macauley to get a
pair of sandshoes (M. going to redeem some articles
of clothing which he had left as a substitute for more
direct payment at Gardner's—at my expense). Coming back the wind was contrary and the waves no
respector of persons; the skipper succumbed quite
early and had to be put down the hatches, but I came
out of the ordeal with more than credit, though I can
scarcely say the same of my outer person, in regard to
which I may further add that my blue knickerbockers,
the pair of flannels and the Bideford monstrosity,
together with one pair of shoes and countless socks
have been put on the shelf some time. M. and I
have struck awe and humiliation into the native popu-
lation by diving from the top of their harbour and
even Mr. ——, with varied success, has risked his
delicately moulded limbs.'

In this letter of forty-two years ago, there is an allusion to a minor trouble which was to become a very familiar one to me later on :

' Bye-the bye, I have been haunted by the bad dream of a lost notebook and I should like to have some assurance of its safety—it's black to look at and hopeless to understand, but if you can discover by some means that it has to do with Greek History, it will make me quite young again, for it contains a good deal that is necessary to salvation in the Schools, and did I leave behind a " Sallust "? '

Well indeed might his mother write of him : 'Sidney came home with his clothes packed up in his top coat and more books than ever.'

His lifelong friend, L. R. Farnell, now Rector of Exeter College, gives us a vivid portrait of him :

' It was towards the end of 1875 that I first met Sidney Ball in a private literary society that was partly an essay-club, partly a wine-club—such things existed in those days—composed of Oriel, Trinity, and Exeter men, and calling itself " The Raleigh." I remember with strange vividness, across the gulf of years, the fascination he exercised upon me that first evening, after which we soon became and remained the closest of friends. Those who knew him only in his later period might find it hard to realise the radiant charm and the sunny brightness which flashed out in daring adventurousness of thought and phrase and act. I soon discovered that my new friend was one of the most popular and best-known men in the University; and his circle included scholars, literary men, and athletes, and especially the literary athlete. For it may surprise many to know that Bell began his University career with an athletic reputation. He won the Freshmen's Mile in the University sports, and he was one of those who started and developed into fame the University Hare and Hounds Club. And he long retained his love of open-air adventure, certain thrilling episodes on flood and field being among the pleasantest experiences we shared. But he had too much sense of humour to be a devout athlete—he was merely the gay amateur, and so he escaped the Victorian obsession of the athlete cult. His humour was then and for long one of his most salient traits, genial and wild as ever humour was, but always tempered with perfect courtesy, grace, and consideration for others; for then, as always, he was the most unselfish of men, wholly free from vanity, egoism, or any touch of morbidness. He had at that epoch the *joie de vivre* in the fullest and highest sense, but at the same time a deep seriousness of intellectual purpose and ideal. In fact, some who were only acquainted with him in his social-practical work need to be reminded that all his life he remained a devoted student, a man of singular intellectual insight. He laid well in those early days the foundations of his true career, the career of an original and impressive teacher.[3]

It could never have entered the head of such a modest man as Sidney that his letters would be carefully kept and might be wanted for biographical purposes. Otherwise, so thoughtful a person would have dated them more carefully. From 1879 to 1882 he was resting from the strain through which he had passed and was preparing in many ways for the work that lay before him. He writes to his mother from his aunt's house at Birlingham, near his old home at Pershore :

'The time I am now spending is such as I shall never get again—besides that it rather helps to clear up my ideas as to what walk of life I am most wanted in and most useful for.'

[3] *Oxford Magazine,* June 7, 1918.

The idea of taking orders was suggested to him as a sure road to a fellowship or a schoolmastership, with a chance of ending as the archbishop of his mother's dreams. One could picture him as a very effective parson in a pulpit, or organising and vivifying a parish, or ruling a diocese, but one could not imagine him subscribing to any articles every one of which he could not keep, or undertaking to expound creeds in every word of which he could not wholly believe.

'Canon Okey wrote me a short note the other day,' he writes, 'in which he drew a very gloomy picture of school inspectorship, and represented to me that I might do considerably worse than going into the Church.'

There is a pendant to this in the description of the opposite attitude of a contemporary who was also looking about in choice of a career.

'He may not stay the semester out and seems to have lost—if he ever had it—all interest in his work —cannot find anything in Germany that would "pay" in a Fellowship exam., and is reduced in despair to reading handbooks of English History. He is going to read for the Church at Xmas if nothing more re-munerative turns up and I daresay if he can once get a comfortable berth, he will succeed in making it still more so, for he seems to have no inconsiderable talent for conforming himself to things, and scruples cost him apparently a less sacrifice than would appear on the surface for he is contented to live and be liberal on ———'s money without taking trouble or interest in making it good.'

'That was the period,' writes the Rector of Exeter, 'when Germany was still the promised land of mental culture, science and music, and its dark future was hid-den from us. Therefore, after our degrees, Sidney Ball and I repaired to German Universities; and we frequently met there.   He seemed to have been specially impressed by Lotze's lectures, for whom he always retained a certain admiration.   At the same time, he revelled in German music and the German theatre and opera, but the many childish incongruities of the latter, especially in the Wagnerian opera, appealed so strongly to his irrepressible sense of humour that it brought us more than once into some peril in a crowded theatre of fanatic enthusiasts.   His innate refinement was sufficient to guard him against any taint of admiration of German manners or political institutions.'[4]

Sidney himself writes to his mother in a vein of great contentment :

' One feels one can really breathe and expand here after such a hothouse as Oxford.'

He is careful to tell her the details of his life and surroundings :

' They have such curious little messes at supper, I make a point of trying all so as to know what to avoid. I have at present selected two as only to be touched in the last gasp of hunger.   The coffee has the signal (and in this case ambiguous) merit of reminding me of home.'   There is a clear little vignette of Lotze. ' If you want to realise what he looks like you must picture to yourself an attenuated edition of Irving as Shylock. In his dressing-gown and red cap the resemblance is most striking—but he is much shorter and walks with a jaunty little swing.   We often see him in a long-tailed coat and red cap sowing or raking in his garden, generally in the company of his old housekeeper and a gardener.'

Sir William Ashley[5] has very kindly given us some recollections of Sidney Ball as he saw him in Germany and during his early days at St. John's.

[4] *Oxford Magazine,* June 7, 1918.

[5] Professor of Economics, Birmingham University.

' I made Sidney Ball's acquaintance at Göttingen in 1880, in circumstances which impressed themselves on my memory. I was reading history at Oxford, and it was the year before my Schools. On the advice of Stubbs, then Professor of History at Oxford, I had gone to Göttingen for a month (all I could afford), to improve my knowledge both of German and of history by sitting at the feet of Reinhold Pauli, to whom Stubbs had given me an introduction. Calling on Pauli, I was received kindly. " But there is a very nice Englishman studying here, Herr Ball. We must find him, and he will look after you." And then Pauli seized his hat impetuously and, with me gratefully in tow, hunted round the little town—dropping from time to time (for he prided himself on his colloquial English) the mildest and most incongruous of expletives—till he ran Ball to earth. Ball took me over instantly, with the readiest bonhomie; helped me to find lodgings; and insisted that I should go off to supper with him. Finding that his cupboard was rather bare, he announced that he must buy some " Fleisch." So he took me to a shop, purchased some slices of corned beef and carried them home in paper in his hand. All this seems trivial enough; to me it was the sacrament of friendship. Remember that to one who had enjoyed few "social advantages" Ball was a brilliant and attractive figure—a few years my senior, full of keen and manifold intellectual interests, distinguished in bearing and utterance, tactfully sympathetic in practical help, without a trace either of condescension or sentimentalism. His very presence breathed forth vitality : in his company existence became vivid and full of hope. And what he then was to me, I am sure he was, then and afterwards, to scores of others.

' Ball had gone to Göttingen chiefly to hear the philosopher Lotze. I marvelled at the easy terms on which he seemed to be with the great man—the quite natural and unforced combination of respect and criticism.

In the intimacy of our friendship I don't think he ever
tried to impose his own views by dogmatic assertion
or purposed argument; he presented himself to one
simply as a man who was thinking his own thoughts,
helped by what others said, but unawed. I cannot conceive of an academic—for that is what Ball was, in the
best sense, through and through—more fitted to open
the minds of younger men, and to help them over the
big and awkward gulf between the receptive schoolboy
and the independent thinker.

'As to Ball's social views at this time, it must be
borne in mind that Toynbee did not lecture till 1881—
that *The Bitter Cry of Outcast London* did not
appear till 1883, that the Social Democratic Feder-
ation and the Fabian Society were not founded till
about 1884, and that the dockers' strike did not take
place till 1889. When, a year or so after our meeting
at Göttingen, Ball was settled at St. John's, and I had
the run of his rooms, it was not socialist economics—
German or English—that he was chiefly interested in.
Curiously enough, it was the later French economists
—of an orthodoxy more strait even than John Stuart
Mill's—he was occupied in reading. I used to be impressed by the whole row of their big, paper-coloured
volumes on his shelves. Unless I am greatly mistaken,
it was Cherbuliez he studied with most care. Cherbuliez has but a faded reputation nowadays : I can
only conjecture that Ball was sent to his writings by
Cossa's eulogy. It may be remarked, in passing, that
the English translation of Cossa's *Guide to the Study
of Political Economy*, in its first and thinnest form
(1880), was one of the very first doors opened to the
English reader from the narrowness of the English
tradition to the ampler fields of European economic
literature. I must confess I have not myself read
Cherbuliez, but I suspect Cossa's advice was not particularly wise. Ball, I have little doubt, was trying
just then to combine the organic view of the State

which he had learnt from T. H. Green and from the
German idealist philosophers, with the old individualist economics; and certainly he went, for the
latter, to its most consistent representatives. Remembering Ball's subsequent writings and sympathies, it is
not without a smile that one reads the characterisation
of Cherbuliez in Say and Chailley's *Dictionary*, and
is reminded that he "montre la stérilité de l'action
gouvernementale pour combattre la misère."'

He allowed himself some relaxation going on a
Hartz Reise with 'the family carpet bag which I carried with me all the way on a shepherd's crook,' but
the temptation of his eager temperament to overwork
'has already earned for me a title to celebrity of
"wunderbar fleissige Engländer," which is a good deal
from such busy people.' And he was always on the
look out for a career. 'Wemyss, I believe, will eventually go into the Foreign or Diplomatic Service, a
thing I should like of all things,' while 'several Americans who are here offered to get me a place in America
which has an enterprising sound about it,' or 'I wish
some enterprising Liberals would divine political
worth in me and "stand" me an election.'

In a letter to his mother, he described a visit which
he paid to his old headmaster at Wellington.

'As I am credited with the gift of having a great
deal to say about nothing, an account of my visit
might take up a good space, for it was exceedingly
uneventful. I lunched one day with Carr and succeeded in getting a good deal of publicity for the fact
that I was in want of a pupil. Davenport offered me
a "regular young scamp" and the ambition of re-
claiming him, but I don't think it will quite suit me.
The Master's children are quite beautiful to look at,
so that I found my attentions to them as much a
pleasure to myself as (I hope they were) to the mother
—they have Wickham's eyes—the second has the

name of William Gladstone. I found my old friend
and rival, Allen, looking fairly happy under the combined distractions of Lower School work and an engagement—on the latter subject he was very frank and
communicative and, at times, poetical. On Saturday,
the school played Charterhouse. Dr. Haigh Brown
offered hospitality to a hundred boys, so we were a large
party. Wickham, Mrs., his sister, the eldest daughter
and myself were met by a pair of horses at Guildford
and, my hat excepted, we did the thing in style. I hope
you are not still concerned about the list. I have done
mourning for my fate some time. Mrs. W. adminis-
tered comfort to my by going through the names of
"great men who got Thirds," and I am sure I feel
quite obliged to Cardinal Newman for the precedent.'

In May, 1882, he tried for a Fellowship at Lincoln
College, and, though he was unsuccessful, there was
a very pleasant outcome in a letter from Mark Pattison.

'ATHENAEUM CLUB,
'*5th May*, 1882
'Dear Sir,
'I much regret that I was unable to secure you as a
member of my College, as I judge from your examination that I should have found in you some of the
love of letters which is mostly wanting in the present
generation of Oxford tutors and professors. I daresay
you will do better in the world without a Fellowship,
but as I know nothing of you but what I saw in your
examination, I will not attempt to speculate on the
subject of your future. Should you again find yourself residing in Oxford or in London, I shold be glad
if you would allow me to make your acquaintance personally.'

This letter led to a friendship with the great scholar,
whose high ideal of a University and of the part that
should be played in one by a College was so like that

of Sidney Ball himself, and with his wonderful wife, later Lady Dilke. Another of the many friendships which were to be such a delight and which opened so many doors into the world for him was that with the large Rathbone circle at Liverpool. That friendship still survives. Miss Eleanor Rathbone has sent us some impressions of Sidney as he was at that time.

'When I first knew Mr. Ball, he must, I think, have only recently taken his degree. He was, I believe, reading for his Fellowship, and he came to coach an elder brother of mine who was working for a Whitworth scholarship in engineering. It was during the summer holidays, and we were staying at Bassenfell, near Bassenthwaite Lake. I was nearly the youngest member of a large schoolroom party, so my recollections are naturally a little confused with those of a later time. But I know that Mr. Ball became immediately popular among us, and that we looked on him from that time onwards as a family friend. He was then, if I remember rightly, a lanky, shaggy-haired youth, with short sight and an absent-minded but ingratiating smile, who accepted schoolroom teasing and impertinencies with placid indifference. He usually carried about with him, even on boating expeditions, a fat book of philosophy which we declared he never read. Probably even his powers of abstracting himself were not proof against our din.

'His special pupil was a not particularly industrious youth, who had a good deal of leeway to make up and was by no means given to enthusiasm for his instruction. The hold he immediately obtained over the boy marked him at once as a born leader.

'One small scene sticks in my mind. Some time after Mr. Ball had left us we were teasing my brother about him and laughing at some of his ways, when a sudden storm burst on us, my brother vehemently declaring that he was the only person who had ever made him want to learn, that he owed him more than he could ever pay, for Mr. Ball, by the time and zeal he had devoted to him, had injured his own prospects in some definite way which I forget—probably by delaying his work for the Fellowship or omitting to apply for some post or other.

'For years afterwards my father consulted Mr. Ball every time he needed a promising young man for any public or private purpose, and however busy with the work of term-time, Mr. Ball always threw himself into the search with his usual freshness and energy. I used to think, that so entirely different in other ways, he had the characteristic one finds in the best and nicest type of solicitor or doctor, of seeming, when one consulted him, to be thinking for the moment of nothing but the question before him and to identify himself with it as the average selfish person only identifies himself with his own personal affairs. And, if my memory holds good, it was just the same when he was a very young man beginning his own career, and so might have been almost justified in self-absorption.'

It is interesting to compare this with Mr. William Rathbone's letter.

'BASSENFELL, KESWICK,
'17th October, 1882.
'My dear Mr. Ball,

'I cannot let you leave us without expressing my warm gratitude for your successful care of Lyle during the last eight months. I was much surprised at what you accomplished in that time. He had idled and amused himself most heartily for four terms at Eton and unlearned most of what he knew, and I was astonished when you proposed he should go in for a scholarship at Fettes, and still more so when he came so near getting it and took his place in school in a form with boys most of whom were his seniors. And your influence was as great and satisfactory on himself as on his work. I hope you will refer to me if at any time my testimony can be useful. I cannot of course speak as your Oriel and other Oxford friends can of your attainments, but I can unhesitatingly confirm what they said of your power, vigour and earnestness, of your energy and conscientious devotion to your work and success in influencing others, of the way in which you grasped and impressed the real point of a question, whether of thought, character, or morals. We all regretted when your work with Lyle came to end, and we lost you as an inmate of our family, always courteous, cheerful, unselfish and pleasant. Wishing you every success in your future work, which is certain to be faithful, useful and good, you must allow me to describe myself in old Quaker language, towards yourself most true as

'Your assured friend,

'WILLIAM RATHBONE.'

'I expressed to an Oriel Fellow—one of Oxford's most distinguished men—my surprise that they had allowed you to leave Oriel. He quite agreed with me, and said others did so too; it was not his fault.'

The autumn of 1882 was spent at the Yorkshire College, Leeds, as temporary substitute in Classical Studies for Professor Bodington. Like all that Sidney did, he did this with his whole heart.

'I can assure you,' wrote Mr. Baines, the Chairman of Council, 'that the hearty manner in which you threw your energies into the work of our classes, in which, from the nature of your appointment, you could only be expected to take a temporary interest, is fully appreciated by the Council, and I believe it will also be remembered by your students.'

The end of 1882 was the end of this probationary time for Sidney Ball. He was elected, without exami-

nation, to a Lectureship in *Philosophy* and a Fellowship at St. John's College.

Archbishop Benson wrote to him :

'I do most earnestly and delightedly rejoice with
you. I am so glad I heard it from no other than yourself. It is a most honourable election and invitation
to congenial work, and I need not tell you I delight
to think that Wellington has so large a share in your
pleasure—that you are glad for the lustre that you add
to the dear place. I hope you will somehow and before
long make your way into this far West. You will be
welcome indeed. With thanks for your letter and
kindest remembrances, in which Mrs. Benson heartily
joins,

'Yours ever sincerely,

'ED. TRURO.'

A less cheerful note was struck by Mr. C.W., of
Wellington.

'I was exceedingly glad to see you had been elected
to a Fellowship at St. John's. You are, I think, the
first O.W. who has secured an Oxford Fellowship.
Don't stay too long at St. John's. Somehow the Fellows there go off their heads after awhile, or something
exceedingly like it. But let us hope you are the beginning of a new order.'

A postscript from a letter to his mother runs : 'I
am not keen about it, as I didn't want to reside at
Oxford. But I hope it may reflect lustre on the family.'

WORK

'Bring me my bow of burning gold!
Bring me my arrows of desire!
Bring me my spear: O clouds unfold!
Bring me my chariot of fire!
I will not cease from mental fight,
Nor shall my sword sleep in my hand,
Till we have built Jerusalem
In England's green and pleasant land.

BLAKE, from Prophetic Books, 'Milton.'

IN OCTOBER, 1890, Sidney Ball was staying at Kebroyde, near Halifax, for some theatricals, in which he was to play one of his favourite parts, that of *Mr. Hardcastle* in 'She Stoops to Conquer.' I also was staying there, but I was trusted with no more glorious rôle than that of prompter. There were two engaged couples among the performers: Maurice Hill[6] was *Tony*, and Berta Hadwen (Lady Maurice Hill) *Miss Neville*. Leonard Hobhouse,[7] then a Fellow of Merton, was *Hastings*, and Nora Hadwen (Mrs. L. T. Hobhouse) was *Miss Hardcastle*. In the following winter there was another performance and, on December 31st, 1890, a third engagement took place. Although it might seem that so very short an acquaintance—something like a broken week of days in all—was scarcely sufficient to justify anything so important as an engagement for life, a certain amount of correspondence had taken place between us during that intervening October Term. After our engagement the letter came daily, and from those letters of his it is

[6] Mr. Justice Hill.   [7] Professor L. T. Hobhouse.

possible to get a very fair idea of what his life was at that time.

I do not think that I was capable then of realising fully his unique qualities of heart and mind and brain, but I began to perceive that I should be helping to take care of an unusually delicate and precious instrument. I can remember my smug reply when Mr. Hobhouse asked me what I meant to do in Oxford. 'I am going to be a mother to Sidney's men,' so I suppose that some inkling of the way in which he accepted his responsibilities towards his pupils had already begun, thus early, to dawn on me.

The books, which formed the excuse for that autumnal correspondence of thirty years ago, began to arrive as soon as he had left Kebroyde. On October 6th he writes from the Savile Club :

'You see I have not lost much time in redeeming my promise. As the book (William Hunt's *Talks About Art*) seems to be out of print, I venture to transfer to you my own copy; and when I assure you that I find it easier to part with any amount of money— "which was his is mine, &c."—than with a book I have once possessed, I hope you will not esteem it less for being worn and old. I wonder whether you would like to see that poem of " The Disciples "[8] (of Mazzini) that I mentioned to you—because I have a copy at Oxford—and I have a mania for lending books.'

On October 8th he was back in St. John's again and I began to get, from his letters, some idea of the life of an Oxford Don.

'Some half dozen candidates are engaged in giving the "answer evasive" to some absurd and unworthy question on grammar. [He was particularly fond of the famous 'answer evasive' story : 'Can you tell me the names of the Minor Prophets?' 'I must decline,

[8] By Mrs. Hamilton King.

sir, to make these invidious distinctions.'] I have not seen Mr. Hobhouse but he has been well employed in electing two of my friends at Merton and we meet at twelve to organise a Toynbee Hall campaign. I am preparing lectures on Ethics.'

He found time to urge me to go on drawing and to attempt some book illustrations.

'Please honour my suggestion and, when your biography comes to be written, I shall be handed down, in the second chapter, say, "At this point Miss Butlin made the acquaintance of a certain gentleman who although himself of obscure talents and inconsistent character, was destined to play an important part in her artistic development—which, indeed, but for his suggestion—and for this alone he deserves to be rescued from oblivion—might have remained dormant. That Miss Butlin awoke and found herself famous was due—we might without violating historical truth say, entirely due—to the no doubt purely accidental insight of a certain Mr. Ball. We have not been able to ascertain definitely whether he was a strolling comedian, or merely an Oxford Don."'

In November he writes of a Social Conference at Oxford :

'I am suffering from an excess of meetings. The great conference is over, and has left me flat indeed, just as if a great roller had passed over me. Your sister (at Somerville College) sat through (I am able to confirm this almost incredible statement) the two "sessions." Mr. Tom Mann's fierce declamations, Mr. Tod's (the bloated capitalist) genial cynicisms, Mr. Courtney's judicial solemnity—all these are "ancient history," not so the fatigue of limb and mind that oppresses the student of social questions,—those bold bad men the haunters of Social Science congresses. However, it really was a success and Mann's

earnestness was very real and went home—I think the
academic mind,—such as it is,—was as much disturbed
as we could wish. In the evening Mr. and Mrs.
Leonard Courtney dined with me—Mrs. Hill came
to meet them—and we talked of Rembrandt—the
greatest man, Mr. Courtney said, who had ever applied
himself to painting, and forgot for awhile the problems
of Labour and Capital. At lunch the "old" and the
"new" Trade Unionists sat down together in peace—
and it was very pleasant to hear them address one
another as "friend"—and a dear old working-man
friend of mine called me "Brother Ball." I could
wish we could change parts more!—that we could feel
more the stress of life, they more the "academic calm."
However, I mustn't pursue this uncomfortable train
of reflections.'

I wonder whether the comrade who called him
Brother Ball was our dear old friend, Mr. Hines of
Oxford, with whom I afterwards became familiar. He
had his moments of unbrotherliness in one of which
he once spoke of Sidney as 'that there Ball, he's nothing but a rusty nail,' but we never knew just what
depths of disgust that signified, and all was soon as
before between us.

On November 5th, when it was a point of honour
to make a noise and to burn something as an expression of the undying 'loyalty' of the College he wrote:

'You appear to be taking a refuge from this present
world of Rudyard Kipling and golf—in that delightful old world which seems to be ever young. Do you
know these delightful lines of Blake "To the Muses,"
beginning

> "Whether on Ida's shady brow,
>   Or in the chambers of the East
> The chambers of the Sun, that now
>   From ancient melody have ceased."

'I have found Mr. Morshead's translation of the "Trilogy" of Aeschylus,—and I venture to send it to you. I am afraid I cannot say it's the same thing as the Greek—but it's the nearest approach to it I know. Jowett's translation of Plato I feel tempted to recommend, *e.g.* of the "Apology" and his translation of "Pericles" speech in his Thucydides. But Tennyson's (most beautiful) "Ulysses" and "Ænone"— Matthew Arnold's "Mycerinus" (do you know his "Forsaken Merman"?) and some others are even better echoes. But there, I am recalled to this present and giddy world, the Undergraduate has left his Plato and is letting off crackers and Roman candles in the quadrangle and I must to my post, and my place. *P.S.*—The loyal demonstration was a harmless and hollow affair, melted into thin air at the approach of law and order.'

We were engaged on the last day of 1890 and on the first of 1891 Sidney had to go to Stourbridge to fulfil a theatrical engagement made long before with his old friend of Oriel days, Mr. Craufurd. His first letters, therefore, chronicled vacation doings.

'My "Noggs" is considered to be very effective. It's certainly rather democratic,—you will be glad to hear I find little trouble with it, though I learn it all at rehearsal. You must begin to exercise wise authority over me by prohibiting my taking part in any more acting, except at Kebroyde, and yet it is through it that we have been brought together. I feel, however, that it has now fulfilled its purpose ... Let your life be full of thought and purpose indeed, but not overweighted by it. The most useful and practical life is often the least consciously so, in being a true woman and in that only, will you be most "practical"; the perceptions of a true woman are quicker and surer than the laboured thoughts of a man ... You know my favourite ode of Wordsworth's to duty, "Thou

dost preserve the stars from wrong "? Have you ever
read Carlyle's essay on "Characteristics"? It's not
the whole truth, but a great deal of it.'

Very soon there came some inkling of the difficulties that beset the path of a 'Reformer' in a Conservative College in those days.

' I was pleased about the President's message. We
are very much opposed in politics and he dislikes mine
greatly, so I am glad to think he appreciates my endeavours to do my duty by him in the College. X——
is the man of whom I told you; he is a man for whom
it is difficult to feel any Christian sentiment whatever,
unless it be one of pity. He has made himself useful
to "the Party" as a wire-puller of a peculiarly un-
scrupulous kind. He is now a Rector in the country
and is using all his efforts to be made Proctor. I am
afraid the contest will provoke bad feeling in College.
I shall have the sympathy of all the people I respect
in College, if the "plot" is successful.'

There was an attempt to prevent his election to the
office of Proctor as this carries with it a seat in Council
and his would, of course, have been 'a vote for reform'
in University matters.

' They, of course, pretend that I have too much work
in College and am likely to break down under both,
but I am really the best judge of that and it's
only a political or really a party move. However, it's
something to be considered "dangerous." I believe
I should have worried rather if I hadn't something
better to think of and I really await the issue quite
calmly and if I do feel any disappointment, it will be
on your account alone as it is, after all, an honour
(the money, £350 for the year, was also a consideration) though a great deal of the work is irksome and
disagreeable enough.'

Mr. Hobhouse seems to have sent a message through me that Sidney Ball should subscribe to 'The Friends of Russian Freedom.'

'Will you ask Mr. H. if he thinks 10/- enough for the purpose? I don't think I ought to give more as I know so little of the practical methods and working of the Society. I'll give more if you wish it,—a readiness to give is generally considered one of my most desperate weaknesses but we must be "practical" mustn't we? I think you might be interested in reading some of Stepniak's books. It is a cause which women, above all, should care about and they have been its greatest spirits and its greatest sufferers.'

By January 15th he was back at work.

'A good many boys are up for the scholarships we have for commoners of the College—they had an essay this morning—the comparative educational value of different branches of study. This afternoon and to-morrow they are examined in their own subjects. Mr. Snow has just made a very happy observation. Mr. Powell, our Junior Fellow, was making his congratulations and observing that I looked changed. I said I hoped for the better. Mr. S., "Let us say he is the same but raised to a higher power of himself." Wasn't that, as you would say, lovely?'

The multifariousness of his duties began to be borne in on me:

'My correspondence to-day has taken up almost two hours,' and he enclosed a letter from Prof. Gilbert Murray, then at Glasgow, 'the youngest professor in the United Kingdom'—'once my pupil and the most brilliant undergraduate of his generation,' after his congratulations, saying: 'Now may I brutally introduce a practical favour which I want to ask of you. My assistant has just died and I am looking for a successor to him. Can you see any likely man and send him to me?' A friend also appeals to me in trouble. Her husband is very nervous and depressed and she wants me to find a young man to travel with him. One of our pupils this term is an amiable elderly gentleman, bearded and bald, a husband and father, and we think we must try and grow a beard between us (Mr. Snow has one). I have ordered my first volume of the *Economic Review* to be sent to you direct. Mr. Smith's review was the outcome of many talks with me, most of the writers are my friends. One of my pupils is ill and I have had to send for a doctor, he came to me for comfort, which I thought was nice of him. Only caught a chill I think. I do like the idea of you taking thought about your gowns because I know it's from the mere love of beauty and I like to think of you rejoicing in beautiful things. Life is after all made up so much of small virtues and graces, and not the least is the art of dress. (Dr. Hill thinks that the combination of our names is the most romantic ever dreamt of by novelists or poets in their wildest moments—I, Sidney, take thee, Oona—!).

'Have just come in from a skate to Sandford in order to get in my letter to you for I go to Miss Pater at 5 p.m., am dining (early) to meet Mrs. Costello (now Mrs. Bernhard Berensen) and shall probably be expected to hear her lecture "On American Women" and in the interval have six Latin Proses to look over. As it happened I found in my rooms an old (and noble) pupil, Lord Alfred Douglas, a very fascinating spirit in whom I take a lively interest, especially as he is always in hot water and is not in favour with the authorities. He came to thank me for having been the means of restoring him to an unappreciative College. I told him of you and it made him quite "shy." The Latin prose came off badly. I was struggling with a white tie when the first pupil came and I had to postpone it. This must not occur again.'

There used to be desperate efforts on his part to

get to the house of my cousin, Miss Read of Clifton, where I was then staying.

'I'm so sorry I talked of the possibility of coming this evening but I am afraid it would have been too great a neglect of duty. My party went off pretty well, I think. The men, however, too serious, *e.g.* Mr. Roberts and Mr. Hobhouse and many like them—except Mr. Wade, who "chattered." Mrs. Fisher,—aunt of Mr. Clauson, née Arabella Buckley, came in for a while. The Latin-Prosers again. Would you care for any more books? I wonder . . . An old pupil came in and this thought is lost to the world. The enclosed will show you one of my engagements.'

'UNIVERSITY SETTLEMENTS IN EAST LONDON.

'Mr. Ball would be very glad to see any gentlemen who would like to meet Mr. Cyril Jackson (of New College and Toynbee Hall) in his rooms on Sunday evening, March 1st, 1—8.30. Mr. Jackson will discuss, "Darkest England,—the Way Out." and will be glad to give any information as to Toynbee Hall, or any other Social Movement in East London in which University men are likely to be interested.'

So runs the neatly printed slip, which he enclosed. He had drawn through 'gentlemen' and substituted 'Members of the College' with a note for my instruction, '"Gentlemen" quite Oxonian.'

'We meet to-night in solemn conclave relieved by Mr. Snow's paradoxes and merry jests—to arrange lecture lists, etc., at 8.30 in my rooms. Mr. Hutton will complain of the cold, Mr. Powell of the existence of the pass man, Mr. Lester of the long journey to the Parks. Mr. Smith of the waste of time—and it will be my duty to sympathise with all and oil the wheels of the educational chariot. And you, have you shopped well and "babbled freely" and read just a little? Clough is a great favourite of mine, don't you like the last poem of all, "Say not the struggle nought availeth"? I think you would enjoy some parts of the quasi-Homeric account of the reading party.'

It was part of the new arrangement of his life that it would rest him to hear me 'babble.'

'The plot thickens about the proctorship. I have suggested that we should make a College order that the subject be not mentioned before 1 p.m. or after 4 p.m. Mr. Snow is simply simmering with suppressed excitement and is greatly elated at the thought that I am not seeking a Government appointment. Mr. Hutton who is shepherding the faithful "remnant" is away, so there is a short lull—there are at least seven electors " sitting on a rail," I think it must come down with them—they are waiting for the President's " nod." I have eight loyal supporters—the enemy only four—but he builds on the rail party. I am glad to say that I am beginning to treat the whole with a certain degree of hauteur—if not levity. I know I am sure of one thing which I value more than office or ducats.'

There were few men, I think, who cared less than he did for place or power or 'ducats' in and for themselves or their possible effect upon his own prospects, but he did care—then and always—for the effect of the actions of his College, in its corporate capacity, both upon its own internal 'character' and upon the men within its walls, and also for its fair fame before the world outside.

'I am thinking,' he wrote a few days later, 'of retiring proudly from the ignoble contest about the proctorship. As a Liberal, I should not represent the College of which Mark Pattison said that it was "eaten up by the canker of Toryism and ecclesiasticism " and then, I really think it wiser not to risk my health and strength—and that for your sake. The Hills strongly

urge this course. We both arrived at it independently.
Everyone recognises that I make a sacrifice by doing
so but it ought to make them more disposed to be
generous in regard to the one thing I do care about.
If I had only myself to think about I should have
fought it out—as it is by withdrawing I give way to
Mr. Hutton, who will, probably, be elected without any
contest and we shall be at least spared the scandal of
X—— The only thing I shall regret is what till lately
I fear I valued too little—the actual emoluments, but,
after all, they might be purchased too dearly. I shall
be able now to give my mind to my work and to our
joint future. It is even possible that we need not wait
so long. They are uncertain about my position—
whether I may not claim to retain my Fellowship.
In equity I ought to, as I am allowed by statute
to marry after seven years' tenure. I have been a
Fellow over eight years, but they tried to prevent
my availing myself of the permission under the
statute by interposing a day between the lapse of
the first seven years of my Fellowship, and my
re-election, so as to be able to say I am elected to a
new Fellowship—a very unworthy dodge, to put it
mildly; and now the anti-married Fellow party think
I am going to claim to hold my Fellowship and are
"uneasy." It is certainly a difficult point, but there
can be no doubt that the College has no moral ground
to stand upon. The President has been speaking in
very high terms of me (and would personally prefer
me as Proctor if I were not a Liberal), and I don't
think they are likely to be mean or illiberal . . . The
President spoke with great warmth and feeling of my
action, said he should like me to know how much he
appreciated my " unselfishness." He has now declared
his intention of voting for Mr. Hutton, and the
X—ians, we hope, are hoist with their own petard.
There is Mr. Snow's little tripping step and gentle
knock, but he only wants to read in my room. He says

he has never known the Common Room so lively; we are indeed a happy family now Mr. G. has gone : it almost seems too good to last, and they are all so loyal and jolly to me.'

A letter from Mr. Hutton, which he enclosed, ended this incident for the time.

'I did not say on Wednesday what you will know I felt; how far happier and better was your renunciation than my enforced acceptance of office. I feel very keenly how *wrong* it is that I should be Proctor, but 'tis no good wearing one's heart on one's sleeve for daws to peck at, so I am trying to carry it off as well as I can with the chief hope that I mayn't be a discredit to you. I have sent my notice of motion to the President. I keep my ears open as to any further news of the Fellowship question.'

I had been laid low with influenza and was rather wretched at this time, so writing from his London home, he tried to solace me for the disappointment and to cheer me up with a story.

'One general turned up, rather a character and secretary of the gardens, in which capacity he had to receive a complaint lodged against the dog of Dr. and Mrs. Bridges, which had destroyed their neighbour's plot. In the course of a chronique scandaleuse of the neighbourhood he referred to a tutor who had married the mother of his charges, but had not been seen since "that row at the Zoo." On being further pressed he explained that — went in for birds, and among others, he possessed two parrots which he fondly believed to be the only specimens of the kind, till he heard of another at the Zoo. He instantly sought it out, and "waiting his opportunity" he seized the bird, put it under his coat and was detected in the act of trying to wring its neck in a secluded part of the gardens. I laughed greatly over this. I hope you may.'

He did most dearly love a ridiculous story. Here is an Oxford one.

'He told me an excellent story about *X*, how he was carried down by a big *A* man in his nightdress, his head under his arm, and produced before a bonfire at *B* College. How the *B* College man required the *A* man to apologise and how he sent to *X* by mistake the very note in which he said he had apologised to " that old ass." How *B* College demanded reprisals and *A* people replied that they considered the apology sufficient. (The *B* men had incited the *A* man in the first instance.)'

Such was the merry behaviour of the youth of Oxford in those days. There were, however, graver moments to record.

'Oxford is stirred to its depths by the publication of an entirely new Greek work by Aristotle, which has made all lectures on Greek history out of date. We have been requiring a new sensation for some time, and this is worthy of an academy. Full accounts were given of it in the *Times*, indeed precedence was given to it over every other news. Jowett once said : " It is not Greek and Latin, but we that are dead "—not bad, was it? But he is also reported to have said : " Art is the bloom of decay." The lecture on Monday is to Honours men on Plato, and men from other Colleges come, so I don't like to put that off ; besides, it is only once a week. Mr. Pater is lecturing on the same subject, but it is said to be an exposition of " Paterism " rather than Platonism.'

'I am off for a round of golf with Mr. Rushforth. I am beginning to take care of myself now—" regular exercise " and that kind of thing—so you see how you are changing me for the better. Mr. Snow goes so far as to declare that my " profil " has changed ! '

His kind old friend, Dr. Birkbeck Hill, had said : 'Of course, I knew that Ball was in love when he had

his hair cut and wore eyeglasses instead of spectacles.'
The eyeglasses had soon to be changed for spectacles
again, as they would not keep on. My sister said that
the special providence which watches over the pro-
prieties caused him to wear them at his wedding and
they did drop off, otherwise he would have recognised
a little crowd of pupils and would have stopped to
shake hands with them all on his way down the aisle,
to the great scandal of the congregation.

This letter contains an allusion to one of his many
forms of activity, which ended only with the merging
of two clubs :

'I have a committee meeting, also at All Souls, of
the Palmerston Club, an undergraduate Liberal Club.
They have asked me to become a kind of permanent
counsellor and treasurer to it. I was one of the original
members and promoters of the Club.'

It was from this Club that he received one of the
few 'presentations' of his life. They gave him a gold
watch on June 9th, 1906, 'as a mark of esteem and
gratitude after fifteen years' service as Senior Treasurer.' Fifteen years seems a lifetime to an undergraduate. In 1899 Mr. Gurney Boyle,[8] then Secretary, wrote on behalf of the Club to thank him for 'his
signal and long-continued services as Senior Treasurer, and would assure him of our hearty appreciation
of the assistance and advice so frequently asked and
so freely given.'

He describes a hurried rush to London :

'To-morrow I appear before a Committee of the
Thames Conservancy to argue a case for a particular
site we want for our College barge, and, as I shall be

[8] Sir Edward Boyle.

in the neighbourhood of Toynbee Hall, I shall probably lunch there. It takes a great deal out of my
work, and I expect I shall find it out when I get back.
Just before I came away I braced myself up to a grand
" tidy " ; what a heap of matter in the wrong place
there was, and how soon it will be there again ! My
friends are amused at my cultivation of young brides;
the truth is I am comparing experiences—the difficulties of getting a house and then getting into it. There
are just now two or three prospective young husbands
hunting up and down every street and alley with a
desperate and newly-acquired interest in sculleries. I
am, of course, still living in hopes of the College
building a house, but also considering the next best
possible thing . . . To-day I appeared before the
Board of the Thames Conservancy—a somewhat
august and venerable body—along with the counter-
claimant, the great Oxford boat-builder and owner.
I was asked to state my case; this was followed by a
statement on the other side, which I again replied to.
We then retired and, in a few minutes, were summoned
to hear the decision of the Board, which was in my
favour. (I always thought I ought to have been an
advocate.) So now I have to plunge into barge-build-
ing; after seeing this through I feel I shall have deserved well of the College, and may retire from this
kind of thing with honour. When I first came I got all
the clubs straight and amalgamated them into a Common Fund. Then I " put through " a Junior Common
Room, and the barge will complete the " reforms " I
proposed to myself. I have already had it designed
by an architect, and I think it will be a " tasteful "
affair; now it only remains to whip up for donations.
All this may seem rather dull, but I am initiating you
gradually into our " College interests." To-night I
dine with a club of choice spirits who are pledged to
put the cause of learning above every other consideration in this University. The " Academic Liberals "

inner circle, so to speak. They had been looking forward so much to my Proctorship and hoped a good time of reform was coming; but the "obscurantists" are too strong, and the interests of the University are in the hands of unlettered Tories and the "assistant-clergy." I shall have to modify your account of me as a "Fabian." I daresay Mr. Hughes and I may not be so far apart.'

A friend of mine, an extreme individualist and disciple of Auberon Herbert, had written regretting to hear that I was going to marry a Fabian.

'The highest socialism is to my mind the highest individualism, which remark, I fear, I have no time to develop. But I want such a state of things as will enable individuals to make more of themselves by association in a common purpose. Did I tell you that Canon Scott Holland wanted me to deliver an address in London on some "Social Question," but I had to plead excess of work. One of my pupils is very ill—inflammation of the lungs : gives me some anxiety. I hope his sister may arrive to-day. Very busy now about the barge, been holding a most amicable talk with my late antagonist.' For the sake of the pelf he consented to become a pro-proctor. 'I am afraid I quite forgot to give you an account of my "rounds," they were quite uneventful, a "blank" evening in fact. We drew two "bars" with no result, and then tramped as hard as we could—at least, I could. The marshal's pace is astonishing, and I came in more dead than alive : could only just totter to my rooms. I go again to-night—chiefly because the snow will not give much chance to tramping. I confess I felt it was a rather mean and unworthy occupation . . . I played golf for the first time this term and enjoyed occasionally the "select" sensation of a "clean drive," still more the brightness of the earth and the views of Oxford. Mr. Hobhouse came round last night. We got into an argument about "the best formula for the moral ideal"; he was rather perverse and lacking in sweet reasonableness. I defended "the Master" against his assaults for some time, and the result probably was that he slept worse than usual, as I certainly did. At breakfast I generally have a pupil, and I nearly always enjoy it except when they talk about football, which I don't encourage. I think they like it too, especially as I get them to talk freely about themselves. I hold what I hope is my last "reception" this term to-morrow in honour of a bride . . . I am going to row this afternoon in the " Ancient Mariners," *i.e.* an eight-oared boat manned by Dons. I have not hitherto been considered worthy of a place in it, but Mr. Smith has asked me to take his place to-day. It is a strenuous performance. I shall leave a little space wherein to describe my sensations, which are likely to be novel . . . I am back again, washed and changed, and feel quite refreshed and invigorated by it. Mr. Farnell was free with his gibes; he has a fixed idea I can't row, but right-thinking and right-seeing men consider that I was a not unworthy member of a distinguished crew. (We were stroked by a Blue and I rowed behind another) . . . I was disturbed in this train of thought by the entrance of Edward Irving Carlyle with his last prose on the eve of Smalls. The Freshmen were taken in a group at the bottom of my staircase this afternoon, Mr. Maxse forming a picturesque background. His social career has been a little interrupted by his swallowing a glass of sulphuric acid instead of sherry. (Now Mr. Maurice with his prose.) Mr. Maurice brought the proses and also a complaint that he had been charged 2/6 for a commons of salmon. Indeed it is hard to keep at the high level of fancy on which I started.'

Part of that Easter vacation was given to a reading party at West Malvern, where he rejoiced in the com-

pany of some of his men in a different relation and in
purer, fresher air :

'Enjoying from the window a wide prospect of un-
dulating and wooded vale, though my imperturb-
ability has been momentarily ruffled by an announce-
ment made by one of my pupils to the effect that he
played whist every night last term! A dreadful case
of depravity following upon his election at the beginning of the term to a Casberd Scholarship. It was
quite hot and relaxing in Malvern; here on the hills
we enjoy blustering winds, besides all the indefinite
blessings of cultured anarchy. After dinner we propose to play a rubber. I didn't play all last term, and
shall enjoy it. We go about unshaven and unham-
pered by any conventional habits, and live as glad
Bohemians. There is said to be a Lady Margaret—
some say a Somerville—reading party in the village.
Mr. Adamson proceeded to shave on hearing this intelligence.'

One of the College, or rather Oxford, legends which
always afforded keen delight to Sidney was the legend
which ran thus and was firmly believed in by generations of St. John's men : 'Mr. Ball examined Mrs.
Ball and fell in love with her before he saw her, from
reading her examination papers. He said that her
mind was "so Greek."'

A possible foundation for the legend lies in this
letter from Malvern :

'I received your letters by first post (I also sometimes wrote twice a day), thank you so much for them
all. Your Greek is very good $\beta = x$ but the Greek α is
not written like the English a; you begin with the
downward stroke from the right α; I have been treat-
ing for a second-hand Pro-Proctor's gown, but failed.
Do you think I could have the velvet sewn on at

Clifton? It would probably be just as cheap and my female relations might like the reversal of the velvet.'

I was not sufficiently capable to sew on the velvet, but I did diversify the study of the Greek alphabet by making, under the direction of a kind cousin, proctorial bands for him.

That Summer Term I was invited by Mrs. Tylden, the President's sister, and as wonderful in her way as he in his, to stay at the Lodgings, as I soon learnt to call the President's house. It was a surprising experience to find myself in, though not of, that mysterious and rather terrifying College.

I had just risen from a rather bad bout of influenza, and it was not easy always to play up to Sidney's idea of me. Mrs. Tylden was goodness itself to me : rather pleased, I think, not to find me the sort of wild—or ' new woman,' as it was then thought funny to call ' advanced women,' that might have been expected of the fiancée of a Don of whose dangerous opinions she could not approve. It never occurred to her, as it did not to many another, to ask what those ' opinions ' were. He seldom had time to spend in explaining or defending the opinions with which the taste or fancy of his opponents credited him. One of the stories of which he was fondest—of a bully at a meeting shouting down a meek questioner : ' *What* does the liar say? Turn him out '—really made in his case a rather deeper appeal than that of a funny story.

On this first visit to St. John's I gained, I think, some idea of what lay before me in undertaking to be a helpmate to such a many-sided man of such multifarious occupations and interests. My chief remembrance is of standing in a window of the beautiful panelled gallery which forms part of the President's

lodgings and runs between the two quadrangles. Here
I commanded a view of the doorway which led to his
staircase so that I could see him coming out and across
the quad. Usually his head, covered with a rather
battered square cap, was bent in earnest contemplation of a letter or a notebook. Very seldom was he
allowed to cross the quad without being stopped by
someone determined to have a word with him. How
many generations of men must remember him, as I
remember him, walking so rapidly, so intently, from the
shadowed doorway into the sun which he loved so
much.

The last time that I saw him in his own beloved
College, I looked down on him from the rooms which
he was then occupying, less than a week before he
died, and saw him crossing from the lodge, stopped
repeatedly by the way and coming towards the staircase, with a swift look upward at me in the window.
He delighted so much in the outward beauty of the
place. 'Isn't it a lovely house? Don't you like staying in it? I do enjoy seeing you against such a background.'

His own rooms, called after King Charles and supposed to have been used by him, had an oriel window
looking down on the garden. He delighted in my
story of the prim young Don who entertained me
(cause as I was of an approaching move out of the
rooms) with the remark, 'Mr. Ball will indeed be sorry
to leave these beautiful rooms.' It throws, I think,
some light upon the typical 'donnish' mind of this
period that the remark should have been repudiated
by him who made it on two grounds: first that he
never said it, and second, that of course it didn't mean
what it seemed to mean (*i.e.* that, on a nearer view of

the cause, she might be viewed as a poor consolation for the rooms), it only meant that Mr. Ball *would* be sorry to leave such beautiful rooms.

I suppose it was a reputation for social maladroitness, founded upon the remarks of such donnish Dons, that caused a worldly Irish cousin to comfort me for my approaching life in Oxford after this fashion : 'I have some friends in Oxford, and they tell me that you won't have to be dependent on the University people for society, as there are quite a lot of *really nice* people living there too now.'

Certainly some of the people I saw did strike me as very unusual, and not of the type to be met with in my native suburb.

'Your fancy picture of Mr. —,' Sidney wrote, 'was life-like. He is certainly a social star of magnitude, and his satellites who attend him to his box at the theatre or upon his drives or promenades, swell his glory—a truly resplendent phenomenon. I shall follow his meteroric career with interest—see whether he falls to earth or dips in a sea of bankruptcy. Last night, being Shrove Tuesday, we had a domestic dinner of Fellows, in Common Room. The President said some caustic things about the pancakes, instituted a comparison—rather unfavourable—with the soles of his shoes and, indeed, they were not worthy of the occasion.

'Our Senior Fellow, "Prince of Liars," was present. He persevered with romances of a most startling character—adventures by land and sea—in the face of the prevailing scepticism and incredulity, and has now the satisfaction of producing a Californian squatter who has seen the spot where he shot an elk; its horns are in the buttery, but no one credits the old gentleman's account of how he came by them. But he's a wicked old man, and is reputed to have " sold his soul to —."

Another Fellow has come from America, who is a man of some parts and intelligence, and was once associated with John Morley, as journalist, now an occasional correspondent of the *Times*. His name is Austin. The Senior Fellow rejoices in the name of Lemprière, more familiarly known as Jerry; he wears the strangest garments: turned inside out they make dress clothes, waistcoat blue with gilt buttons; altogether a "survival" and not of the fittest. Mr. Hutton gave out the "Comminations" this morning in a good round voice, I am told, but I overslept myself and did not get to chapel. Done this twice this week; a good sign, I think.'

The end of the Summer Term brought disappointment in the matter of a College House, which it had been proposed to build for a married tutor. This had been done by some of the more enlightened Colleges as a means of keeping their most useful members still about the College and near their work in it, after marriage. The marriage of Fellows was a new thing in Oxford: the old way had been to put the Fellow who wished to marry into the next College living that fell vacant. The interests of the undergraduates in retaining the services of a good teacher and good trainer of youth had not troubled the older Fellows, who preferred a comfortable berth to the possible discomforts of matrimony. Lay Fellowship, of course, put a stop to this way of disposing of a would-be bridegroom, so that the only way of inducing him to seek his fortune elsewhere was to make things in Oxford as difficult for him as possible.

' The College house has gone the way of lost causes, thrown out by the President's casting vote. He couldn't well do otherwise, as the old Fellows—excepting Mr. Dermer—were dead against it, and — was most offensive. I have no time for more, and am rather at a loss what to do.'

I believe — said that 'he wasn't going to have Mrs. Ball trundling her perambulator in the quad.'

Later on he wrote :

'The College now proposes to "provide a house." I dropped some hints about " going elsewhere," and that seems to have stirred them up. Mr. Hutton proposes a bungalow house. Delightful designs can be built for £900, and seem to have every convenience, both hall and bathroom. It might be put with its back to the racquet court and front to College and President's garden. However, they do seem desirous to do something. The Estates Committee has been actually "empowered to provide a house," and they all voted for that.'

This house was built—nine years afterwards.

He was trying to make up for the loss of the Proctorship money, as an aid to setting up house, by adding some pass examining to his other work, and he describes an 'invigilation' in the Examination Schools.

'Here's a falling off (he used to seize on the hours of invigilation as an opportunity for his daily letter), but I didn't "watch" this morning, and in the afternoon I took in, at Mr. Hutton's instigation, *The Wrong Box* (by R. L. Stevenson), as the result of which I gurgled through the whole three hours with scarcely suppressed laughter, but wishing you could share my mirth, even though it was all at the expense of your letter. Then I came out and had a cup of coffee and a shave, and to-night I take Frances to hear an exciting " private business " scene over the election here (he is writing from the Union), over the electioneering "dodges" on the part of young —; rather sharp practice on the part of that otherwise promising young man. My invigilation is over and I return to a fairly natural life, *i.e.* I shall not write so many or such long letters! Do you read the Baccarat case? Oddly enough I was shown how to play and *cheat* at it when I was at Sir Charles Russell's house in Scarboro'; a friend of his expounded the arts of the game! Mr. Snow is feverishly anxious to get up a table.'

One of the ways in which an impecunious Don who wished to marry could add to his income was by examining a school for the Joint Board of Oxford and Cambridge. This method of raising the wind was employed by Sidney for many years after our marriage, and, as he almost invariably did with most things, he managed to extract some pleasure out of the task. He went to Stonyhurst after being with me at his sister's home, Polstead, in Suffolk, a College living then held by Canon Nance, and wrote of his experiences from there.

'I am, indeed, in strange and interesting company. I dined with the Rector and the Bishop of Salford[9] (who is here for a confirmation). His Reverence was genial and handsome and drank claret "like a gentleman." The Rector had a beautiful face and manner and I really began to feel myself under a spell and to fear conversion. Father Rickaby,—an eminent philosopher—joined us later and knelt to the Bishop and then the master of the school, a clever cultivated man, who frequently takes snuff, took us round, from halls and gymnasium we passed to the playground and then to a sort of Dutch garden, containing observatory and sacred effigies, very beautiful was the glow of the sunset and the distant hills; very pleasant the sight of "philosophers" walking with their teachers. The place includes (1) a school, (2) a university, students called philosophers, (3) a seminary for priests, (4) a preparatory school, all in a world of its own. I

[9] Cardinal Vaughan.

have a nice little room looking out over "the ponds," my bed in a curtained alcove. The College belongs to the order of the Jesuits. I hope I may be able to hold out for a week against their fascinations . . . Got up about eight, had a bathe in the swimming bath, then breakfast with the Master, who afterwards took me another round; it's a wonderfully interesting place. The Library and Recreation Rooms (including billiard tables) splendid. The Sunday is "continental," *i.e.* given up to sports and pastimes,—with an occasional break for services. . . The tennis, with some of my examinees, had been extinguished by the rain,—the boys are very polite and jolly. The Fathers are fascinating and I am almost persuaded to become a Jesuit. I feel it's the real thing and Mr. X—— and the like only shadows. It's rather odd that my Protestant bile is not moved. I much prefer this to the sort of half and half-ness of Mr. X——. Besides, they play on Sundays and regard a tall hat as an unclean thing (which indeed mine is in a material sense). Expect soon to receive a Catholic manual or rosary.'

He encloses a letter from Father Benson:

'STONYHURST COLLEGE,
'BLACKBURN.
'*July 20th*, 1891.

'Dear Mr. Ball,

'You must be sure to let me know if I can be of service to you, in any way, during your stop here. For although I am well-assured that no pains will be spared to make you as comfortable as our people know how; and that your brother, at any rate, was calculated to make himself at home anywhere; still —putting myself in your position—I could conceive that the strangeness of one's surroundings might prove as irksome at the time, as they might afterwards, present an element of the ludicrous. However this may be in your case—consider me happy to be, for the sake of auld lang syne, entirely at your service.

'Very truly yours,

'C. Benson, S.J.'

'P.S.—Later you shall convey to me all the latest Oxford gossip, with which, in recent years, I have become lamentably out-of-date. You are not Revd. I think?'

On July 20th Sidney writes (in pencil):

'During supervision. I am now invigilating for two hours, then I take the form I examined orally for an hour; invigilate again this evening, 5.30—7.30. I have my meals tête-à-tête with Father Gerard, the Master.

'Yesterday afternoon I went a tramp with Brother Newdigate. After a three and a half miles walk we came to a place known as the Black Hole, really a very bright and cheerful spot, where we had a most delightful swim, while at supper (by myself) the Bishop came in and we had a long talk on the state of things at Oxford. He seemed to think it all made for the cause of the Church. I then went to bed an hour too soon by mistake, and so kept an appointment I had made—in bed. The boys are to show their absence of any bad feeling by arranging some tennis for me : they are now doing Euclid, some of them making most artistic designs. The fathers eat in silence, while a boy reads to them; they are now reading a *Life of Lord Houghton* . . . I had five and a half hours invigilation, though I was not strictly "awake" during all the time. I find that the fathers' port woos one to repose. This morning I take the boys, whose marks you added up, in Greek, not a disagreeable occupation for a desperate day. The master is so well satisfied with the results : the first three boys are in the order he hoped. Last night one of the boys went through two recitations for me, and very good they were. The speech of Hotspur and the Walrus and the Carpenter. He is a most versatile creature, has played *Matthias* in "The Bells," *Old Cattermole* in "The Private Secretary," *Baillie* in "Rob Roy." He is the best carpenter in the school : his sketches are excellent, and he is going to be a priest.[10] I enjoy my morning swim, followed by a cold douche. The boys are now doing Algebra ; to-morrow they have French dictation, and I have a horrible fear that I may have to dictate it. Been having a deluge. It might be very good for fishing, if I had only my tackle with me. One of the boys has sketched me . . . I enjoyed my oral exam. Plater was eager and impulsive, Repton measured and deliberate. We had a very enjoyable hour together ; they were very ready with their information, if it wasn't always very exact.

'After dinner the convert took me for a postprandial, in the course of which he gave me the whole history of his difference with the "Anglican community,' and I lost my pipe. He was very great on the heresies of the Bishop of London, and quoted the many "posers" he had addressed to him. A somewhat egoistic display, but curious and interesting. He seemed to think this morning that the discussion had been very much in the first person, but explained that he so rarely got an opportunity of letting off steam upon the "wobblings" and "inadequacies" of the Anglicans. I wish Mr. Hutton could have heard him. We got in rather late, and at 10.15 Father Gerard came round for our customary chat and grog. He regaled me with superb stories of Newman's method of answering inconvenient questions. This morning I had a swim in the rather tepid bath, and concluded with a fresh and exhilarating shower bath. I dine here in the middle of the day ; the Stonyhurst port, which I take with home-made cheese, is excellent ; breakfast

---

[10] The late Father Plater, S.J.

at 8.30 (ham and eggs), have coffee about five and tea (with cold meat) at 7.30 about.'

He was most humanly and frankly interested in his meals. His mother was a pattern housekeeper, and I trembled a little at the prospect of being able, with rather poor experience in such matters, to rise to so high an ideal of comfort combined with due economy. I remember that, when we returned from a moonlight row alone to Godstow, during that visit to Oxford, my sister asked me 'What Mr. Ball had talked about all the time?' and I replied—more or less truthfully— 'He said that stuffed tomatoes were what he liked for breakfast.' It was always one of our stock jokes that he had fallen in love with me because I combined an appearance of fragility with a taste for two helpings of pudding. It was on that memorable visit to the President's lodgings that I first became aware that my fragile appearance was a subject for remark. An extremely portly person had just left the dinner-party which was given in my honour by my kind hosts, the 'Pre' was standing in his favourite attitude with his back to the fireplace, talking over the guests at the party. 'Well, Nell,' he said in his irresistible lisp, 'P— hath grown fatter than ever, and I remember him thuch a thin feller. Why, thirty years ago, he wath ath thin, ath thin '—here he suddenly shot out a finger at me—'he wath ath thin ath you are, Mith Butlin!'

The Michaelmas Term brought with it the hope that it might be his last in College, though there was a definite understanding between us that his marriage should not mean he was any the less 'of' it. The question of where we should live became an acute one.

'Your sage reflections (on the housing question) might well have a solemnising effect (made Chapel in-

deed a work of supererogation). Seriously, I quite
agree. We had better get off our tall horse and get
into a donkey chaise, in which, as you sweetly observe,
we can take up "little ones" by the way, giving them
of our modest abundance. As Mr. Gladstone would
have pointed out, had we asked his opinion, there are
three courses open. (1) A house of our own. Bold and
venturesome and, indeed, hazardous, but involves the
"magic sense of property." (2) A College house.
Dignity and (possibly) economy. (3) A Museum Road
villa. Cheap and—well, safe. (2) and (3) would probably involve lodgings for a time.' And lodgings we
decided it should be, for 'we mustn't talk or think
too much about the College house, everything is so
uncertain. I have just come in from rowing bow in the
Ancient Mariners—we had the eights out to-day. Mr.
Roberts[11] and Mr. Farnell were in ours, and we got
young Howard[12] (of Balliol), one of the Carlisles, to
stroke us, and he kept it lively; so much so that I was
glad of a cup of tea and some very excellent "breakfast biscuits" at Mr. F.'s. Last night I had an exciting chase after a "mystery in a hansom cab" along a
dark country road, but I was pretty done when I got
back, and we failed to catch the mystery; another
attempt to-night. To-morrow we are all assigned
"beats," but don't "sally" till we are wanted. Mine
is about Carfax and Beaumont Street. I can't get
away till Saturday afternoon, but I am going to try the
11.42 from here [my aunt, Mrs. Francis Macnamara,
had asked him to come and see me] if I can, but it will
mean neglect of duty. Mr. Hobhouse and Mr. Hines
have arrived at a compromise, to go on with the dockers
till they can form a local union; but I fancy Mr. Hobhouse no longer delights in the self-willed sweep who,
indeed, gives to agitation what was meant for his wife
and (very many) children. Oh dear, what a life this is;

[11] Ch. Roberts, Member for Lincoln.
[12] Hon. Hubert Howard.

quite put out of my head the cold in yours, and yet I was very grieved (and am now again) and wanted to send you an extra letter; but the post didn't admit of it. I do hope you have quinined and treacle-possetted it away. Here is a certain cure—not whisky and water—inhale ammonia under blankets with your feet in hot mustard and water and put all the rugs and cloaks you have on top of your bed—that's what I shall do to you in future. Mr. Hutton recommends (1) sitting in a draught in order to give plenty of liberty to the microbes, (2) strong dose of quinine last thing at night and first thing in morning. . . I have been trying to make a belated freshman—from Killarney—at home. Showing him about and instructing him in the way he should go. I met Nora going to a concert, and after Mr. Hobhouse conducting a Nihilist who is to speak at the Union. Mr. Wicksteed, Head of University Hall, and an authority on Ibsen and Dante and the 'theory of value' dines with me to-night. He is going to open one of my Social Conferences and I am asking Miss Beatrice Potter[13] to open the other. Am just reading her very interesting book on the Co-operative movement—you must read it. Do you seriously wish that I should get a new suit (for his wedding). I had hoped to get through the winter with that which I have. My "tea" is growing, as it always does—about sixteen—but it must be the last.'

It was, perhaps, the last in King Charles' rooms. He enclosed in this letter one to hand from Lady Courtney. 'Will you keep those delightful rooms?' she wrote, 'It will be hard to part from them.' From the rooms he could bear to part but he could never break himself of the tea-giving habit, and his teas always grew. 'Do you know how many people you have really asked?' I used to ask when the cup prob-

[13] Mrs. Sidney Webb.

lem threatened to become acute, and he would say—
so many—and then, 'I think I did mention it to
so-and-so; he looked as if he would like to come, and
perhaps I did say that we should be pleased to see
so-and-so if he liked to drop in, you don't mind, do
you?' To the very last he loved to assemble his
friends in unknown quantities.

He became a little worried about all the lovely
things which were showered upon him.

'The meeting last night was a great success. "Sim-
plify your own lives and help your neighbours." I
felt rather guilty, thinking of silver candlesticks, etc.
But we will be simple, won't we? And the candlesticks are, after all, severely simple.'

These were the beautiful branches given to him
by Mr. Hutton, who

'has purchased, too, a magnificent Chippendale ward-
robe—and all for your gowns too; it is beautifully
marked and most handsome, brass handles and inlaid.
It is really noble. When I said, "Why, it will hold all
her gowns," Mr. H. laughed at my simplicity. It has
a deep well, and only one drawer (shallow) below. It
would be a distinction in any room or hall. And he
has so far put himself under a restraint, he is going to
add two books of an ecclesiastical bias!'

There was all the agitation as to whom it would
fall to marry us. My relations, his relations, the
College,—the claims of all had to be adjusted. 'I
do think that Mr. Hutton would really like to do it
and I doubt if ——— cares much.' 'I should like
to have said the words of blessing,' wrote Canon
Barnett.

'You must always be very near to us because it is
through you and your work at Oxford our lives have

been so influenced, if you had not kept up the fire of social interest where would Toynbee Hall, and Oxford House have been? May your future grow with the same growth.'

It did really seem as though the difficulty of how to be happy in being married would never be settled, and there was the ever-present difficulty of where to go when married.

'The discussion in Estates Committee was very fruitless. Mr. B. actually suggested that we should be made to go to 10 Museum Road,—finally it was adjourned but the old Fellows did not seem at all inclined to help—took the view that, after all, if I chose to marry I must take the consequences! I am to be Vice-President till it happens—this will mean an increase of duty and of pay—both slight.'

He turned gladly to a more congenial subject.

'We ought to think of books to take to Sercq,— isn't there some new good thing by the author of "Rudder Grange"? I've ordered Nisbet for you. I will bring Butcher "Aspects of Greek Genius," Westcott's essays (on Browning, Euripides, etc.), Church's Dante. I must try to get some good translation of Dante. Dr. Hill's new book, "Writers and Readers." I enclose a sample list of people I might like asked.'

It was always a joke that, our house being small and the guests necessarily limited, he had to curtail this list. He left another amended and annotated list on his much-bestrewn table, 'J. U. Powell (must be asked but sure not to come)' figuring on it and seen by Mr. Powell to his own great joy.

In default of that College House, which was so long in materialising, we began life, after a term in lodgings, at No. 5 Alfred Street, St. Giles'.

Looking back upon it now I can see that it was a really horrid little house, but we contrived somehow to be very happy in it for seven years. The most serious bar to happiness was the taking away of Sidney's Fellowship. It was like him to say that he 'preferred the New Fellowship' with me and the money value was made up to him by the College, which was anxious to retain his services, but he had no seat on the Governing Body of the College and was unable, except indirectly, to control its policy and debarred from any voice in the election of new Fellows. This was a difficult as well as a humiliating position for one whose chief energies and thoughts were devoted to the building up of St. John's into a 'first-class power' in the University. As a considerably lesser evil he was deprived of the use of his surplice—Sunday chapels are 'kept' in a surplice by clerical and lay Fellows alike—and he went, therefore, very seldom to chapel on Sunday. On weekdays he kept as many chapels as he could, both as discipline for himself, in the matter of early rising, and as an example to those who were obliged to keep a certain number. He fought a steady, though always losing battle against 'compulsory chapels,' and more especially against that form of them which allows a man to count an afternoon chapel as a chapel performed, thus putting a premium on laziness and time-wasting for those who wouldn't rise early.

Small and dark and distinctly pokey as was the house in Alfred Street, it managed to be a centre of a good deal of very varied hospitality. First there was St. John's to be considered, and secondly, the various interests unconnected with his strictly professional duties. Each interest brought a circle of acquaintance and Sidney was so much interested in them and so anxious to be friendly and hospitable to all. He was unselfish in his friendships as in everything else; he wanted all to share in the interest and the fun. As time went on, too, he kept a kind of registry office for past and present pupils and a chance acquaintanceship or an ancient friendship between people of influence or importance and the Senior Tutor of St. John's sometimes helped very materially in getting a job for a St. John's man.

It was not until the autumn of 1893 brought to us, in the same month, a series of interesting visitors, that it occurred to me to buy a penny exercise book and to start in it a record of our guests. That book is now swallowed up into two bound and illustrated volumes of the visitors, who meant so much to us and who represented so much that was interesting in Sidney's vivid life. It seems odd now (in July, 1920) to read a letter from Mr. Augustine Birrell, who came to speak at a Palmerston Club dinner and stayed with the Senior Treasurer.

'Nothing would give me greater pleasure than to be present on the occasion you refer to and to find myself in the company you suggest, but June 9th being a Friday it is only too possible that the Bill for the BETTER Government of Ireland may be in Committee and that I may be pinned, if not to my seat, at all events to the precincts of the House. I cannot say that I consider it *unlikely;* on the contrary I think it probable. Of course I might be able to get a pair. You admit Liberal Unionists. I suppose you do not yet invite Tories to your Board. Assuming that I came as I would gladly do, I should of course observe the rules of the game and should prefer to respond to a simple toast, *e.g.* the House of Commons, than to a very restricted one. What literature has to do with politics I don't know. I put myself in your hands and, save as aforesaid, will do what you tell me.'

We began, almost at once, to keep a hostel for early Fabian lecturers. Mr. Hubert Bland came in 1892, before the visitor's book was started, so a picture of him, cut from a Labour Annual, bears witness. Mr. and Mrs. W. P. Byles[14] came in 1893. Henry Vivian, Robert Wallace, Sir Hugh Gilzean-Reid in '94, and F. W. H. Myers, Sidney Hall and Lord Crewe in '95. At Mr. Birrell's second visit in '97, Sir F. Carruthers Gould came too and the book is enriched by a sketch of the one by the other, in a pleasant after-dinner mood. This is chronicled as 'Russell and Eighty Club dinner,' and Mr. A. H. Worrall[15] seems to have been a third guest. I suppose he must have slept in College, for two guests strained the resources of Alfred Street greatly and caused the Master and Mistress of the house to retire to the attic, which froze or boiled its inhabitants according to the season of the year.

In August, 1894, we lent the little house to the sisters of Walter Pater, when they had to return to Oxford after his terribly sudden death. Miss Clara Pater wrote to me at Marburg, where Sidney had a reading party.

'5 ALFRED STREET,
'August 21st.

'My dear Mrs. Ball,

'We came here on Saturday, and all the sweetness and comfort quite cheered our spirits. We cannot thank you enough, it is a real act of charity to have lent us your pretty house. Lodgings are so depressing

---

[14] Sir William and Lady Byles.
[15] Headmaster, Victoria College, Jersey.

and it was so painful to go to see to things at our own house, that we feel we could not have stayed there. We have been looking about for houses in Oxford but cannot find anything we like. And it is very difficult in London too, but I expect we shall finally decide on London, though for many things we should like to stay here. Everybody has been so kind we shall regret leaving all our friends. I hope we do not give your servants too much trouble, they are very attentive and make us very comfortable.'

To Marburg, too, were forwarded the many letters and addresses which came from Roumania in recognition of a meeting which Sidney had arranged in St. John's for the airing of Transylvanian grievances and desire for reunion with the Roumanian kingdom. It all seems strange reading in 1920. Prince Ghika, an old Wellingtonian, came expressly for this meeting, the excitement of our young Roumanian student friend —Démètresco—rose by leaps and bounds as the meeting grew in size and a move was made from Common Room to Hall. 'It is you,' he cried to Sidney, 'It is you who are the saviour of us all!' Language was not easy and a French lady, Mdlle. Delhomme, read Démètresco's impassioned statement of his case. Dr. John Bridges spoke of Kossuth and of his ancient struggle for freedom, but the eager audience misunderstood the reference to the hated Hungarian. When we came home we found that Transylvanian gratitude for so small an effort was not limited to addresses. The men students in Paris sent a copy of Monna Lisa and the Transylvanian women a gorgeous dress —scarlet cloth embroidered in gold and silver thread, for me.

Some idea of the Sidney Ball of this time, as he appeared to the eyes of the Undergraduate world, may be gained from an account of him as an 'Isis Idol,' written by Mr. Adair Hore, which appeared on March 7th, 1897.

'We idolize weekly, and all our heroes are duly ticketed,—idols of the forum who are all but statesmen; oars who will never have a place in the 'Varsity crew. But we can worship other than tribal divinities; and our Pantheon may surely find place for an "all-round" man such as Mr. Ball, who comprehends all distinctions of social eminence in the plastic unity of a fervid personality. Wherefore, gentle reader, look not for our idol in any one niche—he transcends all niches—a *cosmopolouse* of the Academy. Take him as you find him, in the Broad or St. Giles', perambulant or on wheels, a figure not to be hid; equally well seen and unforgettable on the towpath when the Eights are rowed.

'Don, athlete, philosopher, politician and socialist —Mr. Ball is a union of contradictions without confusion. A fervent disciple of the new "muscular philosophy," an Economic Socialist, he has yet never lost the tutor in the man, and within living memory he has kept a chapel.

'Mr. Ball is eminently a man of enthusiasms. Force in his case loses nothing by division. Where another rides one hobby and lets all else go, he has a dozen, and is equally keen on all. He stands out lurid from the gray background of Oxford dilettantism, a Prometheus bent on showing men what real fire is. If only all should catch the spark, what a world were there!

'The willing victim of nearly every society in Oxford, committees are felt to languish without him. He is the most genial of Dons, and his hospitality is known unto all men. In the fine scorn of popular opinion, he has opened his doors to heads of houses and undergraduates alike, and he numbers a chimney-sweep among his intimate acquaintance.

'And this is the key to him. Mr. Ball is above all things our Democrat. It is notorious that there has been no conspiracy in Oxford against time-worn traditions and opinions in which he has not been concerned. He has never refused to take the chair for a red tie, and he has robbed the orthodox Liberal of his last weapon by finding a moral aspect of Socialism.

'His sympathies go beyond even Oxford, in harmony with the great things of the outer world. Unflinching, he lent a hand to subsidize the victims of a Despot, and he has waved a delirious square for the Heir Apparent. But if his energy is great abroad, it is tenfold as great at home. His College knows him as prime spirit in any movement that is afoot, with an exuberance of the perfervid that scares all rivals. He carries his Socialism even into College politics, and as he himself observed recently in a moment of justifiable elation, he is generally to be found on the side of the strikers.

'Finally, Mr. Ball is a philosopher. His exact place in the glorious company has never been defined. But, though he is not to be catalogued, those who have once listened to his nervous emphatic discourse, at times even monosyllabic for very fervour, and have heard his solemn appeal to the unswerving morality of the starry heavens, reiterated with a pathetic persistency that burdens on the sublime,—have not failed to recognize an Individuality. But unique as he is, the Phenomenal is, alas, only fleeting; and too soon he becomes for most of us only the memory of a leader lost, pointing his yearly band of pilgrims to that Green summit of the philosophic faith that only throws back to the footsore climber the echoed confusion of a hopeless "Can't."'

This little sketch of him somewhat distressed his mother, because of that sentence about chapel. She could not, she said, show it to his aunts on that account. I think that the writer himself must have been, probably, a less assiduous chapel-goer than the Senior Tutor. There was some talk about this time of making a move to get his Fellowship restored to him and a letter from his mother throws some light upon the matter. She had been seeing the former Senior Tutor, the great and good ' Bob Ewing.'

' He quite sympathised with Sidney about the Fellowship, but he did not know how Mr. ——— could have done otherwise for it was a serious drawback to the College Sidney never being seen in chapel now he was married, and from what Mr. ——— said to Ethel when he lunched at East Farndon, that influenced him more than the being married. I have always so looked forward to Sidney having a more genial post that it has troubled me to hear Mr. Ewing should think he has done for himself as far as promotion goes by holding the views he does. Mr. Ewing says with his abilities he has made a great mistake. I felt I disliked Mr. ——— very much when Sidney told us of his voting against him, but still I think he is right about chapel.'

In December, 1898, the long-talked-of Tutors' House was built and we moved into it. It was an extreme delight to Sidney.

' I never did think,' he said frankly, ' that Alfred Street was quite worthy of us.'

He enjoyed with all his sun-loving nature the change from the dark, cold, narrow little street to the full sunlight and glorious view, across the President's garden, to the ' towers of Oxford.' Sir Arthur Evans was one of our very early guests and he, looking from our windows, told us one of his favourite stories of the Oxford City worthy who is reported to have said, ' When I survey the aspiring spire of St. Mary's and

PERROTT HOUSE, PERSHORE.

STUDY AT ST. JOHN'S HOUSE.

TWO HOMES.

the spontaneous dome of the Radcliffe I thank providence that, in the course of my civic duties, I have been guilty neither of partiality nor of impartiality.'

Here in the spring Sidney delighted to welcome the mother who had always meant so much to him, who had been so real a mother to me too, and who was to go from us in the coming winter.   Here came old friends and new in bewildering succession; to be entertained so much more easily than in the old house. There is a delightful loggia on the upper floor in the centre of the house; this was the idea of the Senior Fellow, Dr. Lemprière, who had been much in hot countries.   This loggia became a constant joy and pride to the dwellers in the house and a great meeting-place of friends.

'Ball has gone into a new house and is going to take a lodger' ran—or was said to run—the College legend, founded on this rather unfamiliar word. Anyhow, it was a story that pleased the Master of the House.

'It's just like being married again,' he said when he received the following letter from Mr. J. L. Hammond and the chair, which became at once 'the chair of the grateful pupils'; it is now in the Ball Library at Barnett House.

'*January 7th*, 1899.

'You will receive very shortly, if you have not already received it, a very modest contribution to the decoration of your new house. The chair should have been accompanied by a card, bearing the names of Hughes, Gough, Hall, Wakeman, Craig and myself, but owing to a careless mistake on my part, the card was not sent off.

'You will take into your new house the best wishes for Mrs. Ball and yourself, and the warm gratitude of all of us, and it has been a very great pleasure to us to be able to give this very imperfect expression to our sentiments. We all have a great deal to thank you for, and personally I feel that I have even more reason to be grateful to you than any of the rest. We can't pretend that this little gift is anything like an adequate indication of our gratitude, but I hope the chair, when you sit in it to discuss, to read, or nod will revive memories of an ancient year which will be as pleasant to you as they are warmly treasured by all of us.

'I am hoping to spend a Sunday with you sometime next term.'

In March, 1901, there are two entries, one below the other. L. Barbara Bradby, March 9—11; J. L. Hammond, March 8—11. When they left in the same train on the Monday morning after that week-end, I spoke prophetically to Sidney and he pooh-poohed my prophecy. He owned soon afterwards that there are some things which escape the wider manly vision.

I do not think that the College could ever really have felt that Sidney Ball's marriage took him away from his work or prevented him from being to them all that a resident Fellow and Tutor has the opportunity of being to and doing for his 'men.'

There is a pen portrait of him in a novel called *My Father's Son*, by W. W. Penn, prepared for the press by John Harvey and published in *1912* :

'I took my doubts to Mr. Prendergast, my tutor, one of those great men who, I like to think, still conceal themselves in remote corners of my distant native land. He had a wider and yet more secret influence than any man in Oxford at that time. Everyone in the large outside world knew him—everyone who mattered : popular newspapers and the general public, of course, had never heard so much as his name. His lectures were always crowded, but it was his personality, not his theme, which made him a force: no man came under him but went away different and better.

'"What do you think I ought to get in Greats?" I began bluntly, when I had managed to get him to give me five minutes' talk. He was always busier than was natural, even to a man of strong physique and mind as he was: he managed most of the College finance, as well as being chief Greats tutor, and having many duties on University boards and committees; nor did he ever neglect his own pupils, but gave them of his time and brains fully.

'"Well," he said, not looking at me, but industriously filling his always moribund pipe. He hated to commit himself: when he did he was generally right. "Well . . . . ."

'"What I really want to know is, would you think I ought to get into the Indian Civil?" I asked, understanding his methods.

'"Oh, yes," he answered casually, as though he had never allowed any doubt to come into his mind. I knew at once, from the Oxford Standards, that what he meant was that I should certainly get a "Second" in Greats and might get a First, while a low place in the Civil Service list ought easily to be within my reach: anything more, I gathered, depended on the remaining year's work.

'". . . match," he continued, the first part of his sentence being an indistinct murmur; I produced a box of matches, trying not to smile. He could never keep his pipe alight, and never had any matches.

'"Why I wanted to ask you was because I don't know what I ought to do about—about my future."

'"I see."

'"You know, my father wants me——" and I sketched briefly the range of my father's business, and the prospects of it, as I saw them and as I have just set them down.

' "Um," said Mr. Prendergast, relighting his pipe, and looking very intently at it. "You say you don't feel much in sympathy with your father."

' I nodded. "Well, of course, I can't say anything about that : it's natural you should have different ideas. But I should have thought you could have used these ideas in your father's business. You could extend it, get new men to write, take up new lines. I daresay I could—could put you on to some useful men."

[The father of the hero was a publisher.]

' My father's plan over again, seen in a broader way! I shook my head. " I'm sure you can't extend that business except along its own rut, which I hate. You could, perhaps, if you had any capital, but we haven't got any."

' "Well," he said again, blowing through the wheezy stem of the recalcitrant pipe. Then he looked at me directly for the first time, and kept his eyes on me in a most uncomfortable manner. "Well . . . you could combine a good deal of what your father wants with what you want yourself if you could get into the Home Civil. Are you keen on India?"

' "Y-yes," I replied. I had developed a former faint keenness lately : "Mandalay" had just become popular as a song, and the tune haunted me : but there was not much more than that in my enthusiasm.

' "Um, well, but I should think the Home Civil would suit you. You have to work in it, of course, in most offices : but you have leisure too, and you could do a great deal of work for your father in various ways, direct and indirect, without being utterly committed to the business, which is what you want to avoid, I take it."

' It was : I was glad he saw it. He began to speak more rapidly, emphasising his adjectives explosively. "But you have to be in the first thirty or so in the list to be sure of a Home place. You could get the Indian

or the Colonial all right, I should say : there are generally about a hundred vacancies for the three Services,
and most of the best men want the Home."

'"You don't think I should pass high enough for
the Home Civil."

'"Well . . . Do you like the Greats books?"

'"Yes," I answered with manifest sincerity.

'". . . matches again." I produced them. He began
in speaking to put on a queer mannerism of emphasis
which he always used when interested. "I don't see
why you shouldn't . . . It depends how you come on.
You find the work *stimulating*? Its real to you?"

'"Yes."

'"Don't you think you're doing too much other
work? I mean all these club secretaryships. How
many things are you secretary to now?"

'"Football, cricket, athletics, and the whist club;
I've given up the Essay Society and the Beefeaters."

[The Beefeaters was a College club.]

'"It's too much. Can't you manage to resign most
of them?"

'"I could." I did not want to do so. I liked the little
authority these social posts gave me, though they certainly did take up more time than they deserved, because I was a keen and thorough official.

'"You'd better. A lot depends on this coming year
of your work. We want you to do as *well* as *possible*.
The College had three Firsts in Greats last year; we
haven't got so many *certainties* this year, but we want
to keep up the *standard*. Latimer was telling me about
your history work; you ought to do well in that; I
must watch your philosophy carefully. Remember,
Greats is the best preparation for the I.C.S. after all.
Matches; I'm sorry, this pipe won't light. I don't
want you to do what some men are doing now—cutting
Greats work to cram *extra* subjects for the I.C.S. I
don't think its fair to the College, and it doesn't help

much in any case. You ought to think, by the way, about going to a Crammer's after Greats. I should think Sparrow's would suit you best. Now I have to go out . . . meeting . . . committee . . . advisory board. I am glad you have talked about these things."

'"It's awfully good of you to spare the time," I said impulsively.

'"No, no; always come to me whenever you want to. Remember what I suggest about those secretary-ships. We want you to do yourself justice."

'"We . . . ." As I left him, elated yet at ease, I saw the matter not wholly from my own point of view, for once. I saw the College, and, behind it, the University, as a real *alma mater*. I saw Mr. Prendergast considering me from every angle from the standpoint of his duty to the College and from the standpoint of his responsibility for my character and my career, so far as education could mould them. I was no longer a boy, delighting in dreams of the future and the pre-occupations of the moment: I was a man, with the necessity of living up to my manhood heavy upon me.'

To this lifelike sketch of his old tutor and friend there should be added Mr. Darton's letter to me on the day following the death of Sidney Ball :

'I have just heard from Lloyd. I can't say anything I know, which you do not know and feel already far more than I could ever express. But I would like to tell you what he meant to me and to hundreds of other St. John's men and Oxford men. He was the very spirit in essence of all the goodness of Oxford—all the hope and courage and nobility of the place. We got from him not only learning—that plentifully enough : he made the best of whatever was in us, and there could be no ideal we felt which he could not quicken. You know that to most of us in my time he was the College. There will be many better and greater men than I who will tell you this. I feel it too much to say more about that wonderful influence of his—a real influence in England, not in Oxford or in one College only. But to me it is a personal loss just as much. He let me call him a friend, and I shall always be proud of that. It means that something fine and great has gone out of my life—not merely something intimate and friendly, like the memory of old happiness, but some personal strength in which I trusted.'

One of the many loveable little foibles, which heighten so much for those who notice and remember the truth of Mr. Penn's pictures—that constant search for an elusive match—brings back to me one of the few occasions on which Sidney ever hurt my feelings. He came back from a delightful visit to his distant cousin, Mrs. Adam, at Emmanuel College, Cambridge, looked a little sorrowfully at his study mantelpiece— from which he had lately taken two boxes of matches and promptly mislaid them—and rather resentfully at me, and said, 'Adam had *nine* boxes of matches on *his* study mantelpiece.'

Sometimes the far-reachingness of his personal influence and example would be brought home to him by a letter from a parent, though few, perhaps, expressed what many, no doubt, felt with the touching simplicity which must have caused me to secure and to keep the following :

'OCTOBER 28TH, 1908.

'I write to express my very sincere thanks to you for all that you have done for and been to my son Ernest during his residence at Oxford.

'He, too, feels grateful, although he may not express it, for your intellectual leadership of him, and if I may dare to put it, your tender sympathy with him in his struggles after the "best and master things."

You have so infused your spirit into him that his life will ever be richer and fuller and more helpful in the world, by what I deem his good fortune of being brought into contact with you.

'And more beside : I am also a debtor to you; I have learnt much from you through him : for I am a humble student, though not of Oxford, and therefore it has been no little joy in the vacations for me to chat with him about the studies which engaged his attention during the terms. Therefore, Oxford in general and St. John's College in particular will carry in our minds the sweetest memories to the end of our lives.

'I trust that you will pardon my writing to you upon these matters, but I could not help it, as they are much to Ernest and to me. Allow me to add that he is now settled at "Wrens," and lives at 19 St. Mary's Road, Bayswater. He informs me that they work hard, and get through a great quantity of reading; but he adds, it is "drive" and there is "no culture-work." I believe that he has taken some additional subjects, such as Constitutional History and Roman Law. I cannot help thinking of the time, about four years ago, when I brought him to you a "wee laddie" of some eighteen summers, and how you helped us in every way possible, even down to the common matter of advice as to lodgings; but since then you have taught my boy to climb with steady brain and firm feet up the heights whither you yourself were going : hence my gratitude as a father.'

A friend of many years standing has sent the following notes :

'Mr. Ball was part of my first Oxford festivity, an evening At Home at Mrs. Birkbeck Hill's many years ago, and I met him quite frequently during my time at College. As a very green Fresher, I was enormously pleased that he always remembered me, and would come and talk to me, always about something interesting. Once, when he was talking Socialism, I dared to say that I was an individualist. "Ah well, you can't be a good Socialist unless you are," was his comment. I and some of my friends used to call him "Brother Ball"—privately, of course—partly because of his Socialist proclivities, but more, I think, because of his great kindliness. Later on, when he became engaged to the sister of one of ourselves, he seemed to "belong" still more. I remember being extremely flattered when he asked me to make one of a party, including the future sister-in-law and Mrs. Tylden of St. John's, to inspect a house in St. Giles', which he thought "might do." I was much impressed by his knowledge of things domestic and his grasp of the practical difficulties presented by that particular house.

'Another recollection is of a Parliamentary election in Oxford; this was three or four years later, when the Liberals were to have a speech from their candidate in St. Giles' and a torchlight procession after. Mr. Ball, with his usual kindness, offered to take me and two other women tutors to see it. Two things stand out, even now, most clearly: one, the candidate's adjuring his supporters to "vote air-r-rly and vote arrrften," the other, Mr. Ball's sudden decision that we would see the procession far better from the Broad and his sprinting off between Balliol and St. Mary Magdalen Church, with us panting after him. Fortunately, it was vacation, or what might the Authorities have said? But they never knew! It was just like him to think of shepherding us.

'He was very "sound" on all women's questions: the Suffrage, the admission of women to full membership of the University, and so forth. He was one of the stalwarts in the degree campaign of 1896, and it is a real tragedy that he was not here to vote for us again last term.

'He was never without some scheme for helping someone. Of the last, the Serbian students, whom he befriended so fully, have spoken with one voice. In connection with that, he let me give some odd bits of assistance, and it was perfectly marvellous how, in the pressure of work of all sorts, which the war brought upon us, he never forgot the individual needs or desires of every one of the Serbs; how A. liked playing the violin, B. would be glad to hear some good music, C. wanted help with special terminology; and somehow he remembered exactly which of his acquaintances would be able to take on A. or B. or C.

'One calls to mind his never-flagging energy, his power of interesting others in his schemes, his great breadth of sympathy and understanding, but, above all, one remembers his wonderful kindliness—that real and ever-active thought for others which made him talk to the shy Fresher at the parties of long ago, to turn back after a more recent entertainment to reassure a rather inexperienced hostess with "Thank you very much indeed, I really have enjoyed myself," and to spend himself to the last on the stranger within the gate.'

In the autumn of 1901 I was ill, and we went once again for Christmas to Sark and renewed something, at any rate, of that Christmas in 1891. In the spring of 1902 an old friend took me to Italy with her, and Sidney was left to keep house at St. John's with the maids and the cat, Timothy. And here, I think I must say something of what our maids—with hardly any exception—were to us. Without their loyal co-operation it would not have been possible to keep the flag flying as it was kept, for the honour of St. John's, at St. John's House. It is not easy to rise to a high standard of hospitality and to keep open house on small means; it is an impossibility unless the heart of the

whole household beats true to the spirit of the house.
'Like master, like man or maid,' might well have been
said of Sidney Ball, both in his relations with the ser-
vants in College and with those in his own house.
Something, perhaps, of what was felt for him by the
College servants may be gathered from the following :

> 'FROM THE LODGE,
> 'ST. JOHN'S COLLEGE.
> '*May* 24, 1918.

'DEAR MADAM,

'It is a great grief to us in the Lodge to think that
our dear Master and Friend has been torn from us.
We little thought on Saturday that his labours were
so near ending, who lived a life, not for himself, but
entirely for others, and loved by all. Peace, perfect
peace.
> 'Your obedient servants,
> 'H. BROOKS.
> 'H. PAYNE.'

My letter to him, from the Cappucini at Amalfi, on
April 23rd, runs thus :

'I was sitting next to a funny little Italian, who
talked French very hard to me; he had just told me
that the Signorina who used to sit next to him was
"aussi une belle Irlandaise," and I was beginning to
think that, as you would say, "the psychological
moment" had arrived to allude to "mon mari," when
your wire came. It was most dreadfully exciting, and
I found it impossible to explain to my neighbour, in
the French of Stratford-atte-Bowe, the difference between being a Fellow of your College and being nothing but a powerless tutor.'

The telegram brought the news of his re-election as
a Fellow. A postcard on April 23rd from him ran :

'I have only just time to announce an unexpected
bit of news, which will, I hope, give you pleasure. I

have just been elected a Fellow. I had no idea of it, except for a note from Ewing last night. It was intended I should not be prepared. W.G.P.S. has acted a good deal in the matter, and I understand it was not opposed; W.R. apparently has also worked for it, so I am glad to be able to bury that hatchet. I should have wired, but was afraid of alarming you. Timmy is very well, and has been to see me a good deal.'

And on April 24th, another postcard :

'After getting your Sunday letter, I decided to venture on a wire. I was afraid you might hear the news some other way or from someone else than me. Dr. A. told me he was dead against my election, but no opposition expressed at meeting. One of the items for next Estates Committee is a complaint versus the Co-operative Builders in Walton Crescent. Timmy made up to me at first, but has shunned me since.'

Old friends poured in congratulations. Mrs. Arnold Toynbee wrote :

'May I say how pleased I am that you are again a Fellow of your College, as you ought to be; also I shall now have you on my side in my many business quarrels with St. John's!'

The Walton Manor estates, belonging to the College, makes them the ground landlords of almost all the suburb of 'North Oxford.' Mrs. Toynbee was Bursar of Lady Margaret Hall, in that part of Oxford. Mrs. Birkbeck Hill wrote :

'The Doctor has just come down, and he has brought me the most welcome news of Sidney's election as a Fellow at last. The College has at last come to its senses and seen what was the only just and wise course for it to take, and I should like to send it our congratulations. To you and Sidney also, because to have the old state of things go on was very trying to you both, and I hope you have many happy years of life before you in the place you have worked so hard for.'

On Sunday, April 27th, he wrote :

'Had a good many "congratters" written and otherwise. Think I shall celebrate my re-election by going to chapel this evening.'

It was a great relief from the long strain of the twelve years during which he was so largely responsible for the educational side of the College, but had no voice in the management of its finance or of its general policy.

An election to a Research Fellowship in 1904, in which the new Fellow at last had a chance to make himself felt is described in a letter to me, while I was in the country near Oxford.

'Such a triumph. I made a speech which seems to have pleased people. Then —— made a few remarks and spoke of my "generous" speech. Then —— came in and the voting was equal. The poor Pre. looked round and there was a pause. "They are equal," he said, and then, "Will no one change his mind!" A long pause. "Well, I must not consult my personal prejudices. I vote for X——." It was fine of him. Poor —— terribly excited by the tension. The old fellows voted like sheep. None of them had even as much as read X——'s testimonials. I spent last evening in arranging the campaign. We agreed to save time and too much trouble for Y. and Z., to concentrate on X. at once. I had a bad night. No one at home to back me up, and I felt I was beaten. The result is regarded as a personal triumph for me. I hope Z. won't be resentful. I took a very high line, but also a very kindly one. V—— told Mrs. V—— I was "magnificent," but I didn't feel so, and I didn't like having to oppose B——.'

To anyone of his sensitive, almost over-conscientious, habit of mind, such combats between what he felt it right to do and what his personal inclinations prompted him to do, were very difficult. It would have made life much simpler and easier for him had he been able to consult only his own wishes and likings —prejudices he had few or none—and not to think of an election as a matter of even-handed justice to the candidates. Certainly I would not have had him otherwise than he was.

It will seem strange to those who knew only one side of him that one effect of the renewed Fellowship should please him greatly : it gave him a voice in the appointment to those College livings which fell vacant and were not taken up by a Clerical Fellow. His stern sense of balanced justice made him revolt from the tacit assumption that the first duty of a College in appointing to a living was to its own Fellows and Scholars, and only in a very secondary sense to the parish in which they were to minister. Many were the battles that he fought to get the round peg into the round hole. There was still another side to the matter where, as in some instances, the College had property in the parish of which it was the patron. Many were the tales of woe brought to him by some parson who set the claims of the proletariat above those of property, and who was inclined to back those who withstood the petty tyrant of his fields. Thrice complicated was the question when that petty tyrant was the largest rent-payer to the patron of the living. Questions of the kind come up before the Estates Committees of Colleges, and of these Committees the regained Fellowship made Sidney Ball again a member.

WITH OONA MARY.

To face p. 93.

When I say that this sense of regained power was
a pleasure to him, I mean it only in the sense that it
gave him an opportunity of helping to serve the right
as he understood it. Of mere power for its own sake
he had a real dread.

That year of 1904 brought with it an event much
more remarkable than a contested election. Sidney
had always said that, in the hierarchy of his home, he
always expected to rank third : first the Cat, then the
Mistress, then the Master. Now, on June 12th of this
year of many events, he saw himself, he said, taking
the fourth place only, as his daughter had come to
take the first. It seemed to be only appropriate and
right that he should have had to spend the 11th of
June in London, helping to choose Merchant Taylor
Scholars for St. John's, while the early hours of June
12th brought his daughter with them. He took to and
practised *l'art d'être père* with all and more than all
his usual verve and enthusiasm. Oona Mary was born
at 3.30 a.m., and by seven o'clock he had settled that
she should be named after me and my mother and
after his own, and replied to my question, ' But what
shall you call me, then?' 'Oh, I shall call you
Mother,' as though the whole thing had been long
within his knowledge. ' Now we shall really have a
use for this little room,' he said of the Loggia room,
which I had long thought of as mine and as adorned
by my presence. The pleasure and kindness with
which his friends and pupils received the daughter delighted him. Two of his favourite pupils, Shuttle-
worth and Fry,[16] went out at once and bought a silver
cup for her. She was christened in the College
Chapel, and he felt that the compensation, due to Mr.

[16] Killed 1917.

Hutton for not having married us, was at last fully paid. The kind old President gathered his favourite cabbage roses for me and brought them himself to the door. The kindly pleasant world of Oxford friends rejoiced with the man whom it had learnt to value and to love.

Oona Mary was very ill in August, 1905, and all that vacation seems rather like a nightmare in retrospect. Sidney was working hard at I.C.S. papers, and having once secured all that could be secured in the way of doctors and nurses, he settled into the daily toll of work in the loggia until his daughter was more or less herself again.

In 1909, St. John's was faced with the difficult task of choosing a new President. In theory, or under those ideal conditions which this world so seldom fulfils, this should be both a simple and a straightforward matter. In practice, it is not so simple. There are currents and cross-currents setting this way or that, and constantly changing. There are powerful interests to be reckoned with and prejudices and principles— religious and political—play their usual part, and prevent electors from keeping constantly before them the really important question of who is the best man for the place.

Students of University politics, and of the way in which they react on the Colleges, can read in the *Memoirs of Mark Pattison* or in the *Life of Jowett* unedifying details of the way in which such things are sometimes done.

The present President of St. John's College, who was elected in 1909, has kindly allowed me to quote from the obituary notice of Sidney Ball which he contributed to the *Oxford Magazine* in May, 1918.

'He was the life of every gathering, public and private, where he was present; and into meetings where he spoke he threw new life by his passionate eloquence. With such claims upon St. John's, he would have been less than human if it had been other than a disappointment to him not to be elected to the Headship of it on the resignation of Dr. Bellamy in 1909. Some men would have taken umbrage, and severed their connection with the College; but he was too great, too devoted to its interests, to take any such line, and he continued his work for it to the end in what was nominally a secondary capacity, though really of at least equal importance.

'For a considerable time, when Dr. Bellamy's powers were beginning to fail, he had done most of the President's work, and when that ceased to be necessary, he gave his unstinted help in every way to the present President.'

In Dr. James' letter to me on May 23rd, 1918, he wrote :

'Words are quite useless—he was one of the noblest men I ever knew, and our loss is inexpressible.'

Sidney would, as Dr. James justly says, have been less than human had he not felt very keenly the decision of his colleagues. His ambitions for the College, to which he had devoted himself and his powers so whole-heartedly, were boundless, and his almost unerring vision showed him that, with a comparatively young and energetic Head, no limits need have been assigned to its expansion and its opportunities for usefulness. Personally, he was not an ambitious man; he would, of course, have liked the security of tenure and the freedom from care about money which the position would have brought to him. He would have enjoyed the beauty of the President's lodgings and the delight of bringing his friends to enjoy them; but it would have been, as it always was with him, for the good of the College that he would have enjoyed most that part of the pleasures and duties of the Head of a House. He would, no doubt, have made the President's Lodgings a great rallying-ground and a central meeting place for the old and the new elements in St. John's, for that bringing together and keeping together which is one of the ways in which a great reputation for a College can be built up and kept up. The way in which the election, though it may have seemed to some a merely domestic concern—a very small matter—strikes contemporaries, was well expressed in some of the many letters which were written to him at the time.

'I know that your good work was not done with a view to reward; and your card to me shows that you feel on the subject, as I knew you would feel, *viz.* that the interests of the institution come before the claims of the individual. But I feel, and I know many feel, that we have at present in Oxford a growing and unnatural divorce between work done and reward for work done. You are only one last instance in Oxford of a good man being passed over for one who may be better, but who has done nothing in the past for Oxford and may easily prove a failure in doing anything in the future. And can a system which leads constantly to such results be sound and well? I hope that the election of yesterday will justify itself, and I am sure that you will continue to do the best of work for your College. But have a care for yourself. The capacity for work of the best of us may be strained too far.'

The letters of his old pupils struck, naturally, a more personal and, in some cases, a fiercer note.

'I cannot tell you how much I was grieved that you are not to be the new President. Apart from my own reasons for gratitude and appreciation, I feel, as I am sure that very many of your pupils must feel, that there are few successes that might come my way that I should have valued above the pleasure of seeing your splendid services to St. John's recognised in this manner, and the fortunes of the College formally placed under your *aegis*. When I think, too, of the hopes we had cherished of seeing a great leader of democratic and revolutionary opinion occupying this ancient throne, I can only look upon yesterday's work as a very bitter disappointment to the public as well as to the private wishes of your affectionate friend and pupil.'

'It was too much to hope for that we should have you as President. Yet I am feeling quite sick at hearing the news of the election. I suppose it is one of the permanent conditions under which Liberal and Progressive people stand at Oxford. They can permeate the place, but they must never have official predominance. I have always felt that when the Recording Angel begins to ask questions, you are one of the few people who will be able to point to a real life-work. No one can estimate the steady and consistent good that you have done for St. John's and the University. And you will still be able to do the same so that, though your friends feel sore at the moment, in the sum total we can only envy you.'

'It's not merely that you've earned the Presidentship by your work for the College, but you would have made the place really alive and interesting, and, as an old St. John's man, I'd have felt richer for knowing that at last we had the right man in the place. I daresay James has been a very good man, and he may have the remains of a good man about him still; but if University Commissions and internal reforms are to do anything at all, the first thing that they ought to do is to put a stop to the scandal of Heads of Colleges over sixty-five.'

There was a genuine *cri du cœur* from one colleague.

'I have just had a telegram. You know what a bitter grief it is to me. The College will not find another man of genius in a hurry : to serve it for twenty-five years with powers that would have got great positions anywhere else. One cannot hope and expect to have you in College, but I trust that you will not go down. The University cannot do without you—and I cannot, if that was anything.'

Such were the feelings of some members of the College, two of whom had kept the answers which Sidney wrote to them.

'It is very kind of you,' he says in answer to a letter received from one of these before the election, 'to write as you did. I don't know the origin of the statement about X. It is—at present, at any rate—without any foundation. What is true is that X. and others are moving heaven and earth to keep me out, but are divided among themselves as to whether A. or B. is best for the purpose. You have rightly interpreted my own inclinations, but I feel that a principle is at stake, and that I mustn't desert the Fellows who are fighting for it. The opposition has an additional plank in University Reform; it had succeeded in getting the election so arranged that the two Junior Fellows are not able to vote, and it has, of course, a strong candidate in James, of Rugby, to fall back on. Personally, I should not be sorry if, as I anticipate, they succeed; on the other hand, it would stamp the College with a character which I fear would be fatal to all I have worked for. James, though excellent in many ways, is a fearfully narrow man and as reactionary as possible.'

After July 29 he writes again to the same correspondent.

'Thank you ever so much for your warm and generous letter. I certainly had ambitions for the College to which this election cannot but be regarded as a setback, but I am not sure whether I would not rather serve than rule in Philistia. And, after all, I was perhaps fair game—the combination of the Budget and University Reform, for I had to bear the sins of both!—with the Church formed an alliance against which the Gods would have fought in vain, even though the issue was in doubt to the end. We were, at any rate, able to save the College from anything worse. James, if not an enlightened, is a very honest man, and may do some good in that direction. I must, I feel, try to stick to the place, even if it is with rather a stricken heart; for though there is something to be said for the result, there is nothing to be said for the methods employed.'

To a pupil of a younger generation he wrote:

'Thank you ever so much for your warm and generous letter. I certainly had ambitions for the College to which this election must, I fear, be regarded as a set-back. It was a purely political election, and I had to bear not only the sins of a reforming Chancellor of the University, but of the Chancellor of the Exchequer,[17] for whose "Socialism" I was held in some way to be responsible. However, though James is a colossal reactionary, he is an honest man, and may do the College good in that way, and we, at least, saved the College from something worse. It seems, however, one of the permanent conditions under which Liberal and progressive people stand in Oxford that they must never have official predominance, and I was, after all, fair game, and can hardly complain of a fate which has overtaken better men than myself. If I have any personal disappointment apart from the College, it is more than compensated by the kindness of my friends and old pupils.'

[17] The Right Hon. David Lloyd George.

To a favourite cousin he wrote:

'Thank you ever so much for your kind letter. I am sorry for the family that it should not have a President of a College in it; but I had no great craving myself for pride of place, so that I do not feel unduly cast down. In fact, I ought to feel uplifted by the kindness and good opinion of my friends. We have got a very good, if somewhat elderly man for our President, a man, moreover, for whom I have a great personal liking and respect.'

It is eleven years ago now that these letters were written, and it is a strange thing to remember that the then Chancellor of the Exchequer of the 'Socialist' Budget, which made so strange a recoil upon Sidney Ball's prospects, is the Anti-Socialist Prime Minister of to-day. The Socialist Don, with his trained intelligence and his clear vision and foresight, saw even then what was likely to come. He often foretold that the Mr. Lloyd George of Limehouse of that day, the robber of the helpless landlord, the shameless democrat, would live to be the saviour and the sure hope of the propertied classes.

The reforming Chancellor of the University (Lord Curzon of Kedleston) alluded to the help that had been given to him, in his own attempted reforms in Oxford, by Sidney Ball, in a letter to the President of St. John's at the time of his death.

'I was happy,' he wrote, 'in being brought much in contact with Mr. Ball in the circumstances, a few years ago, that attended our efforts to bring about various important measures of University Reform, and I recall with pleasure and gratitude his soundness of judgment and breadth of view, as well as his invariable desire for progress and means of conciliation. There was no good cause in the University with which he was not identified, no reasonable and liberal aspiration which he did not labour to promote, and the success which attended him, as springing from the sincerity of his own convictions and the absolute disinterestedness of his acts, was greatly facilitated by a personal charm that endeared him to all. I should like to join with the College in an expression of the profound sorrow with which it must be lamenting the death of one of whom it had so much reason to be proud.'

There were two letters to me also which must, I think, be quoted. The first is from Professor Dicey.[18] He has given me leave to quote it, and it is only one of the many kindnesses that we have received from him and from Mrs. Dicey. It is written in pencil, and that is in itself a kindness, for writing is a trouble to him.

'THE ORCHARD,
'OXFORD.
'25/6/09.

'MY DEAR MRS. BALL,

'We are all in an absolute state of excitement over Dr. Bellamy's resignation. It is the first time I have wished I had a vote among the Fellows of St. John's. It would be quite at your disposal. If I thought putting up prayers would do any good, I would go to St. Mary's on Sunday for the purpose. I should have no moral difficulty, as I fully believe my wishes would, if fulfilled, benefit the College.

'Yours most sincerely,
'A. V. DICEY.'

On August 3rd he wrote to me again from Hindhead.

'MY DEAR MRS. BALL,

'Oddly enough, I did not see the result of the St. John's election till I came home here from a visit. I

[18] **Emeritus Professor of Civil Law.**

UNIVERSITY
COLLEGE
LIBRARY
NOTTINGHAM

must write you just a line to tell you what a disappointment it was to me, as I am sure to many others of your husband's friends at Oxford, not to see him elected. At my age I can hardly hope to see another election at St. John's, so I must forego the hope of seeing your husband President and sitting in the seat of Laud, though when in due course James is made a bishop I trust, though I may not be there to see it, Ball may be his successor. There is, I have no doubt, with many good men among the electors still a principle or a prejudice in favour of a clerical Head, though James is known to me only by general reputation in the vaguest manner. I presume that, assuming that the President ought to be a clergyman, it would have been hard to make a better choice, and I feel it must be less trying to you than would be the choice of some unknown person chosen only because he was unobjectionable and a clergyman. However, these reflections don't relieve me of my personal disappointment, and I can only wish, as one does so often in life, that things had gone otherwise.'

It was with the help of such letters as these that we got through this bad time of our lives.

I used to tell Sidney that should it ever fall to me to publish some memorial of him, I should do it in the form of a volume of the letters that he received on this occasion. I have given only a very small selection from the numbers that came to him, and those from as many points of view as possible.

I never heard him say a bitter thing about this business, or any other. It fell to him to read the lesson in chapel at the prayers which preceded the election. It is from the 21st chapter of Proverbs : 'Every way of a man is right in his own eyes, but the Lord pondereth the hearts. To do justice and judgment is more acceptable to the Lord than sacrifice,' thus run the second and third verses. When the Fellows had given

SIDNEY BALL IN 1909.   *Photo by Lafayette.*

To face p. 102.

their decision, he said something of what he felt. He did not cast a vote for himself, as some of them urged him to do, as the other candidate was not a Fellow and could not vote for himself. That night he went to Wellington for the Jubilee of his old school. 'I am afraid that they are very disappointed about the election here,' he wrote to me; 'they would have been so pleased to have had me elected.' Unusually and extraordinarily sensitive himself, he could but feel that he had been wounded in what should have been the house of his friends. It was so very easy to wound him, but hopeless to rouse him to retaliation. He could have been a master of irony, but it was almost impossible to induce in him the necessary bitterness.

After the Long Vacation was over, he returned to Oxford and took up again the burden of work for St. John's.

The election of a President who had been so long away from Oxford and its rapidly changing ways and who returned to the College when he had been a Fellow for a short time, thirty years before, to find it doubled in size and importance, inevitably threw an additional strain on the Senior Tutor. He did not allow this to interfere in any way either with his paid or his unpaid work for the College.

There was never, to the last, with him any perceptible slackening of effort. He enjoyed, unimpaired, the old zest, the feeling that he was able to make his life at St. John's House just as useful and fruitful for the College as that of any of those who lived within the walls of St. John's. He loved the big tea parties which gathered round him on Tuesday afternoons, and felt that they were in no way wasted if, through them, only one or two shy Freshmen found their chance of an

informal word with him. Sometimes there would come
'out College' men too, young relatives or the sons of
old friends who came up to other Colleges. He always
forgave, but he could not altogether forget when an
old St. John's man sent his son somewhere else. I
think that the only thing which really rankled in his
mind was one reason given for his non-election, that
parents would be afraid to send their sons to a College of which the Head held 'dangerous opinions.'
No doubt it was hard for the Fellows always to find a
suitable answer to give to irrepressible and tactless
questioners.

He valued and had kept some of the many letters
which came to him from grateful parents. One from
Sir Frank Hopwood[19] in June, 1909, may be quoted
here :

> 'COLONIAL OFFICE,
> '*June 20th*, 1909.

'MY DEAR MR. BALL,

'Many thanks for your kind letter. We were all
very glad that Spencer succeeded in obtaining the
diploma, and I am sure that the subject matter will be
of real service to him in the practical work of the
future.

'But even more important is the experience of life
and enlargement of mind gained during the last two
years in the midst of such happy and attractive surroundings. For this boon to him in life he and I have
to thank you, and we do so most heartily. It was my
earnest desire that he should have the great advantage of good training at St. John's, and when I had
despaired you came to the rescue !

'The boy is very sorry to come down; he wrote
to me on the subject in terms of depression, evidently

[19] Lord Southborough.

conscious that he is leaving behind him probably the brightest period of his life.'

Some of his friends urged him to seek a more congenial post. 'I wonder whether you would like to leave Oxford and come to London, taking, for instance, such a post as they have given to Herbert Paul; you would be a welcome addition to London forces and it would be delightful to have you here helping us to reform Oxford,' wrote one friend. Others urged him to 'go in for' the Vice-Chancellorship of a Northern University. But his heart was within the College for which he had toiled and prayed so long. Even in 1915 he could write with all the old fire on a subject which never failed to rouse him.

'I am just mad about Ellingham. Its true that I never thought so much of him as Stocks and Cunningham did, but if ever there was a first-class man it was Ellingham, and to put him in the same class as Newsam is monstrous. Nagel tells me that they had a surprise First at Trinity, and the men said the list was most surprising; it's like recent lists, and there must be some fatal incompetence about it. E. had to defend a theory (which was really Stocks') on his own, and I was rather perturbed; but tho' he did not, I think, have much respect for me, and cut my lectures, there's no doubt at all that he's as good a man as we have had since Murray, and a Craven scholar to boot. I'm afraid it has upset me a good bit, and I am going to seek a change of mind over the sculptures (Mestrovic). Its a great misfortune no real philosopher was examining. Cunningham thought he would romp in.'

The Visitors' Books record so many interesting visitors and bring back such innumerable memories that they might make a book of themselves. 'Elizabeth' of the German Garden came in 1905 to see her godchild; Mr. H. G. Wells came to us for a Toynbee Hall meeting in 1908, and again, with Mrs. Wells, in 1909; Professor James Ward, of Cambridge, to take an Honorary degree; Miss Mary Hamilton[20] on her engagement to a new and distinguished Fellow of St. John's, Will Crooks for the Oxford Anti-Sweating League, Mrs. Garrett Fawcett to speak at the Union, Mr. and Mrs. Pember Reeves, Mr. and Mrs. Sidney Webb—it was taken for granted that all Fabians came to us—Pat Fisher from East Africa, Arthur Moore from Teheran, Stoyan Vatralsky from Sophia—how little we thought of Serbian complications in 1912. A son of Mr. James Campbell,[21] ex-Attorney-General for Ireland, was at St. John's, and in November, 1912, his father came to speak at the Union and put up at St. John's House. 'That in the opinion of this House, Home Rule would be disastrous to Ireland and a danger to the Empire,' was the motion, and ' Willie ' Redmond spoke sixth. On October 30th, 1913, Mr. Norman Angell was our guest, speaking to the motion that 'Military power is economically and socially futile.' He came again in November, 1913, for a meeting at New College, and then John Raphael of St. John's came with him. The portrait of the latter as the Liberal candidate for Croydon in 1913 faces one of him as a captain in the K.R.R.C. from the Obituary of the *Taylorian* for July, 1917.

There are some letters both from and to Sidney about this time which throw interesting lights on some of the many interests and causes which were occupying him.

'My dear Carter,' he writes to Mr. John Carter (of Mirfield and Pusey House), on May 14th, 1912.

[20] Mrs. Guy Dickens.
[21] Lord Glenavy, President of au Seanad.

'I am exceedingly vexed by the form and tone of the note that appeared in the *Oxford Magazine* in reference to the Bishop of Oxford's strictures on the University. On the other hand, there is something to be said for the substance of the note.

'Frankly, I think it is a pity, and an impediment rather than a help, to those of us who are working on the Bishop's side, that he should appear to ignore the very real progress that has been made in the direction he desiderates, and that unless the criticism which he makes is qualified by a recognition of this fact, it is almost inevitable that it should be regarded as containing a *suppressio veri* and as giving a false impression.

'Within, say, the last twenty-five years I have seen my own College raised from a Pass to an Honours College, and it is, of course, not alone in this respect. Moreover, there is none of the more popular Pass Colleges which does not enforce strict rules as to failure in examinations. With Colleges, struggling to exist, there is, no doubt, a pressure in the other direction, but the students they take are, at any rate, for the most quite poor men, and anxious to qualify for Holy Orders or a profession; and often ὀφμαθείς, this is more specially the case with non-collegiate students who do try to make the best of rather poor ability.

'In fact, it has become increasingly difficult for a rich man to come up, or at any rate to reside for any length of time, simply in order to "have a good time." Nothing is so striking in the recent history of Oxford as the virtual disappearance of this class, and their replacement by rich (if not so rich) men who mean business, and have a profession in view.

'The Bishop knows that I am on his side in this matter, and that much remains to be done to make the University a "Unity of real students." But those of us who are working on this side are not a little hampered by critics who, however right in the main, or at any rate in a large degree, do not take sufficient account of what has been and is being done in the direction of bracing up the standards of undergraduate work.

'I write this *currente calamo*. You may show it to the Bishop if you like, but I hope you will let him understand that I should not think it worth saying if I did not regard his name and influence as of paramount value to the cause we have at heart.'

To me he wrote from the Savile Club (a very favourite resort of his, on the few occasions that he could go to it, and his conscience always pricked him that he should spend so much money on himself. He was on the Committee at the time of his death, and greatly enjoyed the duties of that position).

'*July* 1, 1913.

'I had to borrow change (for porter) from Bhajpai, and then only sixpence.

'Lunch most lordly—Beit's old house—I hope I did not show I was unaccustomed to such luxury. A pleasant party: Birrell, William Jones (who sent his greetings to you), Gladstone and others. Captain Guest looked me up and down a good deal, and was, I think, surprised to find a don so gay. After two or three other courses, I gave up at chicken. Very glad I came. Jones very indignant over the election. I told him that it was just as much political as religious. X—— gone off a good deal; rather nasty about Plunkett, whom he described as most intolerant. Had been meeting O'Donoghue, who spoke of me. I think I shall dine here, very refreshing to feel in the world and out of the pestilential miasma of St. John's. I am writing to Lady Lawrence. W. Jones wants you and me to take tea with him on the Terrace. Though I think Captain G. regarded me as a curio, I think I kept my end up pretty well. X—— ate and drank a good deal.

'I hope Noo is going on well. She seemed to me rather pale and thin. We must give her a good holiday. We might perhaps ask the Reids and Nettletons (American friends) to tea in the Union Gardens on Saturday, or *chez nous* on Sunday. Going to enjoy myself to-day, and hope to get papers done on Wednesday or Thursday. Bhajpai [an Indian friend sent to him by Lady Lawrence] is staying with the Arthur Johnsons.'

It was in December, 1913, in the larger world of London, that he gave sittings to Mr. Stanley Anderson for a drawing commissioned by St. John's. A small piece of 'recognition' which gave him great pleasure. He wrote from the Savile Club :

'I think the first drawing quite good myself. Been round to F.O. seeing L. Collier (who is coming to lunch to-morrow) and A. D. Cooper—nice boys. Big Lascelles, over seven feet, here—the Magdalen giant —knows the Colliers very well. I went up the Nile with his father. Moore and Darton also coming and Mr. Anderson : he has a little son of three, whom he often sketches. Such a nice studio, found it quite restful. Barrow's letters very sweet. Very busy and tired, but feeling very well . . . I was done yesterday, but results satisfactory on whole. Lunch at Savile. Barrow (in window), L. Collier, W. A. Moore, Darton, Anderson, L. C., son of painter, nephew of Leonard Huxley, F.O. office, came to give Barrow tips (I had been to F.O. and secured them). Proved most diverting—a stammer gave all the more point to his rather caustic epigrams. Anderson much pleased, I think, liked Darton very much. Moore introduced me to E. M. Forster, who sat by us. I told him you were an admirer and spoke of " Elizabeth," &c. Taxied to appointment with Cavendish Association, where I was given an early cup of tea, then 'bussed to meeting with Aves, &c. Aves kept me after the others had gone : wanted me to dine, but kept my engagement with J.L.S., one of few people not dressed. I was late but dinner was later, and I couldn't keep awake during speeches. Saturday appointment with Mr. B—— and Rolleston, but also saw much of the Graves, whose son we are having; his mother was a Miss V. Ranke. The son has had poems in *W.G.* and *Spec.* One of F. Porter's (a cousin and Master at Charterhouse) boys. Pt. says, " Your cousin seems a very useful man for us." Graves in his letter said he wanted his son to be under me ! Gave Anderson another sitting, then lunched with Aves at Royal Society, back to studio for a final sitting. I was afraid he might want me to-morrow. Three studies : (1) very dignified, side face, which he prefers for pose, etching possibilities, &c.; (2) and (3) more or less full, the third one the best and may possibly be preferred, as giving more of me, to (1).'

These drawings are now at Barnett House. No. 3 was reproduced as an etching. No. 1 was reproduced in 1918 by photogravure, by Messrs. Ryman of Oxford.

In June, 1918, Mr. Stanley Anderson wrote thus to me :

' Mr. Ball's splendid qualities were impressed deeply on my mind despite the fact that the good fortune of a long acquaintanceship with him was not my portion. During the short period during which I executed his portrait drawing, I realised the depth of his altruistic and splendid sincerity. Not only you and St. John's, but also the whole nation has lost one who can ill be spared at a time such as this, when Europe has taken leave of her senses.'

One of the two ' sweet ' letters must be given in full.

Monday, 15/12/13.

' I must thank you for the kindest of letters, which I have just received, and I cannot be too grateful for your advice, which is the greatest encouragement to me in the course I proposed taking : and also for your hints on tackling Greats.

'In fact the amount I have to thank you for, arising from your letter, is enormous : but it fades away before my debts to you incurred during my time at Oxford, especially latterly. I don't know if Senior Tutors get much gratitude from a thankless generation; but, if it doesn't sound an affectation, I'd like to say that I really feel my chief loss in going down is that of the inspiration to be derived from you—inspiration not in a sense confined to better prospects in the Schools, but in the very widest sense of the word.

'I shall, of course, take your advice, which I was glad to find confirming my own ideas. I'll probably come up about a week before Schools in the Summer Term.

'I am writing to the President to make him an apologetic bow of farewell : but I suppose he already knows about this from you.

'I am sending you a wire, as I expect you want to know finally before the College meeting this afternoon : your letter only got here this morning.

'I think its very probable that I shall be in Oxford on Friday. If so, do I stand a chance of finding you in at any time? Don't tie yourself down for me in any way, as I'm uncertain.

'Lastly, I hear that an etching of you is being, or going to be, done. I should very much like the refusal of a copy, or to have my name down as subscribing for one. I hope this is possible, and that it will be a success.

'I'm afraid I owe you too much for me to be able to thank you for it : so I shan't try a lame conclusion of that sort.

'Always yours,

'GEOFFREY BARROW.'

In June, 1917, there came a 'faire part' for the wedding of Geoffrey Barrow, R.F.A., with Mdlle. Clothilde Séjalon at Lyons. 'En raison des évenèments actuels et d'un deuil de famille, la cérémonie religieuse a eu lieu, dans la plus stricte intimitè, en la Chapelle des Soeurs de Bon-Sécours, le 6 Juin 1917.'

In December, 1918, his friend, North—we always thought of those two as North-and-Barrow—came to Boars' Hill to see me and told me of Geoffrey Barrow's death in Paris of influenza.

Sometimes, when circumstances were unusually trying, the outlook very dreary and the sense of possible failure almost overwhelming, a letter from someone who seemed to understand would come almost as if directly inspired.

'Those who came to you on Ethics last Term,' wrote Mr. Prichard, 'would like to continue to do so, and the following are anxious to come to you on Kant . . . I meant to have written to you last term to try to thank you for your lectures to (*inter alia*) the Trinity men who came to you, to tell you how very enthusiastic those to whom I spoke were about your lectures —as you know that sort of testimonial is rare—and it makes me feel very grateful. I hope you won't think that very impertinent, but the difficulty of finding that, in books or otherwise, which will make fellows keen on the subject seems great, and that is my only excuse for writing this.'

Mr. F. T. Barton, of Leeds University, writes of these later years :

' My old friend and tutor, Sidney Ball, was no ordinary College tutor, to us undergraduates of 1912 —14; he was rather like a personal friend and guide to every student whom he knew, and he made it a point to know all. You always met with the same genial encouragement and meticulous care at his hands, whether you were asking his advice about a set of rooms in College, or receiving from him congratulations or a touch of the spur.

'He lectured to us, for Moderations, on Plato, coming into his study with pipe and tobacco pouch, not with cap and gown, though no Don was ever more dignified and lofty in all his demeanour. In his presence and conversation you forgot all the sordid side of life, and were able at once to understand the spirit of Plato's "Dialogues." Sidney Ball had a marvellous eloquence; his speech, pithy and rapid, often summed up in a rare and inimitable metaphor or two what any other man would have expanded into many sentences. A choice privilege indeed it must have been to partake of the company of Sidney Ball, Gilbert Murray, T. C. Snow and others, a company to which Sidney Ball once referred, at an Essay Society meeting, as the "Snow-ballers."

'What struck me especially was the many-sidedness and real enthusiasm of Mr. Ball's many activities. I have heard him speak on "What Universities can do to promote International Peace" (1912), on the Renaissance of Italian Literature (in argument with Ezra Pound), on the new Socialism (the pervading topic when I was at Oxford) in defence of democracy, Christianity (*i.e.* the real Christianity), and (at the Oxford University French Club dinner) of modern studies. Though a Hellenist, he did incalculable service to the cause of the belated modern humanities at Oxford. At the Union, at the Torpid training breakfast table, as our host in chapel, at our Essay Society, everywhere his influence was active, beneficent and uplifting. He was loved by every member of the College—Rhodes Scholars, Dons, Freshmen, all. Never was his study "ragged" in any Guy Fawkes celebration! Rather was it a keen delight to bear him round the quadrangle enthroned on our shoulders. Undergraduates at St. John's can never have that privilege again. We who knew and loved him shall ever have him enshrined in our hearts. He was a philosopher-saint, higher than a philosopher because utterly free from sophistry and fatuity, nobler than a saint because unclogged by cant, sanctimoniousness, or obscurantism.'

FULFILMENT

I.

AUTOUR DU MONDE

He who binds to himself joy
Does the winged life destroy;
But he who kisses the joy as it flies
Lives in Eternity's sunrise.

Blake's *Opportunity* in *Ideas of Good and Evil.*

THE summer of 1910 brought to Sidney Ball one of the great chances of his life. The Vice-Chancellor was asked to nominate, on behalf of the University, ' a candidate for a travelling Fellowship of the value of six hundred and sixty pounds, the holder to travel for one year in Europe, Egypt, India, East Indies and America.'

These Fellowships had been founded for some years past by M. Albert Kahn, of Paris, and members of various European and other Universities, including a friend of Sidney Ball's, Professor Anesaki, of Tokyo University, had been elected to them. The foundation was, however, being put at the disposal of English Universities for the first time.

On July 19th, when we were enjoying a peaceful domestic holiday at West Bay, there came a telegram from Sir Henry Miers to tell his old friend that he was elected to one of these Fellowships.

He was working at full pressure in Oxford, guiding St. John's, which had only enjoyed two terms under the rule of its new President, and he was still hard at work in the Hebdomadal Council on the work of Lord Curzon's ' Reform Bill.'

' Anyhow, I am most grateful for all your great trouble, and congratulate you on your Fellowship,' wrote Lord Curzon, while later on, with introductions to many people of importance in India, he wrote : ' I am delighted you are going, for I expect that after all your strenuous work you stand urgently in need of a holiday.'

' Since I have been away myself,' wrote an old friend, ' I am more and more convinced of the policy of " Sabbatical years," but how are we going to get on without you in the University for a whole year? There is no one who can do the work you have been doing. I have watched with pleasure and admiration the way in which you have worked for conciliation and mutual understanding and good feeling, and all without forfeiting anything of the confidence of your old associates in reform movements of all kinds. I suppose, however, that people will think you are leaving them in the lurch; take a good holiday, sure that you will be accompanied by the unqualified good wishes of all your friends.'

His old friend, Mr. T. C. Snow, wrote :

' The Albert Kahn Trustees knew what they were about when they gave this Institution such a magnificent send-off. I know nothing about it. How long does it go on. I am afraid I am thinking of the desolation of the College, more than of the good of the world, but I hope you will get a good deal of pleasure out of it, and enlighten dark places with the authentic vision of the philosopher king.'

My uncle, Dr. Charles Macnamara, came from Chorley Wood to see him and to give him valuable advice for the care of his health in India, while my

aunt sent him with an introduction to her cousin, Sir
Charles Bailey, then British Resident at Hyderabad.

Any time that could be snatched from his work had
to be devoted to the very unusual task with him of
caring for the adornment of his person and the getting
of a suitable outfit, and we got for him what he had
long desired—a pair of Zeiss field glasses. They went
later to the war with the Oxfordshire Hussars and
were never returned.

They accompanied a very happy master on their
first journey. 'Glasses working magnificently,' he
wrote of them. When once he had laid down for a
time the burden of work and responsibility, Sidney
was able to enjoy to the full his new liberty. His home
circle was seldom far from his mind, and he sent back
volleys of lovely picture postcards, letters packed
with those intimate details which bring the traveller
to the senses of those left behind, and beautiful gifts
for the home-keeper. There were many debates and
plans, financial and otherwise, for the possibility that
I might have gone with him. The problem of going
abroad to take care of the father or staying at home
to guard the daughter was well talked over. The pithy
remark of the latter, 'Father doesn't approve of staying at home, but mother and I do,' helped to clinch
the matter. She furnished him with a photograph of
herself, a small black cat mascot which survived everything and is still with us, and favoured him with an
occasional letter.

Letters came in return :

'MY DARLING NOO,
    'It is now nearly a fortnight since I saw my little
girl at the station, and Daddy seems going further
and further away from her. We are now near to

Egypt, and begin our journey to the Red Sea this evening. I hope you are following the *Warwickshire* on your map. I hope you had a very happy Christmas and had not more presents than you knew what to do with. You must tell me all about them. Daddy thinks of you very much, and hopes you and Mummy are making one another very cheerful, now that there is no college to worry about.

'With ever so much love and ever so many kisses.
'Your loving,
'DAD.

'All the babies on board are doing very well.'

A picture postcard from Ceylon says:

'There are some sights you will, I hope, see for yourself some day. I think you and Mummy and I must someday make the grand tour. I am carrying about your good luck and getting it, too.

'Much love from your loving Dad.'

He was always anxious to add to his possible usefulness, so that when 'the doctor began a series of classes in first-aid and bandaging on the after deck (after lunch), I attended among others; the theory seemed simpler than the practice.'

The *Warwickshire* sailed into a regular storm, but the accounts of it in the English papers made more impression apparently on those at home than on the traveller.

'A nasty day,' he wrote on 16th December. 'Seas sweep over. My cabin is a fair-weather one, as it is a good deal exposed and is part of an island which is not easy to cross to. Moreover, big waves get in, and I was visited by one as I was going down after lunch. Had to be moved for time being to a two-berth cabin on port side. Really quite rough weather, but the boat seems to stand it well; was able to take dinner last night; felt a bit chippy this morning.'

His first thought on getting to Ceylon was to secure the help of two kindly and experienced fellow-voyagers in getting moonstones for me.

'I have just sent you my voyage diary, such as it is; also what Mrs. Walker and her daughter thought a very choice thing in moonstones. She drove me to the place and was very kind about it.'

He then started direct to fulfil his trust and to see and hear all that he could outside the usual tourist round.

'I arranged to be met at the Peredinya Gardens station; saw over a tea and rubber factory and estate. Spent large part of afternoon in hearing a murder trial at the Supreme Court.'

He began at once to strike the trail of former pupils, or of men with whom his many interests and activities had brought him into relation. 'W. M. Hailey wired (from Calcutta) to let him know my future movements.' 'Newnham cycled up (at Anaradhapura) in a beautiful white silk suit and straw hat.'

'Had tea with Newnham and then Bell took me in a bullock cart, in which we had three easy chairs, to some of the most interesting things.' On his return to Colombo he 'looked up Bishop Copleston (an old St. John's man), who asked me to dinner to-morrow. Found Harrison Jones at hotel.'

In 1918 Mr. Harrison Jones (then wounded and in hospital) wrote to me:

'I have looked upon Mr. Ball as the greatest friend I had in Oxford, greater even than any of my own age, and among those I have some good ones indeed. I do not remember what his views on Carlyle were, but I know that Mr. Ball inspired hero worship in me. He has always represented to me the true Oxford spirit and the true spirit of humanity. He was the "under

graduates' don," because he had a youthful spirit which
sympathised with youth; hence my youthful confidence in him and love for him. It was always my
greatest source of pride that, for three years after I
went out to Ceylon, but before he came on his Eastern
tour, he wrote to me every year, numerous though the
calls on his time were. I was so proud that I was able
to entertain him for a day in Colombo, and almost
jealous of my great friend, poor John Raphael,[22] because he shared the honour of knowing him well.'

It was in such a spirit of real admiration and affection that he was welcomed as soon as his presence in
India became known, and that he became the guest of
governors, missionaries, British Residents, Bishops,
Roman Catholic and Anglican 'Fathers,' and was
equally at home with and anxious to learn all he could
from all.

In Madras he stayed with an old pupil and former
colleague at St. John's, and now a professor at the
Christian College.

Here, at dinner with Bishop Whitehead, he met and
had some talk with one of Gokhale's 'Servants of
India,' and, the next morning,

'I persuaded Corley to take me out to Mrs. Besant's
place, the headquarters of Theosophy. He had never
been there before, and was a little doubtful of his reception. A lecture was going on, but we persuaded
one of the lady teachers to show us round (Mrs.
Besant in Bombay, unfortunately). The people (from
all countries) and the lady's conversation rather weird.'

From the hospitable care of Mr. and Mrs. Corley
he went on to the Residency, Hyderabad.

'Here I am in the odour of official sanctity! A
magnificent and indeed palatial residence (supposed to

[22] K.R.R.C., killed June, 1916.

be the best in India). Received at the station by an Assistant-Secretary, Colvin (nephew of the man to whom I have introductions at Abu), where Sir Charles Bailey's son is also stationed.' Here he experienced his first and last elephant ride, 'half-an-hour of which I found quite sufficient,' motored out to the mine of Golconda, saw some old friends and made some new ones, played bridge and saw something of the usual round of Anglo-Indian Society life.

A postscript to this letter, is interesting in the light of later events.

'The Baileys gave an entertaining account of the Crown Prince's visit, an ingenuous and engaging young man. He thought it would have done his father a great deal of good to have been out here; very energetic and gallant.'

In Bombay he found many old St. John's men, and he also found time to call on a prospective parent. St. John's had even provided him with a 'parent,' a native ruler as a possible friend, but the Prince of Morvi was too unwell to receive visitors, so that experience was denied to him. He dined with the Governor, then Sir George Sydenham,[23] and stayed in a delightful bungalow, hanging over the sea, with Mr. and Mrs. George Crump.

At Ajmer, Mr. Van Wart, another old pupil, 'had a suite of rooms in a separate bungalow and they had also been prepared for you! Each with our own dressing room and, in the middle, a large room largely filled with Holland's kit.

'Van Wart gave me a very good time. He is in charge of a young native prince (eight years old) who is at the Chief's College. The Principal (Waddington, to whom Macdonell gave me an introduction) intro-

[23] Lord Sydenham.

duced me to some of the masters, among them Fanshawe, of Queen's, of whom I knew something. He had read of my tour in the *Oxford Magazine*.

'In the evening I left for Udaipur. Waddington had given me an introduction to the Resident and also one of the local Rajahs, but both were away.

'In evening visited the Palace and, by boat, the Island Palaces,—very beautiful.

'Next morning found a messenger from Rajah laying carriages and elephants at my disposal, but I had already arranged to go on.'

He was already beginning to feel that the unavoidable lateness of his start must hurry him unduly, if he were to see a tithe of all he would have liked to see in India.

At Delhi he would dearly have liked to linger with the kind friends at the Cambridge Mission, to whom he had been sent by his friend, John Carter, of Pusey House, Oxford.

'Here I find myself,' he wrote, 'in most congenial company, in spite of the fact that, like J——, I found kneeling at compline in their small chapel rather cruel to my knees.'

An allusion to a favourite story of a former pupil who 'liked Cuddesdon awfully, except that I got white swelling in my knees from kneeling too much.'

Then there was 'a delightful time with Maynard,' at Lahore and a visit with him 'to the Arya Somaj College, which is supposed to be a hotbed of sedition, a most interesting visit, and Maynard (an old pupil and now an Indian "big-wig") had never been there before.'

In the meantime, French (another pupil), Chief Minister at Kapurthala, had written to say that he was coming with his five years' old daughter to the Kapurthala house, at Lahore, for a week's rest after the Kapurthala wedding.

With the French's he drove to Amritsar and so on to Agra where :

'I am occupying a tent in the Bourdillons' compound. She is a splendid cicerone, so enthusiastic about everything. She drove me round the burning ghats, and gave me views of the Taj, which she is reserving for to-day in moonlight. We had some pleasant (love) rubbers at bridge, Mrs. Bourdillon being my partner, we won hands down easily. Meanwhile I had arranged to hire a motor to Siddri (Mrs. B. and B. being evidently delighted to accompany me, they spent their honeymoon there). A most delightful morning. It made all the difference having them with me. It is one of the most satisfying things I have seen and done.'

Old friends and pupils were competing with Rajahs for the pleasure of having him as a guest at Benares, and meanwhile he had a quiet week in camp with the parents of a man who had already come into residence at St. John's, and to whom I was strictly charged to show marked attention. This was in many ways the best part, where all was so good, of his Indian tour.

'I am writing in the Collector's Court Room, having ridden on in front (with a small escort) on a beautiful white Arab, which I afterwards fed with bread. The road, which was partly grass the whole way, ran along the canal till it turned off into the camp. It was very enjoyable. Yesterday evening Gracey and I went into the village to have a talk with some of the cultivators,—the man who counts. We sat on a square verandah, outside the agent's house, upon bed frames of wickerwork for our seats; below a kind of village square with people drawing water from the well and bullocks feeding around, nearly the whole (male) village gathered around us, one of them was a Pundit and was just marrying his niece. We afterwards met the young bridegroom who had come to fetch her, in a very neatly decorated ekka. I wish a picture could have been taken of us for you.

'It was so pleasant yesterday and this morning on the canal. Here we are again under a grove of trees. I enclose some pulse blossoms I have just picked for Noo. The village Pundit squatted on his knees and told all about his profits, his rent, his fees for funerals and marriages, his family, etc. As we left, Gracey told him that I was also a Pundit, at which he salaamed more profoundly. I should say that I am generally reputed to be a Professor of Sanskrit. We have two more stages, the last into Etawah. I am having a glorious time,' and again, 'My camping ended on Friday, and was most enjoyable from beginning to end. I rode every morning after I last wrote, and finally into Etawah.'

Indeed I wish that he could have been snapshotted, for me, as he rode on that white Arab, he must have looked so amazingly happy and content. A good horse to ride, some broken water to fish in and some deep water to dive into, those were three of the boons he would have craved, had he ever thought of asking for good things for himself.

The next letter is from Queen's College, Benares, where he stayed with an Irish friend, W. S. Armour, of Jesus, a former President of the Union. He had spent a day in Cawnpore, 'very dusty, finishing up by going over a cotton mill under the auspices of two such nice English fellows, one of whom had come out from Lancashire, and were acting as kind of foremen.' He was torn in many directions.

'I hesitated a good deal whether I should not run up to the Exhibition at Allahabad and see Dick

Sorabje, as I also hesitated about going to Aligarh (where Sabonadiere, an old St. John's man, was hoping to see me), but I decided that, in view of the weather which was getting decidedly warm, I had better not.'

At Lucknow he was back in a world of friends again, and could hardly tear himself away for Benares, where

'I was met by both Armour and Gwynne.

'Gwynne having ordered the police boat for me we sat on chairs on a kind of house boat and visited the various ghats,—on the whole the most Indian thing I have seen. Saw everything, the bathing and the burning of the dead, and visited the temple. Very misty at first (very wet yesterday), but sun came out and it was certainly a most wonderful sight, a great sweep of river, lined with Rajah's palaces and temples, rising one over another and with steep steps leading down to the river.'

Writing about Sidney Ball in the *Pioneer of India,* in June, 1918, Mr. Armour said of him :

'A few years ago he undertook a prolonged tour in India, and in a few months he seemed to have grasped more of its problems than many who have been a life time in the country.'

In the evening he met the staff of Queen's College, 'all very able and interesting men. Venis, of Balliol, the Principal and the first Sanscrit scholar in India.'

'I had a very jolly time at Benares,' Sidney wrote from Calcutta. 'The Rajah's carriage (with outriders) was placed at my disposal and Armour said he felt quite exalted in the eyes of the school and his servants. I visited the Hindu (Mrs. Besant's) College, she was not there, but I enjoyed my visit and saw Woodhouse (C.C.C.) who has joined them from Elphinstone College.

'Rode with Gwynne on Sunday morning and afterwards had a call from Venis, such a good man. Tell Macdonell I am anxious he should be brought to Oxford by a Readership in Indian Philosophy. I think the Endowment Fund might help and there would be a good deal of support.'

A letter came from Mr. Armour on the day that Sidney died enclosing a memorial notice of Mr. Venis for insertion in the *Oxford Magazine*.

The good time in India came to an end at Calcutta, where he stayed under the auspices of Mr. Hailey, who was himself staying with the Lieut.-Governor at Belvedere.

'Hailey has put a Government servant (in red uniform) at my disposal and he generally accompanies me driving. Hailey drove me to a meeting of the Council at Government House, introducing me to Gokhale in the Lobby. I spent two hours listening to a budget debate in which Gokhale took part among others,—much interested. Dined with Hailey at Belvedere in almost solitary but impressive splendour. I then attended a State Concert at Government House (white waistcoat and white rose buttonhole from the Belvedere Gardens) a brilliant affair, the first reception under the new (Hardinge) regime.'

Among the multitude of interesting things that were packed into these full days he attended

'A more or less public dinner given by Sinha (a leading barrister, member of Viceroy's Council), about sixty will be present, mainly prominent Indians. I owe this to Bannerjee (Balliol), who is most pleasant.'

He had later on a long talk with Gokhale at his own house.

At Darjeeling he ' " saw the sunrise " on the whole range of mountains, view remaining quite clear for three or four hours. I thought it better not to attempt another moonlight ride, but went on what was considered a spirited animal, after breakfast, and failed to see Mount Everest.'

At Darjeeling he first came across Mr. W. T. Ellis, of Swarthmore, whom he was to meet again further East and then to stay with him at his own home and to welcome in 1918 at St. John's. On this occasion Mr. Ellis had 'got an interview with the Grand Llama, but having missed his train and an appointment with the Viceroy, he tried to interview me!'

On his return to Calcutta he met Mr. John Raphael and arranged to meet him again at Kioto, and, on March 29th he sailed for Rangoon. Here there were more old pupils waiting to welcome him and he also received here an invitation from Mr. Hubert Murray to visit him in New Guinea, from whence he wrote,

'I shall be very glad indeed to have the pleasure of showing you our attempts at civilisation in Papua. I could take you across to Thursday Island where you could catch the Japanese Company's steamers. I hope you will be able to arrange the Papuan trip as I think it would interest you.'

He received also, from the father of an old pupil, a pressing invitation to visit him in the Solomon Islands, and a young German friend, Herr Stubel, of St. John's, would have given him a cordial welcome at Herbertshöhe, in German Guinea.

It did indeed seem as though he had the whole world for his friend and his only trouble was to decide amongst so many delightful alternatives. It was an unusually hot summer, all over the world, that year, and it was inevitable that this, intensifying the tropical heat to which he was now subjected, should have begun

to be too much for him. He missed too the services
of his Indian servant. His letters were still wonderfully vivid and enjoying in tone, but there was not
the splendid buoyancy in them of the Indian budgets.

There were more old pupils to be seen in Singa-
pore. Mr. Claud Severn[24] put him up, took him
about and started him on his further way with many
introductions and much first-class advice.

At Rangoon he fell in with Lady and Miss Lawrence, and Miss Percival.

'I introduced myself to them after dinner, while
they were playing a trio at auction bridge. Of course
we found we knew all the same people. I also discovered that they were bound for Java,' and he remained with them on and off until the end of his
Eastern journey.

These voyages were not without incident.

'We came upon three Chinamen on an overturned
boat. One swam to the ship, another tried to, but had
to keep himself afloat till a boat (after some time)
picked him up and the owner, who had stuck to the
boat. They had been two nights in their position, as
Chinese are too superstitious to rescue one another.
We raised a subscription for them and sent them off
with the coolies.'

The 'Asia,' by which he had once thought of sailing,
was wrecked on her way to Shanghai and he had the
melancholy satisfaction of passing the wreck, while
her ship-wrecked passengers filled to overflowing the
'Mongolia,' on which he was a passenger.

'We had quite a pleasant time at Canton,' he wrote
from on board her. 'We were there on the night of
the rioting, the papers reported that we were detained
and would miss our steamer from Hong Kong, men-

[24] Colonial Secretary of Hong Kong since 1912.

tioning the Lawrences and myself as among the passengers so situated; as a matter of fact we got away all
right and were lucky to see so much of Canton, as people
coming next day could only visit certain parts of it.
It was rather exciting, though I wish I had been able
to get nearer the scene of action. All we saw was the
reflection of the fire. I daresay you will have read
about it and will know more than I did or do.'

His 'side trip' to Java he enjoyed most thoroughly.
He had been in many minds about going as the season
was so far advanced, but his generous Founder had
himself lived in Java and had expressed a wish that
his 'boursiers' should visit it, and that had great
weight with Sidney.

'I am really glad I came this way,' he wrote from
the Dutch boat, 'on which only the chief steward has
any knowledge of English. I now feel quite furnished
with impressions. I feel quite revived by Java.'

He gave picturesque descriptions of the food, the
baths and the customs of Dutch Javanese life.

'Various regulations as to hours (different) within
which gentlemen or ladies are required to be dressed,
quite a large liberty of undress.'

In Japan he pursued, perforce, the more ordinary
tourist route. From Nara he wrote to Oona.

' MY OWN DEAR LITTLE DAUGHTER,

'Daddy is so busy with Japan that he finds very
little time for writing, but he feels he must write something like a letter to the dear little girl he has left
behind him. After such a queer little lunch in Japanese
style, in which you must picture Daddy sitting on the
floor and trying to eat peas and rice and cuttlefish and
such like things—some very funny and some quite
nasty—with chop sticks, we went over a palace of the
Emperor with Mr. Raphael and his cousin. We always
have to take off our boots and walk about in socks or

soft slippers, all the rooms being covered with exquisitely clean matting, the walls and ceiling are all wood and the rooms surrounded with beautifully painted screens, representing pine trees, herons, tigers—all very quaint and pretty. This is a very nice hotel overlooking ponds with boats on them—azaleas in the garden and beautiful hills all round. I have just been a walk round Nara with Miss L. and Miss P., but by the time we started it had begun to drizzle, so we did not go up to any "points of view." We saw some picturesque temples, all situated in woods and there were rows of stone lanterns along the avenues (I have got you a model of one made of deer's horn as a souvenir) and beautiful tame deer were skipping about, expecting to be fed. But it is now raining rather steadily, and we were reduced to rickshaws before we got back to lunch. Up till to-day we have had perfect weather and have been lucky—as Japan is a very rainy country and that is why the people walk about on raised sandals to keep out of the mud; they look as if they were walking on short stilts, and they make a clatter when they run in them. *Monday, May* 15*th.* We have just been to the Aoi Festival, a celebration performed by the Imperial Household in honour of a local shrine, *i.e.* by a certain number of local nobles, appointed by the Emperor, a very old festival. We saw the procession from the corner of a bridge and afterwards saw the service in the temple, including a very old dance, but we did not stay for the horse-racing which the festival includes. To-morrow Miss P. and Miss L. take me to one of the famous places of Japan, Amano Hashidate—isn't it a long name? We stay the night at a Japanese inn and I suppose I shall have to sit on the floor and eat with chopsticks.

'I hope you are having a nice Summer Term and I hope you will see the Coronation Procession, it will be so nice for you to tell other little boys and girls about it when you are an old lady.

'I am afraid you will find all this very dull, but I thought you ought to know what Daddy is doing.

'Ever your devoted,
'DADDY.'

'I am afraid my letters are not so resonant of spirits as in India, but I have got a bit tired and perhaps you would not like to feel that I don't get homesick at times and have a longing to see you and dear little Noo again. I hope you don't miss me badly too—a great thing to look forward to the time when we shall meet again. We must all go together on any fresh travel. I had a rest yesterday, and am feeling more in form to-day. It's hardly to be expected that I shouldn't get a little tired at times of hotel life.'

He wrote from Nikko, when he was still hoping that he might be able to go to Pekin.

'I hope the Pekin trip will prove interesting and enjoyable. I shall have a sea trip both ways to Tientsin and back and am reducing the mere journeying as much as possible. I shall be very glad when I can feel nearer home and cannot help feeling rather homesick at times.'

And at Yokohama, where he had some longed-for letters:

'I was much bucked up by your letter and dear Noo's card. (She had written to say that she would "feel more comfortable when you are on the next continent to me.") How wise she is,—we shall all be more comfortable when I am only on the next continent.'

Once more he was to experience the wonderful goodness of the friends that his own genius for friendship had attracted to him. He was to have stayed with Mr. and Mrs. Walton, but a tornado unroofed their house, so he went to rest at Kamakara, by the shore of the Pacific Ocean, which he was not fated to cross just then. Here Mr. Sansom, of the British Embassy, with extreme goodness, joined him and helped and sustained him through the disappointed days which ended his time in Japan, while taking off him all the burden of preparation for leaving it.

On the last day of June he turned back and sailed for home on a Norddeutscher Lloyd boat. I was able to catch him at Colombo with a word of cheer, and he to reply, 'telegram comforting,' and kind Sir Henry Miers wrote to assure him :

'You need not worry about your undertaking to the Trustees. You are not bound in any way to pursue any particular route; and if you come back, as I hope, quite set up after a long sea voyage, there is no reason why you should not put in a little quiet travel in Europe. I only beg you not to let St. John's tempt you back to any work in Oxford before your year's leave of absence is out. I had with me a few weeks ago Professor Penck, of Berlin, who is one of the German Travelling Fellows, and he told me that he had never got round the world at all, but was obliged to return home when he had completed only about two-thirds of the journey. Your Indian journey must have been a great success, and M. Kahn, who was in England last week, was very pleased to know that you had had so pleasant and profitable a time there. Come back well and jolly and don't trouble about journeys and reports or anything else until the year comes to an end.'

I met him at Southampton, in appalling heat and the middle of a railway strike, but a combination of train and motor soon brought him to West Bay, where everyone was a kind and understanding friend and where there was even an old pupil waiting to see him. Here he rested and recovered and then, with renewed hope and with all his old splendid courage, he began to plan his journey to the West.

On October 14th, 1911, I saw Sidney off from Euston for his crossing to Canada. His kind friend, Sir William Osler,[16] had seen him in Oxford, had furnished him with many introductions on the other side and had specially charged Lady Osler, who was sailing also on the *Laurentic*, that she should 'look after Ball.'

On October 29th he wrote to his little daughter on the back of the portentous dinner menu of the ship:

'MY DEAREST NOO,

'Here is the dinner we had to-night. Don't you think it must make us all very greedy? Daddy thought a little about the frogs legs and how Timmy (the cat) would like them, but he took a Punch Ice instead. I am having such a nice voyage, and am enjoying it much more than the voyage to India—partly because I used to wake up in the morning thinking I shouldn't see my little daughter for a whole year and wondering whether she would have forgotten me by then. I play a great deal of shuffle-board, generally with three nice American boys, one of them not much older than you —(I had to interrupt this)—to resume (you will be learning some new words) a game of bridge—the smoking room was so hot that we took a breather in between times—and saw the lights of Anticosta. Daddy won 'hands down.' Much warmer to-day and I didn't need my new gloves. I am sending Mummy a diary, which I daresay she will read to you. And how are you getting on with your lessons and your little friends? I hope you are doing nicely by both of them. I shall be quite sorry to leave this boat, everybody is so nice and there are not too many of us. I sit next the Parson, who is particularly nice, he often stays at Oxford and is going

[16] Late Regius Professor of Medicine, Oxford.

to stay with the Vicar of Cowley in December. There are some nice little girls on board about your age. We are now in the river of St. Lawrence, you must look it out on the map.

'Your loving DAD.'

His letter to me summed up some of the passengers in his usual vivid little vignettes.

There was the baronet who ' sits next to Lady Osler at the Captain's table, was at Christ Church for a term, then went out to war in S. Africa—was afraid Strong had been trying to make the House a reading College; going out to see a sister at Vancouver, has expressed a willingness to play bridge.'

' A Montreal man at our table was going home on account of his boy's illness (typhoid) received a Marconi wire last night telling him that the boy was getting on nicely and congratulating him on his birthday (of which he was not aware). Result, great standing of drinks and demoralisation of play (he was my partner). He has offered to personally conduct me over Quebec.' But that would not have made up to Sidney for the demoralised game—he was a very Sarah Battle among bridge players. There was a sequel too, 'Mr. B——, the man from Montreal, made me drink his health so often last night that I felt quite chippy this morning, but he can't have another birthday or, possibly, another wire.'

Canada rose to greet and entertain him in most friendly fashion. Mrs. Charles Macnamara, who had sent him to her cousin in Hyderabad, had given him letters to another cousin in Montreal and Mr. Peterson, of Montreal University, had rooms prepared for him. Here, too, was the ubiquitous St. John's man, one whose home was in Vancouver and who ' was sorry to hear of your illness which prevented you from carrying out your original programme according to which I should have been at home to welcome you in Vancouver last month. I was sorry about my Third, I feared it was inevitable when it was already too late to mend matters. We all felt very much at sea in the Summer Term without your cramming classes to steer us through the confused mass of the Ethics.'

Here, too, he fell in with many of the 'Round Table' contributors and helpers—a venture in which he had from the first taken a great interest—and 'young Dale came in to see me, Professor of Education—had been a great ally of Mansbridge in the W.E.A., a very good Fellow and a Liberal.' At Ontario there was his old friend, Mr. James Bonar, looking closely after him and taking him, among much else, to his first Harry Lauder Concert, 'and then on to Shortt—beautiful house—wife and he and I sat before a log fire in a panelled room, had been a pupil of Caird's—very interesting.'

At Toronto there were old friends and a new one, 'a contemporary of mine, from Worcester, who astonished the world by beating Montague and the rest of us for a Fellowship at Merton. His young brother, also a favourite pupil of mine, who died some time ago. He has a daughter at Somerville. Ask her out some time.'

'Sir Grey Wilson, a relative of Grey's—Governor of Bahamas—has asked me to go back with him and be his guest. He is trying to feel and stimulate opinion about coming into Dominion Confederation.'

'A pleasant dinner at Professor Wrong's, two boys who are coming to Oxford (C.C.C. and Christ Church), already has one at Balliol.'

At Niagara he stayed with Dr. and Mrs. Grant, sent to them by Sir William Osler, in 'a delightful house and grounds, covering the top of a hill overlooking the rapids. Dr. Grant a great friend of Plunkett's.

Plunkett sent him his book on Ireland and I am lending him Rural Problems book. Altogether had a most
satisfactory day. It has, of course, made all the difference my seeing the Falls under such conditions.' He·
wrote on the train to Chicago, 'Certainly Canada had
"done him well,"' and he left it for the States with
high hopes for his time there.

He stopped over at Detroit and Ann Arbor, piling
up friends and kindnesses as he went, and then came
to anchor for a time with Miss Jane Addams at Hull
House, Chicago.

'I never saw such a place—or so many "activities"
—boys' clubs, athletic tracks, workshops, needlework
classes, free library, music and, finally, a neighbourhood party, mainly women, recitations, songs, coffee
and dancing in a large hall. I couldn't have believed
so much could go on in the same place, and yet Miss
Addams told me I hadn't seen half. Saw the rehearsal
of a Masque to be played to-morrow afternoon.'

He fell in, most appropriately, with a visit from the
Irish Players and saw the ' Masque of Seasons at Hull
House—delightful, especially the children's dancing.
How Noo would have enjoyed it. Evening reception
of representatives of various settlements, addresses
from a Dr. Graham Taylor (whom I seem to have been
kind to at Oxford) and other "returned" people from
England, mainly about railway strike, also from myself, fifteen minutes, on my reminiscences of Toynbee
and the foundation of Toynbee Hall. This seemed
to be much appreciated and the Editor of the University Magazine tried to get me to dictate it afterwards
for publication. I was very glad to do it for the sake
of Miss Addams and also pleased for her sake it was
so well received, it was only an informal talk, but
seemed to be quite "new" to everyone.'

Truly a great tree to have grown from the tiny seed,
sown so many years before in his room at St. John's.

He had only this fault to find with America. 'I enjoy the food, especially the salads, though I miss my morning and—generally—my afternoon tea.' This was rather comforting, as other wives whose husbands had travelled to America, told me that they could talk about nothing except their preference for American food over the food which their wives provided at home. There was also that other comfort of home-getting,— boots blacked without further thought about those who blacked them. 'I get my boots blacked at the barbers,' he wrote, after many a doubt as to where and how they should be done.

At Madison, he wrote from the University Club and enclosed, as his habit was, many welcoming letters. One, from an old pupil, pleased him particularly, a Telegraphic Night Letter from Minneapolis:

'In long months I have seen nothing so inspiring as your well-remembered handwriting, if by prayer and fasting I can assure your coming then I will fast and pray that I may feast the better when you come; absolutely you must. My home is Maryland Hotel.

'WENT.'

And there were two letters of introduction from Professor Dicey, one of which ran thus:

'MY DEAR LOWELL,

'I have the greatest pleasure in introducing to you my friend, Sidney Ball, of St. John's College. He is one of the best known and most efficient of Oxford tutors. He is at present travelling in America in virtue of a Travelling Fellowship for which he was appointed for his merits, not of course by going through an examination, but because he was known to be a man who would turn such an opportunity to good account. You will find him an extremely pleasant fellow and he is most anxious to know you, being

already acquainted with your works. He represents
very favourably the turn of younger Oxford men
towards what in my youth would have been called
Socialism, but may be more fairly described now as
an intense desire to benefit the large body of wage-
earners combined with the belief that the power of the
resources of the State may be advantageously used for
the attainment of that object. You will find no one
that gives you a fairer and more favourable view of
the modern Socialist who wishes to be fair to rich and
poor alike. It would be the greatest pleasure to me to
hear that Ball has been able to see you. My only fear
for him is lest he should overwork himself in studying
America.'

He had a great time at Minnesota with old pupils
and even got on the track of a possible new one.

'To see an editorial writer,—Mr. Gray,—recently
candidate (Democratic) for Governor, a very clever
wife, decided almost on the spot to send a clever boy
to St. John's.'

He got enjoyment out of everything. 'Harrisburg,
12.40 p.m. I am enjoying this journey,' he wrote on
the train back to Chicago. 'Retired early, a lower
berth, certainly more convenient but very stifling until
I got the astonished black porter to open a window
and let in some frosty but agreeable air. Up rather
early at Pittsburg as I wanted to see the line between
Pittsburg and Philadelphia. Breakfasted, rather before 7.30, spent most of morning sitting on platform (al
fresco) of observation car at end of train. Very few
shared my open air contemplation, it was certainly a
little chilly, especially to the feet, but most enjoyable;
a broad railway with four tracks and all among mountains and rivers. Read a chapter from "The American
Scene" and "New York Revisited," and enjoyed it.'

He enjoyed to the full his own visit to New York,
seeing American life from as many angles as possible.

'I reached K——s house by a complicated car route, in which I was assisted by a fellow passenger. Very friendly, but it was the Nurse's Sunday out. Two boys and what I took to be a doll on the sofa, which turned out to be another boy two and a half months old. Mrs. K. left after a time to tend it. They were considering the problem of how to know the undergraduates, being lately put in charge of them (about eight hundred). I recommended " Barbara " to them.'

'Then to a grand " musicale," " high-toned " music, everyone much dressed, had I known I should have donned my white waistcoat, but Hartley Withers (who is learning American business methods with one of S.'s brothers) kept me in countenance. After concert, supper and small talk, at which I discussed Bergson and other matters. One lady talked most composedly of Oxford with its King's Chapel and Mr. Waldstein, etc,. had taken lunch with Hobhouses, greatly admired Emily Hobhouse, wanted Nora's address to send her " Twenty years at Hull House." Supper consisted of delicacies of which (and the champagne) I partook as a man should.'

He found echoes of very ancient friendships :

'Osborne Taylor's greatest friend is your friend Potter, it seems also that he was a student at Leipzig at the same time I was and he told me (as I thought) that my American friend in those days, of whose scholarship I thought a good deal, is Professor of Greek at Harvard.'

He notes : 'A few moments with Lady Gregory, who is staying at an hotel next door, her company seems to have done well last night though there was some hissing.'

He had an interview with Mr. Roosevelt, and he met Mr. Taft at a great meeting of the Economic Club, but a meeting with Woodrow Wilson was not to be.

'I am sincerely disappointed to find that our movements are arranged hopelessly at cross purposes. I shall be in New York Wednesday evening and through Thursday. If there is any chance of your coming back to Princeton next week will you not let me know? I should be very glad indeed of an opportunity to see you. 'In haste, with sincere regret,

'Cordially yours,

'WOODROW WILSON.'

In view of all that was going to happen later, it would indeed have been an interesting meeting if these two, whose ideals were in many ways so alike, could have met.

After this packed time at New York he went to Mrs. William James, at Cambridge. Here Mrs. James looked after him with extreme kindness, 'a large beautiful room with bathroom, and for the first time I found my clothes rather creased, a Press Clothes Man has come, he is pressing my dress clothes for dinner and a grey tail-suit for another tea at town hall "why surely."'

Here he began a 'quiet time' by lunching with President and Mrs. Lowell and going to the Yale and Harvard match with them, sitting between President Lowell and Dr. Grenfell of Labrador, and being decorated with a red Harvard carnation as he was unfortunately sporting a blue (Yale) tie.

After the match he plunged 'at tea with a young student' into a group of old friends, Mrs. Osgood, Bob Barton, of Glendalough.[17] He was to meet the former in 1912 at the home of the latter, and here—staying at Newton Centre—he came full circle again to Lady and Miss Lawrence from Japan by Honolulu.

'I am having ever such a good time,' was the burden

[17] T.D., County Wicklow.

of his Cambridge letters, 'morning tea and breakfast when I like, and a radiator in my room which I can regulate at will.'

He saw fellow-philosophers, among them that great and good man, Professor Royce, whose portrait now hangs in our room beside his own; he went to see the Fiske Warrens, talking of single tax and many other matters. Mrs. Margaret Woods was staying with them, seeming like a piece of the Oxford which was her home for so long. He experienced a real American Thanksgiving Day and he was not too much wrapped up in the new life to forget the home problems.

'Saw result of Greek vote in Springfield Republican; it was what I expected. What a ploughing of the sands it all is. I don't see that there is any chance of keeping a Commission at bay. Rather excited and concerned over the Foreign Policy crisis, but I hope Grey and Morley have between them steadied things.'

At Philadelphia (Swarthmore) he was most hospitably entertained by the friend of his Eastern voyage, Mr. W. T. Ellis. He attended a great dinner, sitting next to Mr. Wannamaker, and—

'I had eventually to make a speech (which people afterwards described as a "gem," though I think they were only flattering me). After lunch (the next day) received compliments on my speech (of which the Chairman, by the bye, said "that if we had only closed our eyes we might have thought it was Mr. Bryce speaking to us!").'

He visited Bryn Mawr. 'I was so taken with the beautiful grounds and buildings that I told them I should seriously think of sending Noo there for a year, while we might travel round.'

At Washington he 'had a very pleasant breakfast *tête à tête* with Bryce, though he ate most of the porridge thinking I should have no taste for it. I found him very behindhand in certain things, and he didn't seem to read his *Times*. I think he was really glad to talk with me, and was very kind.'

On Christmas Eve he wrote from Richmond, where the Lawrences joined him :—

'I had no time to write this at the Club, as I had promised to write a memorandum on Women Students at Oxford for Mrs. Mumford, a friend of the Graham Brooks, who wants to start a Women's College at the State University of Virginia. The matter comes before the State Legislature on January 9th, and my statement will be put in on Mrs. M.'s side of the case.

'Colonel —— came to see us in the evening, a great character : had fought for the South and been a personal friend of Tennyson, Browning, Swinburne, etc., on one hand, and of Wolseley, Evelyn Wood and Roberts on the other. Also a great friend of C. D. Fisher[18] (Christ Church), a tremendous talker and not a little of an egoist but, with his swear words, quite an entertaining one. Asked us to a picnic lunch (wife ill and had to see a sick man at Johns Hopkins Hospital on Sunday). In morning went about with Miss Lawrence and Miss Cust; governor not at home and most things "closed down." The "picnic" consisted of oyster cocktails, partridges, etc., with Madeira and champagne ! '

It was something of a vexation to him later when he was not able to return to his American friends all the good things with which their means and their generosity had enabled them to regale him.

'We must do our very best for them,' he used to say, 'they did such a lot for me and gave me such *very* nice things to eat.'

[18] Drowned, Battle of Jutland.

He enjoyed so much, too, the businesslike, time-saving methods of America.

'On getting home (December 23rd) found a wire from Dr. Frissell, Head of Hampton Institute, claiming us on Sunday. We decided to leave Richmond Sunday afternoon; went round to the Colonel to get an introduction to a Colonel of Garrison, as we thought our only choice lay in staying at the Grand Hotel at old Point Comfort or Fort Munro. It was all I could do to send a night-letter-telegram to Dr. Frissell. This morning Club, then back to meet Vice-Consul, who had seen our names in papers, and another man Scribner, who thought he knew Miss Cust. Long distance call from Dr. Frissell, telling us he expected us all to stay at Hampton.'

Here, at Hampton, he spent a most memorable Christmas.

'Reached Hampton about six, met by Dr. G.; a big carriage seated like a brake and a cart for kit; then to Dr. F.'s house, a charming "old Virginian home," where the ladies have beautiful rooms, while his son took me to my quarters at the Treasury, generally reserved for Trustees, a perfectly charming suite, including parlour and bathroom. Then went to service. A negro led about six or seven old slave songs (fascinating), an elderly trustee gave an address, and I was called upon. Contented myself with wishing them a happy Christmas in a few sentences, which the Lawrences thought few but fit . . . Then talk and smoke in Dr. F.'s library. He is a great friend of Sir Horace, has often stayed with him, also of Graham Brooks. Sadler had been here and written a report . . .December 25th Carols began about 2 a.m., and there were intervals of chimes afterwards. Breakfast at eight, then I had a good talk and smoke with Dr. Frissell. He is about as good a man as I have met. Young G. then took us to Old Point Comfort and Fort Munroe as far

as Hotel Chamberlain, where we were to have stayed.
Hotel very spacious and contains a beautiful swimming pool, in which we all disported ourselves; my
high diving admired. I also went down a shoot with
some trepidation, shower after. For dinner grape
fruit, turkey with cranberry sauce, a fruit salad, mince
pies and cheese, almonds and raisins and coffee. We
afterwards attended a Christmas tree gathering for the
Indian students; songs and recitations and then a dis-
tribution, the visitors getting sweets. Then we retired,
ostensibly to write letters, actually for a siesta. At
4.30 service in memorial chapel. The boys were lined
up in sections and marched in. Capital choir and
beautiful singing, so we are really having as season-
able a Christmas as we could desire; buglers are now
playing tunes on the Campus and a beautiful sunset
over the water (we are on Hampton Broads, the big-
gest naval station in the U.S.A.), with a young moon.
Now for supper. Quite a nice one, and smoke and
talk in Dr. G.'s study; then at a "Social," where all
the students meet, and talked. Then two of the most
prominent negroes came round to study and regaled us
with songs and stories; one of them had been at the
International Races Congress—altogether a very pleasant and interesting Christmas Day. This is a very
human place, and I am very glad Fisher put it into
my head to get this much acquaintance with the South
and the coloured problem.'

The wonderfully delightful American time came to
an end with the Economic Congress in Washington,
where he saw some of his friends again. The four
charming young men, in whose 'chummery' he had
been made so welcome on his former visit, received
him again, and

'Those dear boys won't take anything for my keep.
Curtis is going to motor the Lawrences and me to
Secretary of Treasury's reception this afternoon.

Attended a meeting on Immigration this evening, very interesting; Miss Addams and Miss Hamilton were there.'

He crossed on the *Olympic* and enjoyed to the full that floating wonder. He wrote from Plymouth :

'A very fine voyage, though not much sun, and a beautiful day for cruise to Cherbourg and back. I thought I might as well have the trip, though most people are getting off here. Dibblee and Mr. and Mrs. Austen Leigh have been my table companions. Pierpoint Morgan on board, though name not down. Also seen a good deal of Stokes, Secretary of Yale University, great friend of Biddle. Had gym. and swimming bath every morning before breakfast. In joyful anticipation.'

As a returned A.K. Fellow, he had both duties and privileges. It was not until October that he was able to settle down to fulfilling his duty in writing a report of his journey. This was not to exceed fifty pages, and he found it very difficult to boil down all his crowded impressions into so small a compass. His luggage bulged with all the literature, descriptive of such varied activities, that enthusiastic friends had thrust upon him. We went to Abinger Hatch, with his diaries, his memories, his letters to me and a selection of the literature accumulated on the journey, and there he completed the task.

In 1918 he was able to enjoy the Cercle of the Autour du Monde at Boulogne-sur-Seine, of which he became a member.

'Came on here by boat : very pleasantly received, given an excellent déjeuner. Mons. Garnier, the Secretary, a returned boursier and myself. All three spoke English, the boursier excellently. They after-

wards took me round Kahn's beautiful private garden, after I had sent in a card. He himself lives in a
kind of cottage close by. Gardens perfectly wonderful : reproductions of Vosges gardens, a more or less
perfect one of Japan (including tea houses, bath
houses, lanterns, etc.) and a Chinese garden. I am
now writing in the library, which has a copy of my
report. (I am sorry I spoke rather disrespectfully of
the French in Indo-China.) Altogether a great success.'

II

AUSTRALASIA

'Magnanimity in politics is not seldom the truest wisdom; and a great Empire and little minds go ill together.
My hold of the Colonies is in the close affection which
grows from common names, from kindred blood, from
similar privileges and equal protection. These are ties
which, though light as air, are as strong as links of iron.'

BURKE (Speech on moving his *Resolutions for
Conciliation with the Colonies*, 1775).

ON the last day of June, 1914, Sidney Ball sailed on
the Aberdeen liner *Euripides* for Australia, where he
was to take part, as Vice-President of the Economic
Section, in the meetings of the British Association.
Never, I think, was there a 'British Ass,' as he delighted to call himself, who started out with a more
thorough intention of making the most of so great an
opportunity.

By the Pâquebot post came a picture of the ship
and :

'Ma chère petite—ecrivez moi une grande lettre
française. I hope you are having a good time with
Mummy and Mary and Peter, and with your lessons

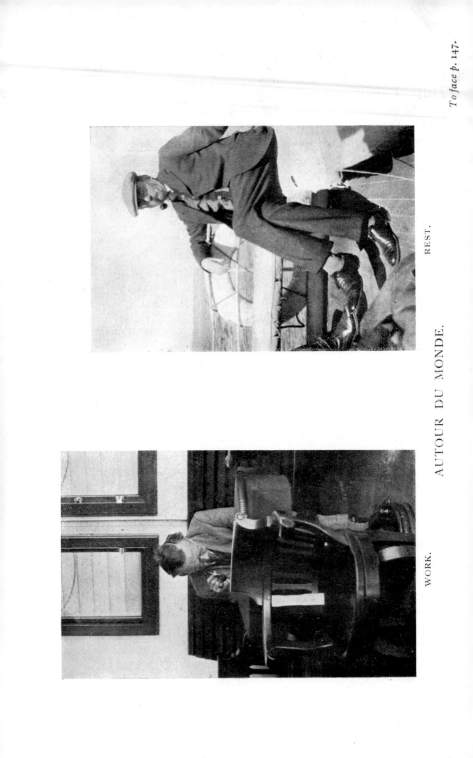

WORK.

REST.

AUTOUR DU MONDE.

To face p. 147.

and friends. I dreamt of you last night—on Boar's Hill. I shall miss our "mixed bathing," but expect you to swim out to meet me on my return.' And from Cape Town: 'You must come round the world with Mummy and me when you have been "educated," and see all the nice places. E.R. very like you, though not really so nice (rather "spoilt"). How many strokes can you swim now?'

To me then came a card from the Cape.

'Had a splendid time here, people astir betimes to see the sun rise on the Cape—a perfect day and quite warm. Our party and Dr. Kimmis were allotted the Major's car, went right round Table Mountain (as on card) and spent a long time at Rhodes' House (now Botha's). Miss Hobhouse's name quite a talisman. Lunched with Sir Henry Juta at Club. Saw Professor Ritchie—an old contemporary—after lunch; very glad to have had a sight of Cape Town to such advantage.'

He soon became friends with all on board, and was made Treasurer of the Sports Club, with Professor Seward, of Cambridge, as President.

I had managed to secure Mr. J. A. Hobson's new book, and Mr. Graham Wallas's, in London, and to catch the boat with them at Plymouth; and those, with his paper to write and an article promised to the *Yale Review*, gave him serious occupation for the voyage.

'Sir Charles Lucas reminds me that we shall have been a week on board to-day; ideal conditions continue. We returned fairly early to the ship and the launch bobbed about a good deal. Some people stayed up in hope of seeing the Peak; some of them think they saw the base. Made some progress with my paper yesterday on the verandah, and had a trial at deck tennis before lunch. After tea some quoits and

Hobson; after dinner a dance on the upper deck, which you did not see. Rubber of bridge (auction) with Sir T. Holland. Our coffee party after lunch and dinner generally consists of our four, Rutherford, Rebavel (an amusing person and aviator amongst other things) and Sir T. Holland; must try and get another light book . . . tried *Woman Thou Gavest Me*, and sorry I did. Came out this morning in my Chinese suit. *Much admired.* Rutherford and others making flattering enquiries.' [This was a tussore suit of which he was inordinately vain.] 'To-night a rather novel kind of game, called War Bridge . . . . War Bridge put off, one of the crew having succumbed to heat or to heart seizure; he was buried late at night . . . . we shall probably raise a subscription, he has left a wife and six children . . . . had some interesting talks with some of the young fellows (third class) going out as farmers . . . . War Bridge last night—rather fun, three people represent a nation. Sidgwick and I and Miss Swallow represented Holland. We won for our section of the world. I play off the final with China (Mrs. Hopkinson and others) on Monday. Delightfully cool again. Now just on the Equator (July 12th, 12 p.m.). Did not keep a chapel this morning; nice to get a really Sabbath morning, and I think I have fairly broken the back of my paper, but I don't find composition so easy on board as at Willowgate . . . . Was able to finish *For the term of his Natural Life*, a grim book . . . . Soup has come in again instead of ices. Reading after lunch and after tea, also some quoits. To-night we have a meeting after dinner about the seaman's family, Sir C. Lucas presiding, and I play off final in War Bridge; certainly a very pleasant and restful life : one can be as solitary or as sociable as one likes, and one hears very good talk over coffee after lunch and dinner. I think one reason why I am so content with myself and bucked up is that I got an ocean letter off to you last night—it is to go by the *Themistocles*, but we are not likely to meet her before to-morrow early . . . The prizes are to be given away to-night by Mrs. Hopkinson, and I have to make a speech on behalf of the Committee in reply to a vote of thanks . . . My speech last night seems to have been a distinct success. Sir Everard said I was the hero of the occasion, and most people seemed to think it was the only lively element in the proceedings. Sir Charles went so far as to say that it was the best speech he had heard, and Mrs. Hopkinson the best speech she had heard for a long time. One lady made the not very happy remark that she had no idea I could be humorous! Everyone seems to have been equally pleased and anxious to say nice things about it, so I am glad that I made the not very serious effort. It certainly does seem against nature that the College I have established should have made it necessary for me to establish myself among strangers. Everyone seems to suppose that I must be something else than a mere College drudge, but can't find me in *Who's Who*, so they fall back on calling me Professor or Dr. Ball. With S. and T. on board and also M., a Sheffield friend, I suspect people know that I have been rejected by St. John's and mentioned for Sheffield, etc. Anyhow, I get quite as much consideration as is good for me. By the way, Druce told me that someone said of my speech—it is the Oxford manner, but it falls from heaven! Not a very good night, but feel bucked up this morning and did a good deal of fair copy.'

Echoes of this speech came back to me from Mr. Druce and Mrs. Hopkinson and others, but no one could ever tell me just what it was that so impressed them all.

On July 24th. ' I was so absorbed in a novel which Layard lent me by a young friend of his, *When Bonds are Loosed*, though it was more grim than convincing, that I forgot to write my daily letter. Had rather an active day yesterday, down for half-hour's tennis on the time-table. Dixon, who was one of the four, said I must have the best man available to play with me to equalise matters, and selected Tizard; as a matter of fact, I played *quite* as well as Dixon and almost as well as T., so we won four sets in the half-hour—a record. I am writing this in working hours, so shall continue it before Hall . . . began Murray's *Euripides*; kept a chapel; X. keeps company with a Miss Y., and spends some time in cutting out a German "glad-eye," as such people seem to be called . . . Must tell you something that will please you before I forget it. I was just beginning to speak about Oxford novels, when Im Thurn said the best he had ever read was that of two ladies who paid a visit to Oxford; he was interested to know why you took the name of Barbara Burke. He had it in his library at Fiji. We must ask them to stay. He wants to take a walk in Bagley Wood. You must be up there now. Its nice to think what a good restful time you must be having too.'

August 3rd. 'Medical inspection to-morrow, at 6.30 a.m. I expect we shall go on again about noon. Lucas has given me an introduction to the Governor of Fiji, which I have sent on. I am due there September 1st. It will be very nice to have a few days with you and Noo before term, and a week-end at Willowgate. I hear that we shall just miss the mail at Adelaide. In fact I don't know that it will be any use posting before Vancouver, but Sir Everard calculates that I can just get in another letter from Melbourne by Tuesday week, which would reach you at end of September. I daresay I may hear from you at Honolulu, *via* Siberia. I may be tempted to send another ocean letter.' And to Oona: 'I have just won a croquet match at the last hole. My partner, such a nice and pretty girl, a daughter of the Archbishop of Australia. She won a prize as the "Scotch Lassie" in the fancy dress ball. There are some very nice children on board, mostly very young, and they seem to be enjoying themselves highly; also several dogs who would, I think, much prefer to be on land. I wonder how you did in examinations? I hope you may be having some French lessons on Boar's Hill.'

Then there is a blurred scrawl:

'4th August. All much excited and disquieted last night by war rumours. In the middle of a dance, rumour from Perth that war had been declared between Great Britain and Germany, and fighting taking place in North Sea—you may imagine our doubt and dismay. This morning another rumour about two English and nine German ships being sunk and of action in Russia and in France. If any of it is true it may mean that the meetings of B.A. will not take place. Hope we may hear it's only a rumour. Very glad to have got this letter off. . . .'

There was a picture postcard too—he just missed the old pupil who had awaited him now, in every other quarter of the globe.

'Cecil Andrews was here yesterday with a West Australian party—sorry to have missed him. Wild war rumours, but no confirmation.'

Confirmation came in Port Adelaide.

'August 8th. A deputation came on board to welcome us, including Prof. David (W. Scott's friend), a delightful man whom I missed at Oxford last term. He gave us a most lucid account of the course of events. What a truly "infamous" proposal Germany seems to have made.'

In Adelaide he went to see a very old friend of ours —she had sailed alone for Australia in 1910 at the age of seventy-seven.

'After lunch called on Emma, a nice little house right on the park before and behind. She came out of the house to greet me, looking very well I thought; very pleased with the big photo. Introduced to her niece—mother of a large family—who gave me tea, second cup of which I upset!'

Emma wrote three times that summer to tell me all about the visit and her pleasure in seeing Sidney, and the photographs of Oona Mary. In 1918 she wrote:

'I cannot tell you how grieved I am to hear of your great loss in the death of your noble husband . . . I have many times thought of his kindness, more than four years ago, in coming to see me, and the beautiful look he gave me in saying goodbye, when leaving Adelaide for other states in Australia. I could never forget that look.'

At Melbourne he stayed with kind and hospitable people, and he also vastly enjoyed a visit to Maryville.

'We are up here with a small privileged party of seventeen, including the Batesons and some of our Euripides folk, Mrs. Hopkinson, Dixey, and others, and four local people attending and guiding. Had a wonderful day, including picnic lunch and tea in the bush—an immense forest with beautiful streams and falls. Its by far the best excursion, and I owe my place in it to Henry Balfour, who had been drawn for it but could not spare the two days. We saw a very rare thing—a lyre bird in her nest at bottom of a tree; one egg only, but we saw the bird. At Melbourne took tea with Dr. Leaper (Behan's friend), old St. John's man, friend of Edmond Holmes and Sir W. Ramsey.'

When he got to Sydney he had a brother to see. They had not met for some twenty years.

'He seemed just the same old brother,' wrote Harry Ball to me in 1918, 'but I thought he was very thin, and I did not like the way he had to strain his eyes to read. The family will never seem the same without him. Its a great thing that I was able to see so much of him after such a long separation. I remember Sir Charles Lucas out here telling me that Sidney was quite the most popular man on board ship, and that they always liked to get him to make a speech, as he was quite the best speaker on the ship.'

It was into the hands of this brother that he had thrust his watch and chain, to comfort him on first going to school, some fifty years before.

At Sydney he 'saw a good deal of Fisher, the Labour premier, and W. M. Hughes, who asked me to see him here, the brains of the party, introduced me to Sam Turner and Dr. R. B. Gray.'

Here, too, he 'called at the shipping offices : was more than half minded to get away by P. and O. *Malwa*, but I couldn't get them to release me from my tickets *here*, and as I found Mrs. Hopkinson going by *Makura*, I finally decided to stick by *Makura* and go on meanwhile (for it does not sail until September 4th) to New Zealand for a week. I suppose this will mean that I shall arrive just too late for beginning of term instead of just too soon; but you must tell the President and Powell that I am held up by the war. Saw some of Harry's friends, including brother of Gilbert Murray; also Mrs. Todd and Dr. Todd (at *Evening News* Office) very keen on my seeing the Solomons; parents of our Solomon (the poet). Saw Hooton.' More St. John's men !

There was much gathering together of links on the *Riverina*, which took him across to New Zealand.

'Captain Webb, who runs the steamship company to N.Z., is one of the family I knew. He ordered the best berth in *Riverina* for me and to myself. We have a table to ourselves, Mrs. Hopkinson and I and Dr. and Mrs. Clowes (from Euripides), Ferrar from Egypt (had played tennis and poker with Hugh Jones—an old pupil), X. and Mrs. X., we saw arriving at Fenchurch Street—rather sombre, played quoits a good deal—an American Professor of Eugenics from Long Island (Davenport), Allorge (once at Oxford), Hobson, once of Madrid, now at Sheffield, and Woodward (geologist). Stocker, of B.N.C., also Gold (the meteorologist) and his wife (the Irish Pedlar of the Euripides Fancy Ball). I like them both. They play bridge . . . Auckland. Reached here Sunday. I made a speech which roused much enthusiasm on behalf of the B.A. Rutherford insisted that I should make the speech of the occasion, so a phophet has honour everywhere save in his own country! I have practically joined forces with Mrs. Hopkinson, who is very generous. But I shall be glad now to feel myself getting nearer home, tho' I am very glad I came on here. Please explain how I have been held up by the war and have been making ' imperialistic ' speeches in the interval ! '

Once before he had sent on to Honolulu the kindly-given letters to the Governor and to Mr. Frank Dawson, which were to ensure him such a pleasant welcome in Hawaii. That time illness prevented him from calling there. This time, though he crossed the Pacific in safety, the activities of the *Scharnhorst* and the *Gneisenau* made it unsafe to put in at Hawaii.

' Off to-day at five o'clock and hope to be home in about thirty days. We may, if it's quicker, try and transfer at Honolulu for San Francisco; if so I will wire, but I want to lose no time in getting home. A good time at Rotorua and the Governor gave me a railway pass, so it did not cost so very much. Spent one night at Waikaroa and went as far as Lake

Taupo. Found *My Father's Son* in a shop there and gave it to Mrs. Hopkinson.'

Mrs. Hopkinson has, with very great kindness, allowed me to quote the following extracts from her diary of that journey round the world in 1914.

'July 16th. Amongst those on board were Sidney Ball, the distinguished Oxford Scholar, who ranked high amongst our Euripides contingent.'

July 19th. There were one or two excellent speeches, especially an exquisitely witty one by the Treasurer of the Prize Fund—Mr. Ball. He is a quaint looking man but none suspected the depths of a charming wit. From beginning to end he kept us in fits of laughter.'

'Rotorua, Sept. 2nd. I write now sitting in a wide balcony gazing at the setting sun over the low green hills. Mr. Ball near by reading and also enjoying the peaceful scene. He is most attentive and good and kind. I shall look upon him as an Oxford brother; the other two are too solemn, but I am afraid we two laugh too much—all the experiences are so very odd.'

'Oct. 5th. I must record that, as we were sitting in the ship on Saturday, two journalists interviewed Dr. Ball and me. We wired in for all we were worth about the loyalty of the Colonies as we had passed through our Dominions. We thought it wise to get this broadcast. If it gets to German ears so much the better. It was very amusing being interviewed. This microcosm of a ship has lost its interest but Dr. Ball always remains the same, cultivated and kindly and, I am sure, of great and good influence on the young. Certainly Mr. Went, sub-editor of the *Nation*, adored him and spoke of him as 'the salt of the earth.'

To Oona he wrote, 'This is Single Tree Hill, where we motored on Monday. Had a splendid week at Rotorua among geysers and the Maoris. I have got

you a Maori charm. But I am really glad to be set
once more homewards as I want to see my little girl
badly and hope I shall not be made a prisoner of war
on the way. I hope you are very patriotic and following the war. DAD.'

So he sailed the Pacific at last. Saw Dr. and Mrs.
Logan (parents of a St. John's man) in Vancouver, in
1914 instead of in 1911, when he meant to have come
back that way, crossed the C.P.R. but had to go down
to New York for a boat and so came full circle home
once more.

III

WILLOWGATE

'The door of Death is made of gold,
That mortal eyes cannot behold:
But, when the mortal eyes are closed,
And cold and pale the limbs reposed,
The soul awakes, and, wondering sees
In her mild hand the golden keys.'

BLAKE. *Dedication of 'Blair's Grave.'*

SIDNEY had always taken the greatest delight in being
able to escape sometimes from the relaxing air in
Oxford to the hills which lie on either side of the
Thames Valley. For some years we had a small house
in Headington, which we bought chiefly as a home for
my old nurse. We spent some vacations there and had
one or two reading parties in it, but it developed in
course of time into an extremely popular lodging
house and the rooms which we furnished and kept,
in theory, for ourselves were constantly wanted. Also

as bicycling grew more general and distances diminished, we did not find it far enough away for the
absolute peace and quiet which are the essence of a
short 'breather.' When Sidney was examining in
'Greats' he took his papers up to 'Hedderleys,' a
lodging house known to and loved by many generations of Oxford men, on Boar's Hill. Here, on the
edge of a sandy ridge, one can look in all directions,
back upon Oxford, or to the Chilterns, or right across
Berkshire to the Wantage hills, to Dorchester, or to
Farringdon, or westward to the Mendips.

Here, in 1902, we had bought a very tiny piece of
land which was being sold, though we had but slender
hopes of ever being able to build. Finally, however,
a kind and valiant American friend bought the land
and built upon it the very house of our dreams, which
we were to take over from her should she cease to want
it and we be able to buy it.

In 1913 we began to take it over and to go there as
often as we could. Sidney took the greatest pleasure
in the little house, in making new friends on Boar's
Hill, and in welcoming the old ones from Oxford. A
few days before his death he was able to make arrangements for the final purchase of it. It was here that he
was badly ill in the autumn of 1915, and we stayed
on the hill through that term. The Boar's Hill friends
rallied round him and showered kindnesses upon us.
His old friend, Sir Arthur Evans, proved to be then,
as always, the best and most helpful of neighbours,
taking us into his own beautiful house while some
alterations were made at Willowgate, and bringing in
the breadth of a larger life and wider interests. Dr.
Robert Bridges came to see him and I will give here
the letter which he wrote to me eighteen months later.

'It is little consolation that one can hope to give in such a sorrow as yours, but I must write to assure you of my deep sympathy, and of my affection for Sidney, who always came to us as a friend rather than a visitor. The universal anxiety that was shown in Oxford during his last days was more than respect, and everyone must have admired the courage with which he faced his serious illness, and his unremitting activity when he could be of any use. I fear that may have provoked his sudden breakdown, but it is very noble to think of and will be a halo to his memory.'

One of the new Boar's Hill friends—Mr. Ernest Stenhouse—has sent some impressions of Sidney as he knew him during those last years.

'The outstanding impression which an all-too-short friendship with Sidney Ball left on my mind was of his great kindliness. This was very plainly no mere eupeptic amiability, for he was essentially sensitive and critical, but a steady impulse—as eager as it was unobtrusive—to help others whenever he could. Numberless instances of this occur to me, but not one case of hesitation or reluctance, even when his physical strength was obviously failing, and all effort must have been increasingly irksome.

'He was intensely interested in humanity, both in the mass and in individuals. I know little, except by hearsay, of his manifold public activities, but I was struck by the keen interest he always showed in the social life of our little community at Boar's Hill, his evident pleasure in keeping in touch with all his acquaintances, and his sympathetic concern in their affairs. This contributed in no small degree to the delightful character of the Sunday afternoons at Willowgate, when the Balls kept open house. The unaffected welcome accorded to casual acquaintances and personal friends alike, the host's genius for putting even the shy undergraduate at his ease, the good talk, made these gatherings a lasting pleasure to the memory. He enjoyed bringing together people he thought would be congenial. I remember many occasions when he called to say, "We are expecting so and so on such and such a day. If you are free you might come along. I think you would like him." I generally did "like him."

'It always seemed to me characteristic of the man that he found a great pleasure in expounding the subtleties of bridge to several of us who were mere novices, while he himself was a brilliant player. His invariable good humour and patience—even when his partner made glaring mistakes—his appreciation when any of us showed improvement, his triumphant chuckle on winning the odd trick with a small card everyone else had forgotten, are all good to remember.

'In conversation he was always striking, but curiously irregular. Quietly thoughtful remarks would give place, unexpectedly, to an animated torrent of speech, not always followed easily by those who did not know him well, and again to gentle banter as shrewd and penetrating as it was kindly. He was an appreciative listener, nodding or giving a characteristic grunt of acquiescence when he thought the speaker had made a point. He would often sit silently for a while, and then sum up the whole situation in a few terse phrases, with an unerring instinct for the *mot juste*, especially among adjectives.

'Ardent politician and sociologist, cultured scholar and polished man of the world as Sidney Ball was, he will be remembered most vividly, I think, as one who compelled the admiration and won the affection of his associates by sheer goodness.'

To the depression of his illness was added the sadness of the death of his sister, Mrs. Nance, the first of the family to go. Both his illness and her death must be added to the gloomy lists of war casualties on the home field. It seems difficult, now, to think how any-

one with ordinarily sensitive feelings survived those
days at all.   There was not even the excitement of
battle, or of new occupation, for the older people, only
the dull dreadful waiting upon events.   The death, in
July, 1918, of Guy Dickins, who seemed destined for
such a career of brilliant usefulness in his own subject
—Classical Archæology—and in the service of St.
John's, was a terrible blow.   It fell to Sidney to com-
pile the College 'Roll of Service.'   The short bio-
graphies of the fallen which appeared each week in
the *University Magazine* brought a good deal of comfort to the poor parents and were well worth the care
which Sidney spent upon them.   It was a horrible
thing to sit by and watch the ruin of so many hopes
and the piteous end of so much love and so many
years of careful teaching.   Sidney would have liked,
as it was his nature to like, to be 'in it' even in the
smallest possible way and, as late as March, 1918, he
offered a course of lectures to the Y.M.C.A.   The
official response was, however, rather damping :

'I communicated with France regarding subjects
that you suggested, but I find that the military authorities would not consider the History of Political Ideas
suitable. Of course we are obliged to avoid anything
like political propaganda, and I suppose that you did
not intend to introduce anything of the sort in connection with the subject that you sent in. Their caution
is extreme, however, but I fancy it must be some nervousness on that score which has influenced their
judgment.'

During the Summer Term of 1917 we stayed altogether at Willowgate, letting St. John's house to Mr.
and Mrs. Sanderson Furniss, of Ruskin College, while
Sidney went back into College during the week and

came up to us for week-ends. In the autumn, Oona Mary went to Miss Isabel Fry's Farm School, at Mayortorne, near Wendover, and Sidney's letters to her give glimpses of his life at that time. After he had taken her to school he writes:

'I had a good journey back. The Serbians considerately abstained from keeping their appointment, as I had heaps of letters to attend to, and a row between our pacifists and a new Canadian soldier student, crowded lecture—arranging for cadets at the Union. Article by me in to-day's *Educational Supplement* on Theological Students at Oxford. A great many women at my lecture this term.' He spared time every Sunday, and sometimes in the crowded week, to write to her with advice and sympathy. 'I don't see why you should not do some German. It is a useful language—though not very popular just now—and is rather hard at first but very easy afterwards, not so difficult to speak as French. I am glad that you are resolved to be a good Irish girl. You will get muscle in time and, meanwhile, I am glad you are getting some Latin, and also that you take mild "ragging" in good part. You shouldn't, however, hate Miss ——. She probably only wants to keep you up to the mark and is "cruel to be kind." I will try to tell you about Trinity Hall, Dublin, but don't you mean Trinity College, or is it the Hall for Women Students? Don't be more "flabby" than you can help; you will find yourself getting stronger and stronger at school.'

'Thank you so much for your jolly letter, in spite of its signals of (financial) distress. I enclose a book of stamps—as they certainly seem to be needful. I don't know whether I ought to send you as much as 10/- besides, but (1) it is difficult to send less; (2) I did offer it to you before if you had not enough, and (3) you have been a very good girl from our point of view. You should learn to keep regular accounts.

Nothing like it to "prevent waste." You certainly write a *very good letter*. I was asked by some of the Home Students to see some delightful plays they were acting for the Women's Hospital; two were by one of the Cherwell Edge Students and the last one (by Miss Jennings) called 'Poached Eggs and Pearls,' describing a romance and other doings in a Duchess's canteen, made me weep with laughter.'

He never lost his love of the play, and he was keenly interested in Oona's account of the '*Iphigenia in Tauris*,' which was being performed at Mayortorne.

'You will do the herdsman all right. Do it dramatically and don't be afraid to speak out. I have been looking at the play again and Mummy and Mary are reading it. You haven't got a very easy part but you must try to be *jubilant* and *excited* and give the long monologue all the character, intensity and variety of effect you can.' Then, in the P.S., which was such a familiar feature of his letters: 'Buck up, speak up and out (and not too fast)—as much "dramatic gesture" and variety as you can. Much disappointed I can't be there. Will meet you at Oxford.'

'I did so enjoy our visit to Mayortorne' (in March, 1918) 'and to the Miss Newby's (it seemed like a chapter out of Cranford). I liked all your friends, but scarcely saw enough of them to make invidious comparisons. I may come with Mummy some week-end to see you and then I may be able to give you my opinion on some of the people I have seen, but you know I am full of charity and goodwill and don't dislike more than I can help. Most people have something to like in them.'

'Write me as one that loves his fellow men' had always been his attitude towards life and it was still his at the approaching end of it. He took a frank pleasure in welcoming 'persons of distinction,' and perhaps an even greater pleasure in bringing others to meet them.

On Shrove Tuesday, 1918, he wrote to Oona about what was to be the last of many jolly teas that he had given in the Common Room at St. John's.

'Did Mummy tell you of my tea in Common Room? W. B. Yeats and wife, Mrs. Bretherton, Mrs. Masefield, Andrèic̀ (especially to meet Mr. Yeats), Godjevatz, Iovanovic and others,' and he sent her a little vignette of a chance meeting on Boar's Hill, where Mr. and Mrs. John Masefield had come to live just across the road. 'Mr. Asquith was at the Masefields last Sunday, and I had a few moments' talk with him. He said he had been told (by the maid) that Masefield was feeding the rabbits and asked me if this was "probable."'

Mrs. Michael Howard and her twin babies were then in St. John's House and he chronicles a visit to them.

'Mummy and I had tea with Mrs. Howard and the twins the other day—you should have seen me supporting both of them on the armchair.' That was to be the last time that I was with him in his own study. He sat in the chair which we called 'The Chair of the Grateful Pupils' and we placed a twin on either arm. It is a pleasant picture to look back upon.

Perhaps, of the many forms that his hospitality took, the one that gave him the greatest pleasure was to have the chance of giving a good time to anyone who had been able to give a good time to him. Such a chance arose during these last months of his life and he was able to welcome Mr. William T. Ellis, whom he had met during his Eastern journey and in whose home in Swarthmore, Pennsylvania, he had stayed. He brought him to Willowgate, took him to lunch with

Sir Arthur Evans, so that he might talk to him on Near Eastern matters—he had just returned from Russia—called together the friends and neighbours on the Hill to hear him talk, and collected some representative people from Oxford, including two American doctors; then he took him down to St. John's and gave him the best that war time Oxford could afford.

On May 10th, the Sunday before he was taken ill, he wrote his last letter to Oona :

' My Darling Girl,

' I am very remorseful to feel that I have left your jolly little letter so long unanswered. But I have been particularly busy with Serbian " collections " and other business, a " Citizens'" Association and Juvenile Organisations' Committee, a great many women pupils and others, and arranging for receptions of our American allies. Last Sunday, too, I gave a " talk " to a meeting of the Socialist Society (including Bilić and Mrs. Petersen and her daughter) on Karl Marx, the great German Socialist, on the centenary of his birth. Miss Fry may tell you something about his theory of value and " iron law of wages " (just been rung up by an American). Tell Miss Fry that the books I recommend on Political Economy are *Gide* (this is a large book), Symes' *Political Economy* and Ely and Whicker's *Elementary Economics* (last edition Anglicanised)—also Clay's *Economics* (very fresh and readable, but rather off the lines of the ordinary and conventional text-books). I think it would interest her. I could lend her any of these books—*Gide* perhaps now, when my boys go in for their diploma on June 3rd. I had got for you *Tommy's Tunes*, but asked Brooks, an old Tommy, to look it through for me, and we came to the conclusion it was too " vulgar " in parts for Mayor-torne, so I sent you Kipling instead. Have you read his " Recessional "? You should. Yesterday, I came up early—had tea with the Foxes (Stenhouses also there). Mrs. Fox wanted to make me envious of her garden, which I told her I was already at first sight. I then went down to the Stewarts, had a cigar with him in the garden, and then played him at golf. Mummy came in afterwards and we had a foursome. Mrs. Stewart and I beat Mummy and Mr. Stewart rather easily. I played unequally, but creditably on the whole. Here's some news : the whole Walker family came in to tell us, with much jubilation (just down to the P.O. to collect Sunday papers and heard some more news, of which more later), their good news, that he had got an appointment at Portsmouth (where he goes on Wednesday) with a commission. They are wonderfully pleased and, if Ian gets into the Navy, it will be perfect. Ian felt very sorry he might not see you before he goes (you might write him a line). Now for the other, less good, news. I met Mr. and Mrs. Bretherton in Sou'westers (been to see the pigs) and they told me he had received a telephone order to go to Dublin to take charge of a depot. Mrs. Bretherton would like to join him, but won't venture the children again on the sea. They may be coming into tea with her mother. The Grahams also are coming so we must avoid Ireland. So glad you are taking so much to Italian and French. You will find them both a great resource in every way. Greetings to Noel and fondest love from your ever loving Dad.'

He was very busy with, and much interested in, the arrangements for the visit to Oxford of some members of the American University Union in Europe. His old acquaintance, Mr. Anson Phelps Stokes, of Yale, was Chairman of the Union, and Mr. Van Dyke and Professor Nettleton were on the Executive in Paris. It was always a great delight to him to come into any connection with, or to be able to be of any service to,

Americans. The League of Nations' Society asked him on May 9th to serve on a Special Committee to 'consider the possibilities of interesting those concerned in Education in the principle of a League of Nations.' He had been helping with a private conference of the National Housing and Town Planning Council, convened by Mr. Shawcross. The Secretary of the Society of 'New Ideals in Education' wanted his help to settle her plans for a projected Conference in August. He was in full correspondence with Father Hodge, of the Cowley Mission, over the City of Oxford Juvenile Organisations' Committee. He was throwing himself with all his old vigour and energy into the founding of a Citizens' Association for Oxford. He was preparing four of the Serbian Undergraduates for the Diploma in Economics, and was giving much time and thought to the committee work connected with the Serbian Settlement in Oxford and, as always, taking a keen personal interest in the welfare of the students. He was constantly asked by the Women's Colleges to take their students as pupils and he could not bear to refuse. Above all, and through all, there was the terrible strain of the war and the daily dreadful toll of life which was the inevitable price of that victory which Sidney Ball was not to see in this world. He promised that in July we should go away together for a quiet holiday and he would really rest. Perhaps we might go to Caswell Bay, where we went in 1917—'It was such a success.'

He came to Willowgate in the evening on the Saturday before Whit Sunday, after a full day of teaching, of Committees, and of many engagements. One of the last things that he did in Oxford was to show Miss May Morris, at the Union, the photographs of the

frescoes painted on its walls, so many years before, by
her father and his friends. The heat was terrible and
he was tired after his long hot ride up the hill. He
enjoyed that evening to the full, the hot bath, and the
change, and dinner in the garden. Of all things that
he loved, a good story for hours of relaxation came
first, and I have always felt grateful to the unknown
friends who wrote the stories that pleased and satisfied
him. Over his pipe that night he read Miss I. A. R.
Wylie's *The Flight of the Duchess*, and put it down
with a little sigh of pleasure—'Quite a good story.'
On Whit Sunday he spent his usual half-restful, half-
strenuous, Sunday morning. Sir Arthur Evans came
in to talk about the Serbs, and a good neighbour on
the Hill with news of her son. After lunch he sat out
in the shade of the house making notes in Bagehot's
Economics for his next lesson with the Serbs. Then
he came in and put down the book with his pencil
between the pages and the beloved pipe beside them.
'I don't feel very well,' he said quietly, and then he
fainted and fell.

I do not think that he had any hope of his own
recovery. He knew that he had fought a great fight
and that the battle was not for him any more. Sister
Leah, from the Serbian Hostel, came to be with him
the first night and gave him all her great care and
skill. His old friend, Dr. Collier, came in consultation
and gave us faint hope that he might be spared to us.
His only anxiety was that messages might be sent
about his lectures which Mr. Duncan Hall, of Sydney,
most kindly undertook to read for him, about the many
tasks which had to be laid down and engagements to
be put off. The heat was stifling until a great storm
of wind and rain and thunder beat over the house the

night before he died. The goodness of friends is a wonderful thing to look back upon and a sure tribute to the memory of what he was and of what he meant, and will always mean, to so many. All the history of that time seems to be written in terms of his great goodness and unselfishness, of his constant thought for others, of his utter selflessness. His thoughts were for the difficulties and troubles of the world that he was leaving, for the College to which he had given so much of his life, for the Citizens' Union, for and through which he had hoped that strength might be left to him to do so much. He had words of praise and thanks for the doctors and the nurses—'Each so good in her own different way.' 'Is there any chance for me?' I heard him ask Dr. Gillett, but I do not think that he hoped for, or wished for, a definite answer. Later on, Dr. Collier wrote to me :

'I want you to realise that what is your loss was, most probably, his gain. When one found, as one did on May 21st, that he had an inflammation of his heart sac, the pericardium, one felt that, if he recovered, he would have been almost certainly crippled for the rest of his life and would have had to give up active work. When one remembers what an active brain he had, and what an active life he led, one felt that death to him would be more merciful than a life of invalidism.'

Towards the very end he spoke of all that it had fallen his lot to do, hardly at all of what he had suffered. 'They have their majority,' he said once, and he cried out, 'I was dreaming, was I dreaming?' He was conscious to the last. Almost at the end he gave a great cry—'I feel my energy returning.'

One of his last and greatest interests lay in what he was able to do for the Serbian students. He had

spent most of his last vacation with them at the Hostel
in North Oxford. An address illuminated by one of
them, ' To our Great Protector from his boys,' had
given him extreme pleasure. So far as it was possible
for them to do so they made up to him for his lost
pupils. He wrote the motto of his old school—
' Heroum Filii '—on a notice of some sports for them
at Youlbury and hung it on the gate of Willowgate as
they passed by. The following letters show, more than
any words of mine could do, how they felt about him.

The Serbian Minister in London, M. Iovanovic,
wrote :

' It was a great blow to me, and to all my country-
men, to hear so unexpectedly that your husband had
passed away. We lose in him one of our best and most
helpful friends and I do not see how he can be re-
placed as head of those in charge of the boy's colony
in Oxford. You will forgive this being the first thought
we had on hearing the sad news, but I can assure you
that our sympathy with you is most sincere, and if there
is any way in which I can show it I shall consider it a
privilege to do so.

' I was just expecting my Government's approval of
my proposal to award Professor Ball a Serbian decoration[19] in recognition of his untiring efforts, and when
the Order arrives I shall venture to send it on to you,
as you may like to keep it as a souvenir.'

Gradimir Kosamarić wrote :

' In the name of all the Serbian undergraduates in
Oxford, may I be allowed to bring these scanty expressions of our profoundest regret, unspeakable afflic-
tion and unexpressive pain. All are griefshot.

' Painfully conscious of what the irreparable, irre-
missible loss of the greatest friendship of the most

[19] The Third Order of St. Sava, the Scholar Saint of Serbia.

sincere friend, Mr. Ball, conveys to us, we cannot conceive of it.'

Kosamarić wrote also on behalf of the Serbian Literary and Debating Society :

'Our deepest sympathy with you. There is nobody to encourage, nobody to help : our dear Vice-President has left us for good, great as the loss of our Honorary Vice-President is we are unable to express even the smallest part of what we feel and think.

'We are so very sorry to have heard of Mr. Ball's surprised death; of the death of our *really* second father, who all the time has been working for every one of us and always was showing us the greatest care and interest in us and who never stopped showing it equally well, until he absolutely could not.

'Our second father and his brilliant deeds we can never forget and one should never forget; for what he has done for common good of us all is more than anyone could expect, of such an aged man.

'He indeed has left us in an exceedingly deep sorrow, that we cannot at all express and analyse it at such a rate that we feel it.

'There really are no words which could express our sorrow and could offer our deepest sympathy.

'We all have a photograph of our benefactor in our hearts and shall all preserve it until we shall meet in heaven.

'Again we most deeply sympathise and send you our kindest regards.'

The members of the St. Sava Society.

Alexander Bilić, one of the four who were reading with him for the Diploma in Economics, wrote :

'I do not have enough the words how to express my deepest sympathy on the loss which has befallen you and your daughter. You know quite well what the late Mr. Ball has been to us, namely so much that, if

WITH THE SERBIAN STUDENTS, APRIL, 1918.

Photo by Soame, Oxford.

To face p. 170.

I compare the loss, when I got the news that my father has died, whom I had not seen for so long time, and this loss now, believe me, I could not tell which is the greater loss to me. I forget, perhaps, somewhat easily my father, because I found another one, whom, I doubt, I will ever forget. There are two or three things in this world for which I was willing to sacrifice everything, even my life, and one of them was the late Mr. Ball. By this very unjust death three fourths of all my plans for the future life-work seems suddenly destroyed. I know so much that my future is now not so bright as it was recently, nor even as yesterday morning. The only thing that I would like to ask you is, that you will allow me to share a little part if not more of your's and you daughter's great sorrow. Please will you accept my deepest sympathy and condolence and I do not know what else because I myself need it, because I am weeping bitterly.'

In looking back now over all those twenty years at St. John's House, we went into it at Christmas, 1898, and Oona and I returned to it from Boar's Hill to break it up and leave it in September, 1918, one sees now that the real division of time came there, as it came to so many, in 'Before the War' and 'After the War.'

'Nothing will be the same again,' said Sidney, when the old jolly days in which he could welcome so much young life to his home came to an end, and we went to economise at Willowgate.

On that last day, May 16th, 1918, when we were together in Oxford it seemed, on looking back, strangely fitting that he should have taken me to see the matriculation of the last man whom he was to receive as an undergraduate of St. John's College. Mr. Humphreys was then at Somerville Hospital and

SIDNEY BALL
bed to be brought in his chair to the steps of the
Clarendon Building, where the Vice-Chancellor matri-
culated him.

On May 24th he wrote to me.

3RD SOUTHERN HOSPITAL.

SOMERVILLE.

OXFORD.

VACATIONS AND READING PARTIES

And in my dreams I still may go
To Brescia or to Bergamo;
    To Cortona or Ravello,
    To Urbino and to Spello,
Cushendall, or Achill Island, or Kilkee,
To Albenga and Alassio by the sea;
Or where those blessed islands lie
The Isle of Sark, the Isle of Skye.

Holidays in Retrospect.

NO one, I think, who has ever experienced life in
Oxford, or who has seen and understood what
Term means to a conscientious and public-spirited
man, could or would grudge him the relief of Vacation.
No one so highly-strung, so far from strong, and so re-
sponsive to his environment as Sidney Ball, could have
existed so long as he did without spending what may
have seemed to some an undue proportion of a small
income on change of scene and rest. Whenever it was
possible, therefore, he put the Channel, at least, between him and his work. In September, 1909, he
joined the Booth liner *Anselm* and went to Portugal.
A postcard to his little girl gave a tiny picture, 'Dropping the pilot.' 'I watched the pilot being dropped
last night,' he wrote to her. He must have thought of
Tenniel's great drawing, of the many pilots who have
been unwisely dropped too soon and, perhaps, of the
new pilot just taken on at St. John's.

'We took another up this afternoon from the Lizard
to Havre. I suppose Nanny has gone now. I hope you

are taking good care of Mummy. Daddy finds it hard to keep awake.' To me he wrote, 'All my troubles dropped away at once.'

Sidney's good nature often got us into difficulties, and we returned home from a Christmas at Alassio, where Mrs. Rathbone had lent us her lovely villa, the caretakers of one schoolboy, one priceless gold watch to be mended in London, and a precious bank-book, two large tins of tunny preserved in oil as presents to Mrs. Rathbone, from her Italian servants, and an enormous wax doll.

We travelled in those days with a tea-basket—for the restaurant-car did not exist then—and it brought its own adventures. I remember the tiny custom-house outpost in the Dolomites, on our walk from Primiero to Agordo, and the doubts aroused by the tea, from which the *douanier* took a pinch and sniffed at suspiciously. Another time we made tea for a German gentleman in the train, and he said that the only way in which he could reward such goodness was by reciting to us his own translation of Hamlet's soliloquy, which he there and then did. Sidney delighted, too, to tell the story of our meeting at the hotel Byron at Ravenna with a pleasant old gentleman who upbraided us for travelling with a German Baedeker instead of an English 'Murray.' He turned out to be Sir Lambert Playfair and he had himself written Murray's guide for that part of the world, which he was, he owned, then visiting personally for the first time. He persuaded us to stay at Pesaro and to go with him to San Marino for the half-yearly elections of the rulers of that ancient, though small, Republic. The kind old gentleman was not up to going at the last minute, for we had to start at 4 a.m., but he insisted on sharing the expense of the carriage, and for that interesting and entertaining memory we owe him many thanks.

Then there were our three visits to Ireland, the first in 1892, of which one, who became a great friend, has sent me such kindly recollections.

'In the autumn of "'92,"' writes Lady Byles, 'we were fortunate enough to collide with Mr. and Mrs. Sidney Ball in an ancient hotel omnibus in Londonderry. Before we reached the station we realised, in part, our good luck, and the delightful companionship they thenceforward accorded to us made our wanderings in Donegal peculiarly delightful. Dunfanaghy, Horn Head, Gweedore, the Rosses, Carrick, Slieve League, then across Donegal Bay to Mullaghmore in a fishing-boat diligently cleaned up for the occasion, every step of the way was illuminated and adorned. Mr. Ball jumped into the heart of the Irish question and all its problems with swift understanding and vision. Father James McFadden—a true, wise father of his people—put us in touch with local history and difficulties, and drove us himself along the romantic sea-girt road to the Rosses, where we stumbled into characteristic Irish hospitality. The leading man of the district was expecting Dr. McDonnell, the beloved Bishop of Raphoe, on a pastoral visitation, and the English travellers were forthwith set to share the bountiful meal prepared for him—a feast as great in its carnal way as the intellectual, political and social intercourse with the Bishop.

'We were beset by every sort of weather—the best and the worst—but nothing marred those happy days. One thing sticks in my mind—Mr. Ball's delight on finding on the mountain road to Glen Columbkille an upland tarn called Lough Oona, "named after my wife," as he insisted.'

Our visit to Ireland in 1912 leaves some vivid memories of a visit to 'Sir Horace,' at Kilteragh, of the gathering bidden there to see the aeroplane race across the Mourne Mountains from Belfast, of Æ. and Susan Mitchell, of 'George Birmingham' and Katherine Tynan and James Stephens and many another, of the kindness of the Miss Yeats at Dundrum and of the Abbey Theatre plays to which they took us, of Mr. Lennox Robinson and Miss Sara Algood. Then the visit to Bob Barton[19] and his sisters at Glendalough and the remembrance of bidding him good-bye on his doorstep and of the curious feeling that I somehow saw then in his face a forecast of what was to come. That year, too, we went on to Belfast and saw old Campbell College pupils, and were entertained and looked after by them and their kindly pleasant people.

As the years passed away the host of pupils, past and present, increased and the circle of Sidney's interests widened, each interest bringing with it its own circle of friends. It was seldom that we went anywhere without meeting a St. John's man or, at any rate, a friend of one. Only once can I remember a time when Sidney did not recognise instantly the immaculately dressed man whom he had last seen, perhaps, in a battered cap and tattered gown or in the extremely negligent attire which was at one time 'the thing' in the undergraduate world of Oxford. Or it might be some rather prim curate in whom he was called upon to recognise the dashing pupil of many years before.

Mr. William Snow has kindly written for me about one of the reading parties before my time.

'Though I was not a member of St. John's College, I came to know Mr. Ball through my brother, T. C.

[19] T.D., County Wicklow.

Snow, than whom he had no more devoted admirer. In 1888 we were invited to stay for a week with a reading party which Mr. Ball had at Strands, near the foot of Wastwater; and I well remember that the letter of invitation contained the words, "Mind your brother brings his banjo"! (I had not, and never have had a banjo; but the rumour that I was a performer had somehow spread.) My keenest recollection of the stay at Strands is of an excursion up Scaw Fell on a boiling day in the middle of a very wet summer. Mr. Ball led all the way and negotiated some difficult rocks between Scaw Fell and the Pike in a manner that impressed us all. I am not sure that he was justified in taking a dozen inexperienced youths by such a difficult route; but he probably credited us with his own skill and fearlessness.

'The following year he invited W. G. Salmon, of Jesus, and myself to join his party at Sark, and now, after thirty-one years, some of the incidents of that time stand out very clearly in my mind. Here is one of them. One morning it leaked out that it was my birthday, and the whole party adjourned to the only shop on the island to buy me presents. Among these were a cabbage, a cigar, a bust of General Gordon in soap, and a box of matches. In the course of the morning an old St. John's man arrived on the steamer to pay a short visit. When Mr. Ball saw him he said: "Here's that fellow, Witherby. I'll throw Snow's cabbage at him," which he did, following it up with the bust and the cigars.

'The bathing at Sark is very good, and of course we were in the water every day. I have spoken above of Mr. Ball's boldness on the Sca Fell. He was in his element bathing at Sark. I have never seen anyone make such daring dives, dives which he would not allow any of us to attempt (not that we wished it), over rocks hidden or exposed, from heights which appeared to us impossible.

'Nor must I forget our evenings when work was done, and before whist was started (there was no bridge in those days). H. A. V. Ransom was at the piano, and many and varied were the songs. The chorus in particular, evolved I know not how, was a favourite with Mr. Ball.

> "Then gather the children round the Great Preceptor,
>   And roll the Pupil Teacher on the floor,
> You'll seldom find a person that's inepter,
>   For he's fit for little more than Littlemore!"

The "Great Preceptor" was, of course, Mr. Ball; the "Pupil Teacher" was the late W. G. Pogson-Smith, then a young Don at St. John's; and Littlemore was the Oxfordshire County Lunatic Asylum.

'Only once was the perfect harmony and good-fellowship of the party interrupted, and that was when two men conducted two island maidens home after a concert. Mr. Ball was terribly angry, and said that such conduct was "damnable, damnable, DAMNABLE!"

'I should mention that Mr. Ball had a huge tin of tobacco always full, and that all were welcome to fill their pipes from it.

'Mr. Ball was a kind and wise teacher, a sympathetic friend, and a boy among boys. It was a sad time when the eight weeks came to an end.

'A year later, Mr. Ball informed me of a post for which he thought I was suited, and which would suit me. I obtained it and held it for nearly eight years. And it must be remembered that I was not his pupil, nor even a member of his College, only the impecunious brother of a friend.

'I last saw him in 1915, at Willowgate, where I took my brother, now an invalid, from Oxford in my motor bicycle sidecar. I shall not soon forget that garden in the mellow August afternoon, and the sparkling, allusive, very Oxonian conversation of two great intellects.

'It is a privilege for me to be allowed to lay my tiny wreath upon the grave of so good and great a man.'

Sidney's prowess as a diver was sometimes put to strange uses. I remember vividly the dismay which seized upon a picnic party in Achill Island in 1903, when the key of the food hamper was dropped into the sea, and the relief which followed when Sidney dived for and secured it.

The first reading party after our marriage was in Sark in the Summer of 1892. Mr. Pogson-Smith, who had been one of Sidney's first pupils and was then among the most promising and brilliant of young Oxford Dons, came too, and we went to Miss Robins, at Rose Cottage, where we had gone on our wedding journey six months before. I cannot help thinking, when I review this episode, after eight and twenty years, that I must have been something of an embarrasment and not a little of a nuisance on that party. I remember with contrition that some of the men took me out fishing with them and my persistent and genuine raptures as we heaved gently up and down on the Channel swell met with a more perfunctory appreciation from the rest of the party, while their polite offers to go home on my account fell upon deaf ears. Not until long, long afterwards did I realise that our return at last was a forced one, and that the compliments I received, when safely on land, on my being such a very good sailor, were so charged with meaning.

In the Easter Vacation, 1896, Sidney started off with the party for Broadway, where we had found ideal lodgings, and I joined them later. One of his letters chronicled, ' I told the men that you were coming, and they said, "Oh, good business."' This was cheering and encouraging, and Sidney's letters gave hints of the way in which I might prove to be of use.

'The men seem very satisfied. They found Miss Stanley "wonderfully cheap" and everything clean and nice—except the cutlery—but thought you might brighten it up. They had finished tea, but I had a little and then undid the stores in the back yard. They seemed touched with your attentions'—which must, I think, have been expressed in sweets. 'Johnson is sleeping over the butcher's. He likes the view on "the street," but now thinks he would have liked a room over the farm-yard, from which he could have catapulted sparrows.' And again, 'I found that Johnson had my Politics; he is now catapulting at a cork!' Or 'Johnson looks very nice in his Sunday get-up (he hopes to change in the middle of the day into "something else" —has made arrangements for a *plank* instead of a feather bed.' Johnson was always one of those who enter into life with simplicity and thoroughness, and his residence over the butcher's led to an entry in Sidney's next letter. 'Johnson has been seeing a pig killed.' It was Johnson's splendid old father—Admiral Johnson—who said of this party, when his son had sailed with some difficulty into the port of a 'safe pass,' 'It was that cruise to Broadway that did it; he never would have passed except for that cruise.' There was a very exciting boat race that year and 'we had a sweep on the Boat Race last night. I drew "the Idea of the Good"—Atkinson the extra egg for breakfast—Rogers, Cambridge, which Johnson, having already Oxford, bought up.' Sidney was very near to his own birthplace of Pershore and there were one or two families of cousins living near to it. 'The Shelmerdines have asked us all over to tea on April 7th,' he writes, and 'The men are certainly very nice and seem to appreciate my being here. They are most attentive and often ask when you are coming.' He was just beginning to be very keen on bicycling and on golf. 'Yesterday, we rode to Tewkesbury—sixteen to seventeen miles—then on to Deerhurst—another four —(over ploughed fields as we lost our way), where there is a pre-Norman Church and Saxon Chapel— then back by the tow-path of the Severn (grass and rather hard work, as there was a high wind)—had an excellent lunch at the Hop Pole and saw the Abbey. I had no idea how fine it was. I found myself rather done during the journey back. We left Broadway at 10.30 and were back before five. Roberts and Johnson stayed behind—put in a church and went a long walk. French, Roberts and Hollis, went in the evening and so did I. The Vicar is quite an orator in his way. Miss Tennant had got us fowls for yesterday's dinner, so they were postponed. A large ham lasted us exactly four days. Hollis, Johnson and Atkinson have joined the golf club, so I hope to have plenty of play. I didn't do so badly with the Doctor on Saturday. The men are all practising their new clubs on the Green in front of Miss Tennant's, to the general entertainment. Played "snooker pool" (very badly) with Hollis (very good), Taylor and Johnson last night. This afternoon we had a bicycle ride—five of us—to Winchcombe and Sudeley Castle—very nice. I ran into a drove of horses coming back; the showman to whom they belonged told me I was "a nice sort of fellow racing yourself as well as the horses" and told the others that I ought to be under control. Miss T. caters excellently —breakfast, ham and boiled eggs; lunch, cold meat and pickles and cheese; dinner, a great hot joint, milk pudding and fruit and cheese. The men eat greatly. My article is out; they have sent me two numbers. Would you like one?' (This was the article in *The International Journal of Ethics*, which developed later into his well-known Fabian tract, 'The Moral Basis of Socialism.')

'It is a pleasant party and they all laugh at my

jokes, and generally are very considerate and pleasant, also they are no trouble as they are all reading history.' And again, 'It has been a great success—as pleasant a party as I have had, and they read eight hours a day. Had a quiet morning here all by myself; the men are all finishing their Herodotus—not much abandon at table so far—I do most of the talk and badinage! Atkinson and Taylor ("Science men") are forming a combination against Greats shop, but Johnson rather likes it. A. and T. had a "run" this morning before breakfast. J. has his fiddle with him—piano not tried yet. Some of us find the place "soporific." We saw Mary Anderson just now.' Madame de Navarro had just settled into a lovely old Cotswold house in Broadway. Sidney had once had the pleasure of conducting her over St. John's, when, in the zenith of her fame, she came to Oxford to visit Professor and Mrs. Max Müller.

Capt. Corbett-Fisher writes of his time at West Bay in 1902 : 'It was Darton who told Barrett and myself one night after Hall that we were to join Sidney Ball's reading party at West Bay in the coming Easter Vacation. The prospect of a holiday in delightful country with golf and other games and pleasant companions would have been enough to make the invitation instantly acceptable. But this was not a case for acceptance or refusal. If you can imagine Lord Northcliffe refusing to join the Supreme Council, or an athletic undergraduate declining the honour of a Blue, you can imagine either of us refusing to go to West Bay. For me and, I think for Barrett[20] too, life at the moment had not much to offer. We felt that we had attained one of our highest ambitions and were henceforth numbered amongst the elect. For we were, indeed, being admitted to a very exclusive circle. But, apart from the ensuing odour of sanctity and success, and

[20] Killed, 1917.

above it in our estimation, was the opportunity now first offered of close association with a don who seemed to be regarded as a super-man by the men who read with him. Up to then I had had a bare half-dozen interviews with him, and, of these, two had been more embarrassing than pleasant to me. But the magnificence of his character had begun to influence me even then, long before I knew him for the most gentle, kind, honourable and just of men. It may seem strange that I, who was much more attached to games and other diversions than to anything that might be called serious, should have been irresistibly attracted by a learned philosopher who spent his day at work and was seldom seen without a pile of books and papers under his arm; yet not so strange when I recall the second of my interviews with him, only a day or two after my landing in College fresh from Ireland, like a fish out of water. I was to matriculate at 2.30 and play football at 2.30: and when I asked him, as my tutor, how it was to be done, he told me to get ready and meet him in the Lodge at 2 o'clock. At that hour, when I had been decently disguised in cap and gown, he took me before the Vice-Chancellor, explained the situation, got him to hasten the ceremony, hurried me out again to hand over my scholarly clothes to the waiting boy, and set me safely on my way to the Parks in time for the game. And this was at the beginning of the October term, when Senior Tutors with even less to do than he have only a few minutes to spare for breakfast and less for lunch: and I was a very obscure freshman hardly yet known by name at the College gate.

'Our day at West Bay was divided very much like a day at College: work in the morning, play from luncheon to tea-time, work from tea to dinner, cards for the hour which at Oxford we should spend in the J.C.R.; and work from about 9.30 till bed-time. Barrett and I, for whom Greats were still more than two

years distant, seldom stayed up till eleven. But the
serious worked till about twelve; and S.B. often
stayed later still after his regular work was done, perhaps writing a testimonial for X, or completing plans
for placing Y, who was going to get a Third and
seemed unlikely ever to find a place for himself.
How many hours, when he might have been free, he
spent in helping lame dogs, only himself and the
generations he helped could tell. The junior members
worked in the dining-room—a very pleasant room,
especially on a sunny morning. I can see Barrett now,
at the table making entries in his commonplace book
in the exquisite handwriting which I envied, or absorbed in " The City State," or " The Meaning of the
Good," which he had chosen as his introduction to
Greats. I was generally busy with the little blue-
bound translation of the Republic—I was a poor
scholar. Once or twice each morning S.B. would come
quietly in, and give us a short discourse. At times, a
smack entering the harbour would claim my attention.
The call of the open air was hard to resist. But Barrett
scarcely ever moved from his table between ten and
a quarter to one, when Mrs Harris came in to lay the
table for luncheon. Once, and only once, I induced
him to play truant : and we went out to the third tee,
which was out of sight from the Pier Terrace window,
and played for three-quarters of an hour. At luncheon,
when someone asked whether we found it easier to
work outside, S.B. only said that he hoped we would
not corrupt any of the others. Thereafter, morning
golf had no attraction.

' The course was then a short nine holes, which we
should easily have covered twice between two and four-
thirty. But, good cricketers as some of the party were,
we were none of us golfers; and I believe no one
succeeded in playing eighteen holes without encroach-
ing on the working hours. It might have been done
had the way been all downhill, or the stone wall at the

AT STUDLAND.

AT WEST BAY.

To face p. 184.

second hole provided with more and wider gaps, or the rushes which stopped the hard drive along the ground less thick and well placed. It was at the rushes that the lucky couple who held the niblick for the day easily went ahead. But fiercest of all the obstacles was the quarry, many fathoms deep, which lay right across the drive at the top of the hill. Sometimes we were all in it together, and the clanging of iron on stone must have been heard down at the harbour, particularly when Darton or Raphael was at work : for they were powerful men. There was an easy way round it. But the conscience of the moralists, and the hope that springs eternal even in the very worst of duffers, forbade any to take it. Judging by my own play now and what I have seen on my occasional meetings with some of the others, we did not learn much of the art of golf. But we got a remarkable lesson in self-control. Not even a three minutes' engagement with the rushes could force from S.B. anything stronger than his favourite "Bother." No misadventure—and he had his full share—ever drove him to use violent words or ruffled his temper. In restraint of language I have known only one who was his equal, and that one started with the advantage of a long ancestry whose conversation was chiefly "Yea, yea," and "Nay, nay."

'The hour's card-playing after dinner took place upstairs in S.B.'s room. On my first visit it was whist, at which he, Macrory,[21] Lloyd and Darton were as good a four as one could wish for. Barrett, Hills and myself were also members of the College Whist Club, but played a much inferior game, knowing not Cavendish. Barrett was not really a card-player at all. He joined in for the sake of company, but had no love for any card game. He hated being dragged from his half-easy chair with the book-rest and Marcus Aurelius, to make up a four. Hills, who had taken to cards in his comparative old age, was tremendously keen;

[21] Died a few months later.

but at that early stage in his gambling career, the slowest player I have even seen. Just when it was that S.B. told us he had found a new game for us I forget. I think he produced it without warning as we were settling down one evening. And with the help of a book of rules and a few minutes of his tuition we began a new epoch. Thus bridge came to College. By the middle of the following term it had the entry to practically every room. We played no more bridge at West Bay. I am told S.B. often blamed himself afterwards for the harm he had done. He had little cause to feel guilty more than any innocent agent of an inevitable revolution. I can hardly think that he accepted the responsibility for its introduction beyond our own College. And as to that, though the fever spread, as I have said, and in time, though not in my time, killed whist in its own temple after a great struggle, it never became with us the absorbing time-waster which it presently was at a neighbouring college, where ninety-six men were counted playing on a Friday night at ten o'clock, an hour when some at least of them must have been supposed by dons or parents to be at their books. I confess I played more than was good for me, and perhaps helped others to do likewise. But if any Class was lost which should have been gained, it is safe to say that another game would have filled the wasted hours had bridge never been invented.

'Golf and cards were not our only games. For a quarter of an hour or so between breakfast and the morning's work we took sides at quoits, the materials for which were supplied by S.B. and brought down in his own luggage. At this recondite game there was little to choose between us. If anyone excelled it was himself, who may have got his skill playing at odd moments in the quadrangles of Oriel, as we in our day played bowls in St. John's gardens. Also we bathed. My first year there Easter was cold, and there were days when some of the party were missing at the appointed hour. One morning with snow on the ground S.B. and I went out alone, with much conscious virtue. I think I might have shirked had it not been that bathing ensured my getting early to breakfast, which was important. For there was one who loved to steal a march on all who lingered in bed, and devour their portions. He had a passion for fried eggs. And Mrs. Harris, who was more than punctual, played into his hands. I have it only on hearsay and state it with all reserve, that one morning he put on her kitchen clock by five minutes, and she, unsuspicious soul, put the dishes on the table as her clock struck eight. So he had five minutes alone with them. That must have been a heavy day with him. But, ordinarily, he started level with other punctual folk at eight o'clock. He said that he sacrificed himself in the interests of education and good habits. But poor Barrett, whose Swedish exercises or hair-drill or devotions of some sort always kept him busy till 8.15, could not be made to see it, and after his third or fourth morning of semistarvation the powers were asked to intervene. So, after some remarks about the early bird and the worm, it was agreed that the third attack should not begin before 8.20. So that trouble ended happily.

'Politics were not much discussed, but not because all were of like mind, for Hills was a young Tory, and Crawford and Barrett were of Tory upbringing. Darton was a Whig, Lloyd just then an Olympian, looking down on all parties and jeering at everybody's pet idols. I alone, I think, would have sided with the Chief in a straight vote. For—I speak now of my earliest visit—the famous "Domination" speech in the J.C.R., which sowed the dread seeds of Liberalism in a score of respectable young Tory hearts and changed the course of at least half-a-dozen careers, had not yet been made. Perhaps we had too much time for discussion. Schools occupied a large part of our thoughts.   Only on the Sunday walks did we give much attention to Chamberlain or Lloyd George.   It was on a Sunday afternoon somewhere on the hills that two or three of us got him to talk about Socialism, of which I was then as completely ignorant as the average schoolboy.   Shortly afterwards, he gave me my first text-book, a copy of his tract, "The Moral Basis of Socialism."   But this was not followed up either then or later by any preaching or teaching.   And I must admit that when, at the end of my time at College, I labelled myself a Socialist, I could only with difficulty have passed the simplest examination in the principles.   But I was one of many who would have embraced Buddhism or any other creed merely on the ground that what he believed in must be right.'

ACADEMIC POLITICS

By Dr. L. R. Farnell

A MAN of Sidney Ball's character, with its masterful impulse towards social and constructive work, was certain to play a prominent part in the politics of the society in which he was placed. And it was no less certain that he would be found in the front rank of the party of Academic reform. From his earliest under-graduate days his innate and developing sympathies were with the advanced wing of Liberalism; and, as his studies and experience matured, the reform of the Universities became for him as for many of his comrades a leading principle of a larger national ideal. Nor was he of the temperament to remain content with mere theory and speculation. To take his part in the heat and burden of practical life, at a period when the problems of reconstruction were vital in our Academic world, was an imperious call for one whose social instincts were as powerful as his intellect; and these were fortified by a long and devoted course of post-graduate study, which while satisfying his always ardent interest in pure metaphysics, gradually inclined him to specialise rather in the field of social philosophy.

The Oxford which Ball entered in 1875 was certainly in need of drastic reform, the control of the University by the Colleges being excessive and detrimental to both. And this need was only partially satisfied with much compromise and indecision by the

Commission of 1877, which created indeed, or rather restored, a genuine University system, but left it confronted with the Collegiate without any sure provision for an organic integration of the two. There was certianly much new life awakening and a quickened and healthier energy arising in the Colleges; the somnolence of the eighteenth century that still hung heavily over this place in the first half of the nineteenth was passing away. New studies were arising and finding keen votaries; the ideal of research asserted itself as against the lure of the examination, and was powerfully incarnated in Mark Pattison, who won many admirers and disciples among the best of College Tutors. The system of inter-Collegiate lectures had well started, which opened something of a career to talent and unlocked the prison-bars of the sequestered College. But only the lines had been indicated on which a new life might develop and flourish, and very much remained to be done.

In 1883, Ball was elected to an official Fellowship in St. John's College, and he held this to the close of his life, being promoted in the course of years to the dignity and status of Senior Tutor but not to the Headship, when the vacancy occurred in 1909.

The society which elected him was one where the conservative spirit and the tradition of a past age were strongly dominant, and where a man to whom the role of reformer was inevitable could hardly expect to find complete sympathy and an untroubled life. Yet no thwarting opposition could ever chill or embitter his sunny and genial temperament; his character charmed those who had no sympathy with his academic ideals and disapproved of his social views, and, being always a frank and fearless worker, and through most of his

life a leader, in the cause of reform both within his own
College and without, he won many friends and fellow-
workers and never made a personal foe.

Nor has any man in Oxford ever worked for his
College with more unselfish, unsparing, and enthusiastic devotion than Ball, his influence within its
walls was great and salutary, and that it occupies a
far higher position in our present academical world
than it occupied forty years ago, is an achievement that
must be ascribed in great measure to his service and
his policy.

A College life so arduous and fully charged would
have been sufficient for most men's energies. But there
seemed no limit to his in dealing with causes that he
had at heart, and he early recognised, what some
among us have not wholly recognised yet, that an
Oxford College can only thrive as part of a larger
organism, a vitalised and well-organised University;
this latter has not yet been wholly evolved, but for its
evolution he worked throughout his life with ardour
combined with insight. For idealist as he was, he had
strong practical sense and could well take the measure
of the attainable; he loved this place too well to be a
mere revolutionary iconoclast and the reforms he advocated were mainly those which have already been
accomplished and for some of which many are still
working with some hope of success. Yet his ideals
were not those native to the Thames Valley but
matured from a wide experience of other Academies.

Most of his activity in the politics of the University
was intimately associated with an influential club of
which he was an original member and which started an
'Oxford movement' of a different trend from the better known one. Its history has been hitherto unre-

corded, but it might interest the future historian of University Reform. It was constituted in February, 1889, at a meeting held in Exeter College, which society may claim to have given the primary impulse to the movement. Its numbers soon rose to nearly thirty, and the Professoriate and Tutoriate were at first almost equally represented in it. Most of the original group have died, but their memories are preserved in the annals of literature and science; others are no longer resident among us. The names of such men as Bywater, Pelham, Henry Nettleship, Cook-Wilson, Napier, Onions, John Mowat, York Powell, Arthur Evans, Warde Fowler, W. M. Lindsay, Haverfield and Greenidge, Ray Lankester, Sir John Rhys, not to mention others who are still active in Oxford, give the clue to the ideals of the Society. Its aim was mainly to maintain and develop the character of the University as a home of learning and science, and for this purpose to place the interests of the University as a whole above those of the separate College, to strengthen the influence of the Professoriate and to diffuse the ideal of research throughout the College teaching staffs, to encourage new subjects of study but to keep the examination system within bounds and to exorcise the examination spirit, to act on Academical, not on political grounds in elections to Council and other University bodies, finally to safeguard the Bodleian Library as a centre of mature study. This last point in the programme was rendered necessary on account of the fears aroused by the eccentric administration of the Librarian of the time.

For many years Ball was the Secretary of the Society, and he showed throughout unfailing judgment and energy in propagating its ideas, in framing legislative measures to embody them, as well as in the task of securing the right men for important administrative posts in the University. The Club had its festive side, being also a dining-club; some of its members were gifted conversationalists, the memory of whose talk lightens up for some of us these colder and more lonely days.

The first important measure that emanated from the Club, and was strongly supported by it in all its stages, was the scheme for the establishment of a School of English Language and Literature; and throughout the long conflict to which it was exposed, Ball was its strenuous, though silent, supporter.

It is difficult now to understand the prejudice and opposition that the measure excited. The classical 'Die-hards' regarded it as one more attack on the Classics, and when they found they were losing, demanded that at least Honour Classical Moderations should be the only avenue to the School. Others maintained that English Literature was too beautiful to be submitted to the indignity of an Examination or was a vague and soft thing that would elude the iron grasp of the examiner. Professor Freeman amused us by threatening us with an examination paper on Shelley with the great 'Harriet question' figuring large. 'Nothing so foolish has ever occurred to the mind of man but what it has been made the dogma of some philosopher' is a cynical reflection which *mutatis mutandis* is suggested by many an old controversy in congregation. The English School slowly fought its way through and was at last established by the aid of the compromise that Pass Moderations should be its avenue, a compromise of no value for either side, but which Ball rightly advised us to accept. The reform

party won in the end after strenuous effort, and the
statute concerning the English School was carried in
congregation by a majority of forty. The Club regarded the victory as valuable, not only because of
the intrinsic importance of the subject itself, but because the tyranny of the examination system, which
it was one of its objects to overthrow, is mitigated by
the greater variety in the range of subjects open to
study.

It was becoming obvious at least thirty years ago
that for the strengthening of the educational power of
the University some change in its legislative machinery
was necessary, especially in regard to the constitution
of Congregation. By some freak of carelessness of
earlier legislators the congregation franchise was based
on residence. This worked fairly well till North
Oxford with its suburban attractiveness sprang up,
which resulted in the dilution of congregation by a
large non-teaching element. Their presence was defended on ideal principles by either party, according
as they were felt by either to be an accession to its
voting strength; but it destroyed the rightful claim
of that body to represent the actual teachers and
workers of the University. Many were the conferences, both public and private, on this thorny subject,
to which was linked the equally difficult question of
the reform of Convocation; but it was not till many
years after, when at last the authoritative weight of
our Chancellor's manifesto was thrown into the scale
that congregation was finally purged and its franchise
made a teaching and official franchise. The gloomy
prophesying of some that the change would narrow
its outlook and clog progress does not seem to have
been fulfilled.

As regards the position of Convocation, Ball was in favour of limiting its authority and of reserving to congregation the final decision on educational matters. He was also sympathetic with the idea of imposing a further educational test for the M.A. But he does not appear to have committed himself to any formal proposals.

As early as 1895 he and his associates began to prepare a scheme for the encouragement of research by the institution of special Degrees to be awarded for original work, a scheme which has blossomed into the Baccalaureate and Doctorate of Letters and Science. In the inception, discussion, and pressure necessary for carrying it through Ball was deeply concerned and his advice and activity contributed much to its final acceptance. On the view that the research which these degrees demanded was at least as valuable as the ordinary B.A. curriculum, Ball was in favour of the proposal that this Baccalaureate should lead equally to the M.A. and that the Doctorate should carry with it the franchise. The University, wedded to the exclusive privilege of its junior Examination-course, was not prepared to go so far. But he and his friends had every reason to be content with this realisation in a practical form of one of their ideals. And the system which was mainly their work has born fruit and worked for good; it has increased among us the sense of the value of original work and diminished our reverence for the prize-system, that fatal enchantment that lay heavy on the early Victorian's soul.

They were less successful with a lesser matter that greatly preoccupied them about the same time, the fusion of Classical Moderations and Greats, suggested for the sake of improving the Character of our Literae

Humaniores course, as they believed it would, as well as to diminish the strain of examinations. In spite of the authority of Bywater, Pelham and Stewart, who memoralised the University in its favour, the proposal had no chance of being discussed on its merits; it excited too much resentment among the Honour moderation Tutors to be proceeded with. That every established examination creates a guild-interest is a lesson that the educational reformer has to learn.

About that time certain ideas in which Ball was keenly interested began to be mooted, which even now are still in the air but before long may evoke legislation : as that the Non-Collegiate system needed reforming, so that in the case of maturer students the mode of entrance to the University might be made easier and simpler and its power of expansion increased : that the Boards of Faculties should be given more educational control of the studies and teaching. In fact, the perfecting of a plan for organising our teaching by Faculties rather than by separate Colleges and for securing the more efficient and least wasteful combination of professorial and tutorial instruction was necessary to the ideal of University policy to which Ball and his friends were pledged. To this he devoted much careful thinking and strenuous effort. He played a leading part at two conferences of members of Congregation held in 1903 and 1904 where the problems connected with the better co-ordination of our teaching resources were discussed in detail : resolutions were passed in favour of increasing the powers of the Boards of Faculties and of giving them the right to appoint certain College Lecturers to the status of University Lecturers with stipends paid out of funds allocated to the Board : the proposal to pool a large proportion of the College tuition funds and allocate it to the Boards of Faculties, strongly advocated by Ball and his friends, was too drastic for the majority to accept; but that Conference was successful in adumbrating a General Council of the Faculties, an idea realised at last by the recent Consitution of the General Board, to which high hopes have been attached that may perhaps be realised in the future.

His part was no less prominent in the movement that was on foot in 1907 for the formation of a University Reform Association. A large number of professors and tutors gave in their names and held several seances at some rooms in the High Street, where various schemes were put forward and discussed. The main object of these was the better organisation of teaching, the development of the power of the Boards of Faculties, the creation of a General Council of the Faculties, and the more earnest encouragement of research. All this naturally enlisted the warm support of Ball and his comrades who were answerable for a good deal of the programme of these meetings.

But such gatherings in Oxford are apt to be barren of immediate or apparent result, and this was no excepion.

Early in the summer of 1907 a somewhat violent attack on Oxford was made in the House of Lords by Dr. Gore, then Bishop of Birmingham, and partly to counter the effect of this many of the leading Professors and Tutors, including Ball, openly proclaimed the need of a Commission in a letter to the *Times* (July 24th), and the programme of reform sketched in it was on the whole in accord with his policy. But the suggestion of a Commission, even if Government had been willing to entertain it, was silenced for the time by the authorative pronouncement of our Chancellor, who published his views on University Reform in 1909, and urging the objections to a Commission made a strong appeal to the University to reform itself from within. The greater part of the book strongly attracted Ball's sympathy and he had ample opportunity of putting his views and those of his associates before the Chancellor. Lord Curzon's letters to him are warm and appreciative and in one he thanks him cordially for the excellent advice that he had received from him on an important matter.

HACKWOOD,
BASINGSTOKE,
April 24th, 1909.

DEAR MR. BALL,

Your letter is the very greatest encouragement to me and gives me I think, more pleasure than any other communication that I have received on the subject.

I am particularly glad to think that I have not been unjust to the view of the section with whom you act and who have done so much to bring to the front the question of University Reform.

Yours truly,
CURZON.

Shortly before this, in 1907, Ball was elected to Council and retained his seat there till 1912. A perusal of the 'Acta' of this period reveals, what we should expect, that he was a very active member sitting on many Committees, making many proposals and supporting many schemes, all of them consonant with his ideals of University Reform, but none of them of far-reaching importance or belonging to *la haute politique* of reconstruction.

He may have found, as others have, that the air of the Hebdomadal Council is not favourable to the birth and nurture of daring reforms; gradually also, the conviction grew upon him that Oxford, with its centuries of traditions and the great power of its manifold vested interests and under the spell of what has been called 'the Thames Valley temperament,' could not or would not unaided and by its own effort carry through a thorough and coherent scheme of self-re-organisation.

His last act of public policy before the war which temporarily closed down all legislative activity, was his determined and effective resistance to a measure for changing the constituton of Council whereby the Professoriate was to lose its right to representation upon it. He and his associates, who were specially concerned with strengthening the University and the influence of learning in our counsels, had been inclined to acquiesce in this measure, but on the understanding that the Professoriate was to receive as an equivalent the privilege of a number of seats on the new 'General Board of Faculties,' which, it was supposed, would henceforth possess the chief initiative in our educational legislation. But when the Statute dealing with that Board was passed without allocating any seats on it to the Professors, he and many others determined to try their utmost to save their representation on Council. The fight was arduous and excited some heat. The measure which cancelled their established right had passed all its stages but the last, when by a vigorous effort, in which Ball put forth all his zest and energy, it was rejected in Convocation. It was rejected by an opposition that was devoted to the interests of learning and having long experience of

Council-elections was well aware of the danger with which the University was being threatened, that its chief executive and legislative body might come to consist solely or mainly of 'safe' and popular business men. It is a rare happiness for the reformer to be able on occasions to play a conservative part and to thwart reactionary progress.

Thus through the whole period of his Academic warfare, he was an ardent combatant for the cause of learning; and he was happily able to impress his ideal upon the policy of his college. Yet of his own far-reaching studies he was able to leave behind him scarcely any written memorial. This is the sad necessity of the fighting life, that it can contribute to the cause for which it struggles little but the fight itself, leaving to others to work the richer harvest in peace.

However his views may be judged, a fair survey of his University activity, of which the picture given above is an inadequate sketch, enhances the impression deepened upon all who knew him of an utterly unselfish and high-devoted spirit. Never was his view clouded by the thought of personal gain or personal risk. His long and arduous striving to make things better for us in this place, according to the light that was in him, was thankless and unrewarded save by the admiration of his friends : it was certainly detrimental to his personal career, cutting him off from higher promotion which he would have only valued because of the greater power he might have obtained to assist the University. He bore his disappointments with perfect dignity and self-restraint, and went loyally on his way till he fell exhausted by an over-strenuous life.

If one asks whether a life spent in combat against strong forces of stationary inertia, the bane of all

spiritual societies, was 'worth while,' one asks a feeble
and paltry question. A man's life is measured not by
what he wins but what he strives to win. Something of
Ball's ideal has been realised; the University is growing stronger and broader; much more that he hoped
for may be achieved in the strenuous times that are
calling us and with a new spirit awakening. If a fuller
achievement is won, a few of us who may live to see it
will render a due memorial-tribute to his leadership
and inspiration.

The University has lost a man of courage, devotion, and insight who could have helped her greatly
now in her time of need. And the writer of this chapter has lost a life-friend and counsellor, whom he never
needed so much as now.

UNIVERSITY
COLLEGE
LIBRARY
NOTTINGHAM

SEVERAL SIDES

I. AS COLLEAGUE

By Canon Nance

SIDNEY BALL was elected to an official Fellow-ship at St. John's, for tutorial work, without examination. I do not remember any election at St. John's that was made so quietly and so entirely free from any opposition, and I do not think any election turned out so fortunately for the College.

Ball was a most helpful colleague in College work. It was impossible to have any quarrel with him on account of his natural sweetness of temper. In any matter of discussion he was eminently fairminded. He would press his point at times with incisive and tense energy of argument, but if he failed to convince us, he was ready to yield with grace, even though he might think he was beaten by prejudice or shortsightedness, and there was never any trace of bitterness left behind.

It was no easy task for a strong Liberal as he was, with Socialistic views, to win his way in a College like St. John's, where the spirit of the place was ultra-Conservative, and the ecclesiastical tradition of High Church Jacobitism was maintained by most of the fellows with zeal and pride in the past history of the College. Few men could have done it, but Ball succeeded in winning not only the sympathy and affection of those fellows who were liberally inclined, but also the respect of those whose views were so diametrically opposed to his own. All was transparent and honest in him; there was no suspicion of intrigue or any consideration of personal advantage.

It was especially in times of elections to Scholarships or Fellowships that his special qualities of fairmindedness and insight into character proved useful.

In matters of College discipline he exercised an influence that helped things to go smoothly. His intimate knowledge of the men and his natural kindness of heart tended to throw his weight on the side of leniency in the administration of discipline, and one might be quite sure that any consideration that could fairly be urged for an offender would be made the most of by him.

But the most striking thing of all to me was the influence that he had with the old President. Dr. Bellamy was an ideal representative of old St. John's. He was associated with St. John's almost all his long life, and the traditions of the College were sacred to him. He was recognised in Oxford as the leader of the Conservative party in the University. His wit and caustic humour made him a brilliant and amusing conversationalist, and even those at whose cost a gibe was made could enjoy a jest against themselves when it was as good-natured as it was witty. One such instance may be quoted, as an illustration, that concerned Sidney Ball. The President was just about to say grace at dinner, when he noticed that Ball in a certain absent-mindedness, not unusual with him, had begun to crumble his bread and eat it. So, instead of the usual Latin formula 'Benedictus benedicat' he said in English, with his lisping tone, 'For what we are about to receive, and for what Mr. Ball has already received, the Lord's name be praised.'

Ball's capability as a Tutor, and fine character as a man, completely won the President's regard, and though his views in politics were so distasteful, the President grew more and more to trust him in all matters that affected the management of the undergraduates, so that the College was left almost entirely in his hands. But I am speaking now of what happened after I had left Oxford. What I saw in my own time was enough to make me think that the President was thoroughly justified in his confidence, and fortunate to have a lieutenant so worthy of it.

As I look back to those years in which I was a colleague of Ball's, I do not recollect a single instance of self-seeking or of irritability of temper or selfishness however much we might at times differ in opinion. He was always the same gentle, fair-minded, fascinating personality.

I leave it to those who were his pupils to speak of his influence over them and his power to teach. I have tried to write as one who appreciated him as a colleague and a friend.

II. AS TEACHER AND FELLOW WORKER

By Dr. Davey Biggs

Freshmen who joined St. John's College in the October Term of 1882 found themselves in an atmosphere of accomplished and impending change, change not merely in the composition of the Society which is inevitable every October, but change in the influences which were to mould their outlook on life, and change in the emphasis to be laid on its various interests.

The impression of such change was made on the first Sunday in term when, going with the instincts of an explorer to the University Church, they heard what was, in effect, the funeral sermon of Dr. Pusey, with its summary of his lifelong devotion to the poor from the religious standpoint of 'a servant of God.' And in the following days, as they loitered in the College barge waiting their turn to be 'tubbed' they found the dressing-room table littered with copies of *The Bitter Cry of Outcast London*, in which the interest in social conditions was expressed in terms not of religion but of humanity. Before the end of Term the era with which Dr. Pusey's name had been associated was closed by the death of his great opponent Dr. Tait, the Archbishop of Canterbury; and when we came back after the Vacation it was to find a new fellow in residence, who had been a pupil at Wellington College of the new Archbishop. We soon became conscious that, of the new order of which we had been expectant, our new tutor was the embodiment.

Mr. Ball had been elected at the end of the October term, without examination, as a 'Greats' tutor, but his sympathies and interests overflowed the wide channels of the School of *Literæ Humaniores*. The first-floor rooms on the staircase in the passage between the two quadrangles became the centre and home of an amazingly busy life. The day often started with a breakfast party at which men who had hardly known more of each other than their names were entertained together by a host who really knew how to entertain. Then followed the round of lectures and pupils and meetings, and time was found for interest in the Athletic Club and Debating Society: of the University Volunteer Corps and of the Browning Society he was a keen member, and when one of the evening papers published a sketch entitled 'New Types at the Universities—Bell, of St. Jude's,' the original was unmistakeable. But amid all the tangle of such multifarious activities one thread ran unwaveringly. It was not possible to be long in the company of the new fellow without discovering his zeal for the improvement of social conditions, and presently we found ourselves invited to attend lectures on subjects of social interest by such masters of their subjects as Mr. Fowle (of Islip) or Mr. Moore Ede (now Dean of Worcester). These were given in the new lecture room, and many of us owe our first interest in such matters as poor relief and village councils to what we heard on those Saturday evenings.

Then followed the establishment of Toynbee Hall as a centre at which University men could learn at first hand the conditions and opportunities of life in Whitechapel, and we would be asked to meet the Warden or his wife or curates at some social gathering in Mr. Ball's rooms and take our part in entertaining the visitors they would bring by the score to Oxford on a Saturday or Bank Holiday. But it was in reading for the Greats School that we really came to grips with our problems, for his treatment of Political Philosophy made us understand our responsibilities for to-day and the future. He did not confine himself to the ordinary text-books. I remember him giving me, after a term's work at Greats, the suggestion that I should read in the vacation *Ecce Homo*, *Past and Present*, and a little but very stimulating American work *What social classes owe to each other*. Thus he measured his men as individuals, and gave them what he guessed would draw out most surely their particular power, by its appeal to their particular point of view, with a wonderful insight and chivalry. And of time and strength for their instruction he was unsparing. For nearly a whole term, when through illness I was unable to read, he used to let me go and talk to him for an hour every other night on the topics in the text-books of philosophy, and what I owe to his careful guidance in learning how to estimate and how to express the speculations and convictions of other minds is as incalculable as my gratitude has been unfailing. And what he did for me was typical of what he did for many others. And he valued gratitude. Once when he had taken a reading party to his favourite Sark they had delivered in his rooms some pictures—an artist's proof of 'The Harvest Moon' and the like—for in his austere self-denial he had, in spite of his artistic appreciation, never allowed himself a picture, and the words in which he expressed his thanks will never be forgotten by those who heard them and saw him as he spoke them.

And then for thirty years our paths lay apart, if parallel. I took my degree in 1886, and it was not till 1916 that I was brought back into any sort of frequent association with my old Tutor. But in the autumn of 1916, at the National Mission, an 'Oxford Interdenominational Council for Social Reform,' which had its headquarters at Barnett House, was founded, and he consented to be co-opted as one of the members, and become Chairman of the Committee on Relations between Employers and Employed. He was a hard-working member of the Council and of the Executive, to the meetings of which he bicycled down on a hot summer afternoon in 1917 from Boar's Hill, betraying, by his appearance on arrival, how the physical and mental strain of the War was telling on one who had always suffered from overstrain. But all through the winter of 1917 he went on with his work for the O.I.C.S.R., presiding over a Committee, in which all varieties of Christian opinion from the Jesuit to the Quaker were represented, with a tact and a knowledge that won universal homage, and he was re-elected at the First Annual Meeting in May, 1918. He was not present at the meeting, he had not been well enough to get down, and before the week was out we knew that we should never have him with us again, that henceforth we should only have memories of his enthusiasm and devotion to the cause of social betterment.

Barely a fortnight before we had both been the guests of Father Plater[22] at what now is Campion Hall and I like to recall that on this occasion, the last time we ever met, the exchange of some old reminiscences over dessert led to his explaining to Father Plater that I had been his pupil.

III. AS SENIOR TUTOR.

By A. M. D. Hughes

I first saw Sidney Ball on a winter evening of 1890 in the big chamber of King Charles's rooms, when he was taking the names of candidates for a scholarship. He sat at his table under a shaded lamp in an element of dim stateliness and pleasant firelight, and his manner was as mellow as the scene. In his dealings with us during the examination he invariably repeated the

[22] Died 1920.

charm, and one at least of the successful candidates, when thinking of the days to come, counted him thenceforward among its goodly promises. And when we had gone up to College and Greats was coming on, the personality of the teacher was more a part of its lure. We encountered him during this period mostly in the distance and in the popular legend more than in the flesh; but there would hardly be a member of the society in his first year whom he did not invite sooner or later to a walk or a breakfast. There are dons for whom breakfast-giving is a discipline of humanity, but Ball was born to it, and the little house in Alfred Street, where he lived for some years after his marriage, must be a pleasant spot in many memories.

His talk on these occasions was admirably appropriate. It never left the common ground, or smacked of improvement, and it fetched the shy and mulish out of themselves. The secret of his skill lay in something more than a kindly sympathy with his guests. They attracted him as a subtle critic of human nature; but they concerned him much more deeply as a missioner of a certain school of thought, that is to say of liberalism in its widest and most spiritual sense. I do not mean that he preached any doctrine at his breakfasts, or preached at all. Even in set discussions of political or philosophic views, when his aim was to persuade, he would talk as much for ventilation as for victory, and his passionate faiths were seasoned with abundant humour. Patient as he was, putting his trust in light, and loving not ideas only, but men also, he was no dogmatical propagandist, and was extremely careful in laying hold of younger minds. On convivial occasions he would, of course, sometimes argue for his political opinions, immensely pleased with any res-

ponse, and gentle and hopeful with the most obdurate;
but the subject came in on the tide of the talk, and all
that he was constant in introducing was not the theme
but the temper—his own temper of gay reasonableness. The common ground was plentiful, for he
always had one foot in his youth; politics, however,
were the greater part of it. Those years saw the birth
of the Chamberlain Imperialism; socialism was gathering power both in the University and in the world;
Home Rule was a burning novelty; and Gladstone
was steeping all hearts in hate or love. This was especially the field in which Ball's cordial zest for the
surface and his interest for the bottom of things played
together. 'I fear,' he once said of a political friend,
'that he has a lobbying mind.' He was rather happy in
a lobby himself, in the sense that the personal factor
intensely interested him. Few men in Oxford maintained so much contact with the militant thinkers of
the day and knew so many of them, and to hear him
talk was to come closer both to the stage and to the
heart of the drama. His keen appetite for all public
matters, and for the morning and evening papers, and
his relish of political gossip were phenomena of a profound passion, moral and intellectual, and something
of the ground tone was often audible in his lightest
talk. At election time no man on earth was more alive.
I was one of a party staying with him at the Hostel in
Old Headington when Liberalism fell so ruinously in
1895. Some of the party stayed down in Oxford every
night until midnight for the latest results, and arrived
at his house at one or two in the morning; and each
time he got out of bed and came down for news and
retired to his pillow quite or nearly mute. When we
became his pupils, and so were made his friends, he

cared much for our political souls, and plied us with his tempered socialism and the aphorisms which put it into tabloid form :—as, for instance, 'Socialism is an austere system, and will bring with it no soft jobs,' or, 'Socialism has come not to take away property, but to bestow it.' 'Imperialism,' he would often tell us, 'is the last refuge of a scoundrel.' How deep this political feeling was few men, I believe, ever realised, for he hid it under irony and sunshine ; but I believe I am right in saying that the 'condition of England' vexed him, especially in despondent hours, like a personal distress. 'I don't know how to justify this,' I have heard him say, looking round him in the comfortable study at St. John's House, 'I have to explain to my working-men friends that this is an official residence.' The thought that the comfortable, and he among them, could not justify their comfort was by no means a painless visitation.

I do not think he was a talker who 'said good things'—that is, solvent things that put the matter to rest. He was not an oracle ; his gift was for discussion, and he thought a great deal in arguments. One evening when a man from another College collared the conversation, and like Thrasymachus of old 'doused our ears with streams of words like a bath-attendant,' and the pathetic pertinacity of Ball's 'But then,' or 'Yes, of course, but—'; for a talk was nothing to him if not a rapid give and take. And his constant practise in it, together with his instinct for style, had given him a rare power of apt and exquisite expression, a *flair* for telling phrases, and a habit of trying always for the consummate word. One form of his wit was to cast the account of an incident or the description of a personality or a man's appearance into language a little too dignified for its subject, and to touch us with the combined effect of verbal neatness and gentle mockery. One of us related at breakfast one day how he had spent the vac. in a family somewhere in London, coaching the heir of the house for Smalls, and how the father, who by the way was supposed to have married in spite of a vow or resolution of celibacy, took the news of the boy's failure tragically to heart, sat supper-less at supper and for many days hated the sun's beams. 'I see,' Ball commented, 'he thinks that all this is a retribution for his marriage, and you (turning to the tutor) are guilty of a derivative participation in the original offence.' His repartees were sometimes works of art. A well-known man in the University at that time, a leader among undergraduates, had failed in Smalls. A lady at lunch in Eights Week began to discourse on the pettiness of such an examination, and pedantry that directed it, and how 'an original genius' was above these tests. They were not tactful observations, and Ball was annoyed. 'Yes,' he remarked drily, 'it is rather hard to be original in a subtraction sum.'

The truest thing to say of him as a teacher would be, I think, that he was (in a word that used to dwell on his lips) stimulating. He stimulated more than he directed or formed. So soon as Mods. were over he would summon his new pupils to prescribe a course of general reading for the Easter vac, soft rain for the tender herb. Lecky's *European Morals* was one book he recommended. Pearson's *National Life and Character;* Pater's *Marius the Epicurean; Romola;* and, among many others, especially *Ecce Homo*, a book he loved. I remember we were rather astonished, not to say suffocated, by the length and variety of his list; but in time and in contact with him we learnt the inestimable value of his method, or rather his effect, as a teacher. I have tried to describe it in a few words which I may here quote by the Editor's kind permission from the *Oxford Magazine*:

'Sidney Ball gave so much of himself to social and public activities in the latter years of his life, that those who saw him only at this period are likely to overlook what was after all the main element of his influence— his power, that is, as a teacher and inspirer of youth. A few words on this subject may not be amiss from one who sat at his feet in the early nineties and knew him for many years.

'In those days Pragmatism was still to come, and for Oxford the last words in philosophy were those of Hegel and Green. For most men reading Greats the conclusion of the whole matter was stored up in the *Prolegomena to Ethics* and in Mr. Bradley's *Logic;* for *Appearance and Reality* came out at the end of my time. These were the lines of Mr. Ball's teaching; he was, and remained, a Hegelian, and regarded the Pragmatists, when they came, and what he called their "misological fervour" with no more, I believe, than a vivid interest. But Metaphysics was not his main bent, and I doubt if any of his pupils would undertake to define his beliefs in this province over and above their fundamental idealism. Beyond that point his steps seemed to be tentative and not very willing. Here, of course, the religous consciousness flows into the philosophic, and he was at once too religious and too critical not to feel the inadequacy of "our poor fathom-line of thought." And then he was embarassed by his greatest virtue. His sympathy, his eagerness to be just, and to be all things to all men for truth's sake, inclined him to mediate, to find a balance or a common ground, if, and whenever possible, and indisposed him to be positive. "He that is not against us," he would think, "is on our side." He would talk oftenest of the ultimate reality as "a something not ourselves that make for righteousness;" but at times, as for instance in a lecture on the Myth of Er and the notion of a last Judgement, he used the language of a much more personal conception, and with greater impressiveness.

'In fact, his peculiar ability, as a teacher, was not to train his pupils to a certain doctrine, though that, of course, he meant to do and did, not to mould minds so much as to kindle, and to bring them into living touch with the great thinkers, each in turn, and with the burning issues of the day. He was a sower of seed. And herein the personal equation was most important. Quickly susceptible, and very human, he needed sympathy as heartily as he gave it, and often seemed to us not more a master in philosophy than an elder brother. He always accepted his relation to his pupil as a spiritual bond, so that to read with him was to win, or rather to receive his friendship. And as a friend he was above praise—studious, patient, cordial, tender-hearted even, taking and remembering men at their best, and giving them his. For these reasons his lessons in the study were better value than his lectures. He was made for the tutorial system. As for the lectures, they were highly useful for the Schools, which was their aim; admirable in exposition and summary, and in force of style, for he looked on telling phrases like a lover; but the drawbacks of the dictatorial method are many, and he did not shun them all. Who, however, that went to him with the weekly essay will forget those colloquies, how free he was, with the pipe (that would never go) for the token of freedom, how glad to be heckled and eager to have it out? Better still, a reading party of his was a feast. He took it seriously and kept the men to work; but the holiday in it revealed him on sides of which we saw a great deal, but not enough for us, in College—as full of humour, and wit, and high spirits, keen to enjoy, and every way lovable. Here, in German beer-gardens, or on Dorsetshire downs, in long talks, young and vernal days, it was all fresh and great and full of discovery. No teacher ever spent himself more. All the way to the Schools he watched and cheered us on, caring for us, I do believe, more than we for ourselves. He was, indeed, one of the ardent and unselfish who are well tired when their day is done.

'As I have said, his primary interest did not lie in Metaphysics; it was ethical and political. And there was a striking feature in his attitude on these matters. I do not mean his Fabian socialism; though that, of course, was a big chapter of his influence in Oxford. I mean generally his love of the intense and of all such thinking as is veined with fire. He was constitutionally not only extraordinarily energetic, but daring to a degree. There was a tradition in my day at St. John's of a dive he once executed from some rock or mole in Jersey which made him the talk of the place, and I have seen him shoot down Malvern Hill on a bicycle, and slap through a drove of cows, in a way that stifled breath. And so in theory, "Let your loins be girded," he would quote, "burn with a pure gem-like flame;" "venture neck or nothing." Morality, he used to say, was adventure and evil was dull. He was a "eudae-monist" in the highest sense of the word; and I think that, saving perhaps Spinoza, the Greek Masters were more to his mind than any modern, by reason of the element of rapture in which their ethics are steeped. Put together the spirit of each of the two bits of literature that he oftenest cited—the Epilogue to *Romola* and *The Statue and the Bust*—and you have himself. I have written only from the point of view of a "reading man," but that is half the tale. He was also the passman's don and the soul of College life, whom all sorts and types of the thirty generations that passed before him at St. John's will mourn as a friend, so rich his humanity, and so great his heart.'

I could add many particular illustrations to that account, but memories of the sayings and actions of a friend who was the genius of old and very happy days have an incommunicable value for the bearer of them, and are apt to be insipid to others. But the account does not give the full impression of the consuming zeal and self-forgetfulness of his service as a teacher, or of how very human he was in it, how dependent for his success and his comfort in it on being met half way. The man who listened to him with mental reserve or cold assent, the man with no weak place in his armour, whose essays were 'faultily faultless'—either of these types put him out. He wanted to hold the climber by the hand, and to be leaned on. He grieved with a humorous grief for the lazy and the unprogressive. 'So-and-so,' he would say in deep dejection, 'is still smiling, and will smile to the end of the chapter.' His pupils will remember how he hovered on the stroke of the hour about the door of his lecture-room, if its previous tenants did not quit to the minute with admonitory openings and shuttings of the door, and the air of a man defrauded; but few will have seen him on the afternoon when the Honours' List should appear, flit-

ting restlessly in and out of the Schools or along the
way there. On reading parties he had a way of beginning to expound or debate towards bed time, and who-
ever slept overhead would hear the argument rumb-
ling into the night. One night at Marburg on the Làhn
I sat up late with him to receive a lesson on the Ethics,
and, after it was over, was just falling asleep when a
light in the room waked me. I sat up, and saw him
standing at the foot of the bed with a candle in his
hand and in dishabille. He could not be satisfied that
I had got it well into me, and, standing there, continued his discourse. I have forgotten it all now, except the opening words, which are characteristic of his
mediatory spirit. 'Of course,' he began, 'what I meant
to convey was that Aristotle really said the same thing
as Plato.'

This zeal for others made him a victim, as well as
an exemplar, of the tutorial system. One of his friends
said once that 'he gave up to the Senior Tutorship
what was meant for mankind.' His was the sort of case
at which the critics of Oxford point when complaining
of the small amount of print put forth by many of
those who carry the University on. The undergraduates of my time used sometimes to talk of the re-
muneration involved in his life. Others, and not a few
whom he taught or influenced, wrote the books or led
the policies which moved the world, while he remained
obscure, freely rejoicing in distinctions not his own,
and never thinking of self. Was it right that he should
bother so often about College Clubs, or wasters' debts,
or freshmen's rooms, flitting about the quads in pursuit of these matters, or 'fleeing,' perhaps, in his own
words, 'from an irate parent?' So far as his friends
could tell, this question never troubled him, and there

is, of course, a sufficient answer to it in the philosophy
of which he was a priest. And on the other hand he
knew that the influence he exerted from Oxford was
important, however imponderable. It was no small
performance to stand to many generations of the University for the Oxonian radicalism of which Green and
Toynbee were founders—a radicalism which is equally
at odds with excess and deficiency in the critical spirit,
which modulates the letter and cleaves to the essence
of the Christian faith, and applies it strictly to the
whole life of the State, political, social and economic.
He, more than any other man whom we then listened
to in Oxford, vitalised old thoughts with the fresh air
of present problems. The 'war on two fronts' which
this radicalism wages is a trying task, and Ball's perpetual criticism of the mind of his own class may have
so far estranged him as to make his position of media-
tor between an old world and a new harder than it
need have been. His merit and value were that he saw
so clearly and felt so passionately the need of the
mediation, and gave to it all that he could—the
thought and study of his lifetime, and the glowing
charity of his great heart.

It is upon that greatness of heart and goodness of
nature that the memory of him finally rests—that
'philanthropy' which Bacon says 'of all virtues and
dignities of the mind is the greatest.' It was far from
being a fond or blind goodness, but accompanied the
subtlest observation of moral and physical characteristics, and came to terms with the keenest distaste for
certain types of men. I will mention two out of many
examples that I remember. His help to his pupils did
not always stop at precept or sympathy, but sometimes
he gave or lent the poor among them the means for

further study out of his own none too ample means,
and his manner of doing so was perfect. The other
example is a small incident, and his life was full of
such. I stayed at St. John's House once when he had
invited an awkward and perhaps rather timid man to
dine with him at High Table. His guest, however,
thoroughly enjoyed himself. About nine o'clock Ball
came speeding in from Common Room to see his wife,
thrust in his head at the study, and exclaiming quite
excitedly 'He's altogether happy!' speeded back
again. His pleasure in the other man's pleasure was
irrepressible.

IV. POLITICS AND POLITICAL PHILOSOPHY.

By Ernest Barker

I first came to know Mr. Ball with some degree of
intimacy in the course of 1907. I had written a book
on Greek Political Philosophy; he had reviewed it,
with a generosity which I shall always remember, in
the *International Journal of Ethics;* and henceforth,
if I may quote a great political thinker whom we were
both glad to count our master, '*idem sentire de republica*
was a principle ground of friendship and attach-
ment.' From 1908 we were thrown together regularly.
As Junior Proctor I sat with him (my seat was next to
his) on the Hebdomadal Council; and in the same
capacity I served with him on a committee which introduced certain branches of political science into the
curriculum for the Diploma of Economics. After 1909
I was, for over four years, a Fellow of his College, and

in Common Room and College meeting I learned to know him with a real intimacy.

What I have said about our first connection seems to me exactly typical of him. He was a fountain of generous encouragement to younger men. He had an instinct for mothering; and there must be many who will remember his encouragement as long as they live. He had a quick mind, always seeking, and always ready to welcome, any sign of promise. He had not made a system, or locked his mind upon a system; his thought had, as it were, *antennae* of a living sensitiveness, always feeling for new truth; he had a ready responsiveness, which invited and deserved full confidence. To be abreast of him seemed the same as to be abreast of contemporary thought; when I talked with him, I felt that I knew the progressive spirit of the time; and as I write now, I feel a longing to carry my doubts and hesitations about these perplexed and uncharted days to his study, and in talk with him to learn something of the currents and of my bearings.

I was never his pupil; I knew him only as a colleague; but all that he was to me he was also (and I fancy, even more) to his pupils. I have gone into his room (a simple room, with a long table, and shelves of books on philosophy along the walls), and I have found him, on a summer afternoon, with a group of young men round him, and the teacher's passion upon him, ardently, in his rapid way, pouring out suggestion and stimulus on the eve of schools. (He would look up, I remember, half impatiently—but he was too kind ever to be really impatient—and with a seeming frown, which was really short-sightedness, from behind the powerful glasses which he always wore; and I would hurry over my business and be gone.) This, I think, was his great happiness, as it must always be the great happiness of a great teacher. He was always generously communicative; he could not but give in a large bounty; and the more he gave, the more he had.

It was not only to his pupils in philosophy that he gave his time and himself. He seemed to be father-in-general of all the undergraduates of the College. If the 'Greats' men saw most of him, as their tutor in philosophy, all men saw something of him, as the senior tutor of the College. His room was a place of general recourse, and he must have spent unnumbered hours—gladly, ungrudgingly, and without thought of what he was giving—on an infinity of detail. To many, long after they had left Oxford, he seemed to be the college, and 'Ball' was counted by them as synonymous with 'St. John's.'

His mind naturally ran to action, as a living and eager and generous mind must. He was the least selfish of men; all his instincts were for giving rather than getting. Any good cause could count on something more than his support; it could count on his time, his thought, his co-operation. I should reckon foremost among his good works—and they were many—all that he did in the cause and the service of education. He was long and honourably associated with the cause of University Reform in Oxford; he was a prominent figure in many meetings held to promote that cause, some dozen years ago; and, being at that time a member of the Hebdomadal Council, he played a large part in a number of reforms which were carried during the early years of Lord Curzon's Chancellorship. But it was what he did in the service of working-class education which seemed most essentially the expression and mirror of his inmost self. For many years he was a member of the Council of Ruskin College—a working men's college established in Oxford about 1900—and along with other University colleagues he did much to keep the college in touch with the friends of working class education throughout the University. He had also much to do with the beginning of the Tutorial Class movement, which, starting from Oxford in 1908, has spread through Great Britain, is spreading through Australia and other self-governing Dominions, and seems likely to spread through the United States of America. He read a paper at a conference held in Oxford in the summer of 1907, at which the movement was born, and he seconded the resolution for a joint committee of the University and the workers which gave the movement shape. It was one of the regrets of his last years, which I remember his expressing to me, that his early connection with this movement had suffered an interruption. (He had been absent from Oxford for a year, on a journey round the world; and his absence meant a severance of his connection with various University bodies.) But he found a new channel for his eager activity in other directions, and particularly in the city of Oxford. He was a man to whom one naturally turned for help in the inception of new plans; and as he was the first President of Barnett House, so he was the first President of the Oxford Citizens' Association and the first President of the Oxford Juvenile Organisations Committee. It shows the richness of his personality, and the many-sidedness of his interests, that these three presidencies, which he united naturally in himself, should now be held by three different persons. There could be no single successor to the mantle which he let fall.

He had an appetite for affairs; discussion was meat

and drink to him; he went about asking, suggesting, full of news, full of views, at once receptive and creative. There was something Greek in this; he was fond (as, partly from him, I also learned to be fond) of the passage in the *Politics*, where Aristotle defends the collective judgment of the many—'for some see one side, and some another, but all can see all sides.' He liked to speak in the Congregation of the University, and he spoke with power and emphasis. Fervour came upon him; he carried the question at issue back to its first principles and his own deepest convictions, and, balanced as he always was, he yet made it a matter of passion.

I have spoken of him as always balanced. To some who knew him, who themselves belonged to the Conservative camp, this may seem a hard saying. To them he was a Radical or a Socialist; he carried a red banner; he plunged into all 'advanced' causes. Yet I firmly believe that he always 'heard the other side.' and felt to the full the value of the other case. Sensitive as he was to all currents of feeling, he could not do otherwise. He knew both the defects of his own side and the merits of the other; but he also knew the value of loyalty to a side and a party. This is a knowledge which men of a fine intellect, particularly when they are engaged in the teacher's life, find it hard to attain. They see both sides; they feel the responsibility laid upon them for intellectual honesty, and for keeping their passion for truth at any cost undefiled; and they become but lame associates in any movement that involves concerted action. With him it was otherwise; he was always a good associate. There was sometimes, indeed, a disjunction between the views he would express in private conversation and the steps he would take in associated action; the one would be moderate; the other, if not immoderate, would at any rate verge more to the left. But I always felt that I could understand how he came to think as he did, and how he came to act as he did, on any given question; he thought as a thinker for himself; he acted as a believer in associated action; and I saw no inconsistency.

I am not competent to appreciate him as a philosopher, except on the one side of philosophy we had in common—the philosophical theory of the State. I should say that he belonged to the idealistic school of philosophers, and that he was interpretative rather than critical. At any rate it is as an interpreter of the great thinkers that I remember him most and understood him best. Plato and Rousseau were his familiar friends; they became real and intimate persons as you talked with him; he might criticize them, but he always as it were, took you into the inside of their minds, and his criticism was never external. If he followed any particular thinkers, I should say it was Burke and T. H. Green. Like Burke he was a believer in representative government; he never made immediacy the mark of democracy, and he never favoured any form of direct action. He liked to ask his pupils whether representation was the essence, or the defeat, of democracy; he liked to say that democracy was the best form of aristocracy, for it meant government by the freely selected best. He was a believer, as I have said, in party; and his life was the expression of his belief. Profoundly interested in all labour questions, and a member of the Fabian Society, he always seemed to me essentially a Liberal. In many ways he was the successor of T. H. Green. He was not, like Green, a constructive philosopher; but he was, like him, a

Liberal through and through; and like him too, he interpreted to the citizens of Oxford the Liberal element in the Universiy.

He wrote but little; he gave himself to the world *viva voce*. One of his chief writings was a Fabian Tract (No. 72) on the *Moral Aspects of Socialism;* it is reprinted, along with tracts by Sidney Webb, Bernard Shaw and Sir Sidney Olivier, in the volume of the Fabian Socialistic Series entitled *Socialism and Individualism*. The paper he wrote for the conference of 1907, which led to the foundation of Tutorial classes, has also been printed. He wrote many reviews (some of them in the *International Journal of Ethics*), mainly of books on politics and political theory; and he was for many years the Oxford correspondent of the *Manchester Guardian*. As a Lecturer, he ranked easily among the foremost of those who lectured for the school of Literæ Humaniores. There were two themes on which, at any rate in the last ten years of his life, he generally lectured—the Theory of Knowledge, and Problems of Political Theory. On the first of these themes he gave his last lecture at the beginning of 1915. On the second he lectured regularly in the four terms preceding his death. The war, as was natural, had turned his thoughts strongly to political problems; and I can bear witness to the influence which his lectures exercised on one at any rate of my pupils in the course of 1917.

To live in Oxford is to live in a constant fellowship. It is a place of clubs, of meetings, of discussion. It was his natural home; and in many ways he was its central figure. He was one of the oldest members of the Political Economy Club, and he attended regularly its dinners and debates. He was a member from the first of the Politcal Philosophy Club; and indeed wherever men were gathered together, for the discussion of abstract problems or for the planning of action, he was almost always to be found. He did not lay waste his hours. He spent them at once lavishly and fruitfully. He gave to us all; but he gave most abundantly to his colleagues and his pupils in St. John's. He gave great pains to College business. Tuesday by Tuesday he presided, as Senior Tutor, over the Tutor's lunches at which tutorial matters were discussed; day by day he served the undergraduates as teacher and guide.

As I look back, I recognise more and more what his encouragement meant to me. Encouragement from an older and approved scholar is a very precious thing to one who is younger and untried. He knew well how to give it: and he gave it no less modestly than generously; he was never stiff-necked in his own views; his thought was too flexible, too sensitive, too sympathetic for that. He would seldom say that one was wrong; but he would gently and tentatively suggest other views and other considerations. This was no mannerism; he was generously minded; and he valued what one submitted to him at a higher rate than it always deserved. I leaned greatly upon his help in a work I was writing during the last years of his life—a new edition of the book on Greek Political Philosophy which he had reviewed in its first rude form. We had many meetings and many talks about it—more particularly about the part which deals with Plato; and busy as he was with many things (and above all with the welfare of the Serbian refugee students in Oxford) he always found time to read the proofs and to make suggestions at which I eagerly grasped. He died before the book appeared; and he never saw the acknowledgment of my debt which I sought to make in the preface. 'Words cannot repay the debt,' I wrote (he was still living when I wrote), 'which is not the only debt owed to him by the writer.' Words are now the only currency I can use to pay my debt. Unavailing as they are, I pay these words as a tribute to the memory of one who was to me, in the full sense of every word, a guide, philosopher and friend.

V. AS ECONOMIST.

By Professor F. Y. EDGEWORTH.

ECONOMISTS, especially those who cultivate the science of wealth for the sake of its bearing upon human welfare, have suffered a heavy loss by the death of Sidney Ball. We may recall gratefully his services to the Journal. The reviews with which he enriched our pages and those of the *Economic Review* form part of his claim to be remembered. In these critical writings he sometimes allows to appear, incidentally and unobtrusively, views of his own more valuable than the opinions which he lucidly analyses. Thus, Sorel's doctrine of violence (reviewed 1916) seems rather futile; while Ball's criticism teaches a lesson needed by economic controversalists that there may be a 'soul of goodness' in tenets that are *prima facie* absurd. Blind defiance of economic reasoning was no part of the Socialism which Ball ardently advocated. Rather he agreed with Loria that 'Sociology can only exist and can only attain to the dignity of an exact science by taking as its point of departure the analysis of the economic fact.' As showing his appreciation of abstract reasoning, with some doubt as to its usefulness, or at least as to the utility of its last refinements, his remarkable review (in the *Economic Review*) of Professor Pigou's *Wealth and Welfare* may be mentioned. Stimulating as were Ball's writings on economic topics, he exercised an even more useful influence as a teacher, and as the promoter of various institutions directed to the increase of social welfare.

VI. AMONG UNDERGRADUATE SOCIALISTS.

By G. D. H. Cole

When I went up to Oxford in 1908, I found Sidney Ball the recognised head of University Socialism. The situation then was not quite what it is now; for the Liberal Government of 1906 was still at the height of its popularity, and Sidney Ball found no difficulty in being at the same time President of the Oxford University Fabian Society and a leading member of the Liberal Club. We had our extremists then, organised outside the Fabian Society in the University Clarion Scouts; but all of us, whatever section we belonged to, looked up to Sidney Ball and regarded him as our protagonist in the then stony ground of the Senior Common Room.

I had the temerity, with Kingsley Griffith, to start a University Socialistic paper, *The Oxford Socialist*, in my first term, and I well remember the kindly interest which Sidney Ball took in our venture, and the

encouragement which he gave us. I still have the
letter, saying nice things about our youthful effort,
that first brought me in touch with him. From that
time on, he is closely mingled in all my memories of
Oxford Socialism, except during the time when he was
away on his journey round the world. The last meeting of the O.U. Socialist (no longer Fabian) Society
which I attended—I was passing through Oxford at the
time—was one at which he read an extraordinarily
live and stimulating paper on Marx. That was towards the end of the war, and not very long before his
death. He told me afterwards that he intended to work
up that paper for publication; but he never did so. I
asked for the MS. of it after his death, but found that
much of it was so incomplete that, much to my regret,
I could not recapture enough of what he said to enable
it to be published. Yet, when he read it, it was so
finished a work that it is hard to believe that most of
it was never even written down.

This, however, belongs to a later time than that of
which I want mainly to speak. It was as an undergraduate that I, like most other young Socialists, most felt
Sidney Ball's influence. His house was always open
to us, and we had many a talk and argument there. He
remained to the end a Socialist whose active participation in the movement outside Oxford had been mainly
in those earlier days when the Fabian Society was a
live and vigorous body, exercising a big influence
through the Labour and Socialist Movement. But he
was always very little of a Fabian in the narrow sense
of the term, and wonderfully open to new ideas. I was
a Fabian in those days; but particularly in the development and ideas of French Syndicalism and in the
Guild Socialist theory which was then first outlined

in the *New Age*. I could always rely on getting a thoroughly good talk and a sympathetic view of such movements from Sidney Ball. He grasped at once their real meaning, and their importance for the future of British Labour, and he was even best at understanding and sympathising where he did not fully agree.

Nor was it only for talk that we went to him. In University matters, I never knew him on the wrong side in anything that really concerned freedom. He was always ready to help anyone in trouble, and he never minded doing the unpopular or unorthodox thing if he believed it right. He showed his belief in freedom of conscience by saying his word for the conscientious objectors during the war, although he did not agree with them; and I know how his personal help was valued by some of those who found themselves in trouble during the years of war. That meant a lot for him; for it is an open secret that, if he had been a little less true to his principles, his merely material success in his career might have been a great deal more.

Sidney Ball's socialism was not dogmatic. He was not a fighter or a propagandist by nature, but a teacher and an interpreter. I was never his pupil; but I know that talking to him helped one to understand things—and that is, after all, the best test of a teacher. To us, he was a friend whose knowledge of the past and of the wider movement of Labour, and whose quick though critical sympathy with new ideas was an invaluable stimulus in the days when we were putting our new-found Socialism to the test and finding out whether it was really a youthful enthusiasm or a really grounded faith. He helped us there, because he was not only our counsellor, but also and above all our friend.

VII. AS FRIEND AND COUNSELLOR

By James Bonar

THOUGH nearly contemporaries in undergraduate days we did not I think, meet at all then, or indeed much at all till the Crumps brought us together in London in the eighties. His good work at St. John's, not thought promising ground in those days, was well known to everyone interested in social reform.

For about thirty years he had been to me a valued friend, and latterly a sort of oracle on social reform. We looked for progress and light in the same quarters, but he had a keener insight and wider knowledge of men and 'movements' and books, to which I deferred. His 'enthusiasm of humanity' was tempered by reason. His hopes for it were always high, but he could always distinguish the practicable from the impracticable or too remotely practicable.

I had looked forward to hearing deliverances from him on the present 'condition of England,' to enlighten me as to many things happening now in the Old Country of which one can have no firm grasp at a distance of time and space. I can now only fancy what they would have been, by the aid of memories of long ago.

One gathering at Oxford is particularly associated with him in my recollection. It was in Balliol Hall on the 29th April, 1899, when Edward Caird, then Master, presided. It was a propagandist meeting in favour of Labour Co-partnership. The hard work needed to beat up an audience was done chiefly by our friend Sidney Ball, and one good result from the meeting was that he and Mrs. Arnold Toynbee agreed to represent the Labour Co-partnership Association in Oxford.

Here in Ottawa I had a delightful visit from him in October, 1911, for part of two days. After a sufficiency of serious matters we enjoyed Harry Lauder together. Our friend was in his brightest mood and with no slack hold on life. I missed him and Mrs. Ball when I last passed through Oxford three years ago; but was warned of no mischief. The news of his death was a sad surprise. However good the living epistles he has left, his own presence will be sadly missed.

VIII. AS FABIAN

By SIDNEY WEBB

SIDNEY Ball joined the Fabian Society at the beginning of 1886, some nine months after I did. We know nothing of his action in the Society for some years; and the Oxford Fabian Society was not founded until 1895. But my recollecton is that meetings were arranged in Oxford pretty frequently during these years under other names (such as ' Society for the Study of Social Problems' or something like that—there were all sorts of names), at which I and others spoke. I forget when I first went to Oxford, it was actually on the invitation of Unwin (either Raymond Unwin, the present Town Planning Architect at the L.G.B. or his brother) who presumably wrote as the transient secretary of one of these fleeting societies, *very likely on your husband's initiative.* The lecture was in a small

College lecture room, doubtless at St. John's. The
date of this must have been the winter of 1886-7 I
think; and it was probably the first of our F.S. lectures
at Oxford; and almost certainly due to Ball. I think
he was present at my lecture, and of course we met;
but I do not remember knowing anything of his activities then.

Neither Pease nor I know what turned Ball to
Socialism. The Fabian Society was issuing its little
publications from 1884 onward; but these can hardly
have influenced him much; and his joining the Society
as early as the Spring of 1886 shows that he had been
influenced from other sources.

Of Ball's connection with the Fabian Society you
will find brief mention in Pease's *History of the
Fabian Society*, and in the obituary note in last June's
Fabian News. The tract he wrote for us in 1896 (reprinted from *International Journal of Ethics*) sets
forth his conception of Socialism fully and ably; and
it has remained one of our most valuable publications,
having gone through four editions, and still selling
steadily, as the best exposition of the relation of
Socialism to Ethics and Philosophy.

No one can estimate how much the Fabian Society
owes to him, for his unwearied patience and enthusiasm, and his forbearance with the inevitable
vagaries of successive generations of young people
feeling themselves 'emancipated.' It was undoubtedly
due to him that the Fabian Society was continuously
represented in the University life and thought for
some thirty years; and all these generations of young
men—latterly also young women—have owed a very
real part of what was good in their socialist education
to your husband's always wholesome influence. It was

because we never found the same sort of supporter and colleague at Cambridge that the Society's record there has been very different.

IX.　AS SENIOR TREASURER OF THE UNION

By A. S. OWEN

In March, 1906, Mr. Ball was invited by the Union to fill the post of Senior Treasurer, which had been vacated by the death of Mr. T. H. Grose, of Queen's College.

During the days before the war, there is little that is startling to tell of his work, but that is largely because it was so successful. He was very careful not to obtrude in the management of what he declared to be 'primarily and fundamentally an undergraduates' club.' Even those who held office during his days of financial management admit now that they were unconscious at that time how much of the smoothness with which things went was due to the hours of work done by Mr. Ball with the loyal and assiduous co-operation of Mr. Gill, the Steward. Out of sight and carefully obliterating himself, Mr. Ball was seeing to the successful conduct of the society's affairs, and few of the members of the Union who heard his terminal statement of accounts or the carefully prepared annual budget which he read in each October term were aware of the great debt of gratitude they owed to the society's Senior Treasurer.

At his death he had no more sincere body of mourners than the servants of the Union, one of whom wrote from France that he had lost a good friend, and would never forget the many acts of kindliness shown to him during his long service.

Mr. Ball did not attend the ordinary debates of the society, but he was nearly always present at the chief debate of the term, when one or more distinguished stranger came down to take part in the discussion. Among the eminent visitors of the Union who took part in its debates during his term of office were Mr. Lloyd George, who provided an anxious evening for the officers of the society, as a suffragette attack on the then Chancellor of the Exchequer was anticipated, Mr. Bonar Law, Mr. Walter Long, Mr. Austen Chamberlain and Mr. Philip Snowden, while the Irish question was argued on different sides by Mr. Redmond and Sir Edward Carson.

On one occasion during his term of office the Union took an entirely new departure and extended its invitation to a lady, Mrs. Henry Fawcett.

The outstanding event of this period was the erection of the new North Wing. Mr. Ball was the moving spirit throughout the furthering of this building scheme, and the new buildings stand as a perpetual monument to his energy.

Another acquisition of the Union, which was directly due to Mr. Ball is the collection of caricatures concerned with Oxford celebrities and the events of the sixties by Mr. Sydney P. Hall of Pembroke College, which now cover the walls of the big smoking room.

The officers elected in the Summer Term of 1914 had no reason to surmise that they would never actually discharge their official duties on the spot. But in the long vacation came the war, and with it the complete transformation of Oxford. The Union Society shared the fortunes of the University. Like the Colleges, it was denuded of its members, and among them the undergraduate officers of the society went off to the war. At the beginning of the October term the officers all formally commissioned the Senior Treasurer to act as their Deputy, authorizing him at the same time to make such economies as he thought fit.

For a year things worked with great smoothness. But the October term of 1915 saw a change. The deputy officers who had helped to run the society had gone out of residence, and the Union just at this time incurred the heavy loss of Mr. Ball's services for the term owing to an illness which confined him to his house at Boar's Hill. Despite his serious illness he allowed himself to be visited by some of those who were trying to help the society through these difficulties, and Willowgate was more than once rung up on the telephone from the Steward's office. In January Mr. Ball was happily well enough to resume his work at the Union, a provisional committee of management was appointed and the rules definitely readjusted to fit the temporary war conditions. Throughout the crisis it was a great help to the Union that Mr. Ball was known to have sincerely democratic views; when he was autocratic (and he sometimes had to be) his autocracy was known to be forced upon him. It was a striking proof of his hold upon the members of the Union at the time, that an appeal against the President's ruling was withdrawn when it was realized that the carrying of such an appeal would greatly weaken Mr. Ball's position.

The real vindication of his work was to be found in the smoothness with which the society resumed its activities as soon as the Colleges began to refill in 1919. This account of his conduct of affairs at the Union may be fittingly concluded with some quotations from the letter of sympathy sent by the President, Mr. Wiggin, to Mrs. Ball, when he heard of the Senior Treasurer's death :

'In all the many things he did, he cannot well have ever attained more complete success in the face of greater difficulty. You will, I know, be fully aware of the results of his work there, for they are plain for all to see. But, perhaps, you may not have altogether realized the magnitude of the task which he so readily and generously undertook. . . . He assumed the responsibility of safeguarding the interests of all the members absent on service, and he had to defend them on several occasions in the face of serious and organised opposition. The accounts of what happened form one long tribute to the energy, firmness and extraordinary tact with which he dealt with each problem as it arose. His methods, indeed, were such that he earned not only the respect, but—what he never sought—the whole-hearted affection of all that remained of the society, in circumstances where the ordinary person would have to choose between unpopularity and failure.

For many years before the war the society had, at regular intervals, testified to their gratitude to him for his work as Senior Treasurer . . . When, at the conclusion of peace, it again becomes, as we hope it well may, one of the pivots of the new Oxford that it is to be, his name will be given a permanent and unique place in its records. For the preservation of its traditions, in fact, its unbroken existence, has been largely, if not entirely, due to his splendid devotion.'

X. AS CITIZEN OF THE WORLD

By M. Charles Garnier

C'est en 1910 que furent établies en Grande-Bretagne les bourses de voyage de la fondation Albert Kahn. M. Sidney Ball, d'Oxford, fut élu pour le premier voyage en même temps qu'un collègue de Cambridge. Nous avons eu le profond regret d'apprendre sa fin prémature, survenue le 23 mai dernier.

Si rapide qu'ait été son passage au Cercle en 1913, nous avions été séduits par le charme tres Oxonien de sa parole et l'aménité d'une âme cultivée restée ouverte a toutes les beautés à toutes les bontés de la vie. Plus tard, quand sur lui-même nous avons appris tout ce qu'il nous avait tu, nous avons compris l'attrait qu'exerçait sa personalité complexe, constamment enrichie par le travail, mais constamment maintenue une et simple par l'action.

Fait très neuf aussi, rompant avec une vieille tradition, il s'employait lui, universitaire, lui *gownsman*, pour le bien des *townsmen*, des bourgeois d'Oxford, cherchant à réveiller en eux le sentiment de la dignité municipale et du patriotisme local.

Il fallait tout son charme personnel pour qu'une activité sociale aussi étendue et diverse ne lui suscitât aucune inimitié. Il continua comme homme d'être aimé de tous; mais ses idées alarmaient son propre *College* et, sans trop s'avancer, on peut dire que son attachement à la cause démocratique lui coûta en 1909 la prèsidence de St. John's.

Deux ans plus tard, heureuse diversion, il fut élu
titulaire d'une des bourses de voyage autour du
monde. On peut s'imaginer ce que fut un tel voyage
pour l'homme que nous venons d'apercevoir, ad-
mirablement préparé par sa large culture humaine, son
ouverture d'esprit, sa sensibilité, qui, déjà mûrissante,
gardait une étonnante fraîcheur. Son rapport, dru,
preste et vivant, ne nous montre à l'oeuvre que le pen-
seur et le sociologue, toujours aimanté vers le mieux,
voulant la justice pour tous au mépris des errements
coloniaux les plus invétérés, et montrant une sin-
gulière prescience dans ses vues sur la révolution
chinoise qu'il annonce comme prochaine. Mais le
simple voyageur, qui marche les yeux agrandis vers
une nature nouvelle et des cités rêvées, le fils de la
Terre qui, tout remué de piété, découvre en vibrant
d'une seconde jeunesse les beautes insoupçonnées de
sa mère éternelle, ce voyageur qu'avec une caractéris-
tique pudeur Sidney Ball avait caché aux lecteurs d'un
rapport académique, il révéla qu'il l'avait été, lors de
son passage chez nous, dans l'intimité des libres cause-
ries. C'est sur l'image de l'homme heureux, jouissant
à nouveau des belles visions en-allées, que j'aimerais
à clore cette brève esquisse.

Et puis, celui que Sidney Ball avait trouvé au
Cercle, avec qui choquer la coupe pétillante des
souvenirs asiatiques, avec qui s'échauffer dans le
match des mémoires aux prises, avec qui rire du rire
qui allège, libère et rajeunit, c'était Cornuel, alors tout
frais débarqué du Mexique, ayant encore sur le front
le hâle des longues traversées et sur l'âme la fleur du
grand voyage.

Tous deux aujourd'hui sont disparus, tous deux au
cours de la guerre; l'un en pleine jeunesse ardente,

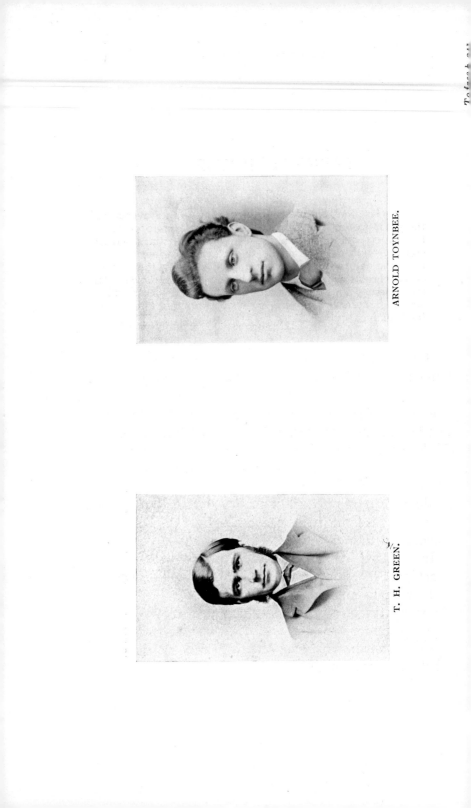

ARNOLD TOYNBEE.

T. H. GREEN.

BARNETT HOUSE.

'Those of us to whom University life is an avenue to the great world, would do well betimes to seek opportunities of co-operation with those simple Christians whose creed, though we may not be able exactly to adopt it, is to them the natural expression of a spirit which at the bottom of our hearts we recognise as higher than our own. In the everyday life of Christian citizenship and its struggles against ignorance and vice, such opportunities are readily forthcoming.'

T. H. GREEN. *Sermon on ' Faith.'*

'I am dining at Oriel to-night,' writes Sidney in a letter to me of February, 1891, 'with my old philosophical teacher, Cook-Wilson, Professor of Logic. Do you know Arnold Toynbee's addresses? He was another of my "formative influences," but Green, I think, most of all. I must lend you his two lay sermons.' That great teacher was just dead when Sidney came to St. John's. Arnold Toynbee was to die in the spring of 1883. Their spirit lived on and their lives and teaching helped and inspired the life and teaching of Sidney Ball.

In an essay on Thomas Hill Green by Professor MacCunn there is the following passage of which Sidney has marked a portion: 'For his was the sympathy of a profoundly matter-of-fact yet ever aspiring nature which worked for popular causes because not all the brutalism of savagery or slavery, nor all the degradation of civilised cities would shake his analytic estimate of what human nature had in it to become. *It was matter-of-fact idealism—that kind of idealism which believes that in beings capable of development the far results are the true realities,* which can see in beginnings the prophecy of ends, and in potentialities the promise of actualities or (to translate abstract terms into more concrete phrase) which can see in a country ditcher or a dock labourer the makings of a citizen.' The words in which Professor Mac-Cunn speaks of the great teacher, who was a chief formative influence in the lives of so many Oxford men, might well be applied to Sidney Ball himself. Professor MacCunn's *Ethics of Citizenship* was one of the books which he knew and loved best and which he constantly recommended for his pupils' reading. It was on the lines of this book, he once told me, that he would have liked to write, had the time ever arrived when the constant serving of tables, which was his lot, should have left him free for the writing of books.

Before he sailed for Australia in 1914 he had helped to start a venture in Oxford which was destined to be in a great degree the focus for many new hopes and ambitions and, though it brought added work and anxiety, it brought also much profit and pleasure to help him through the terrible strain of the years that still lay before him.

I do not think that, when he entered on what was to be one of the last new enterprises in which he was to engage, that he could have had any idea of the immense interest that it was to be to him. It became, in a really wonderful way, a rallying point for old memories and for new hopes. Those revered friends Mrs. T. H. Green and Mrs. Arnold Toynbee supported the idea with all their instructed faith and with their accus-

tomed generosity and joined with Mrs. S. A. Barnett in
helping and extending all the good works which had
been the connecting link between them for so many
years.

I do not think that Sidney Ball's life had many
brighter recollections than that of the Sunday morning's post which brought Mrs. Barnett's letter to tell
him of Mr. George Cadbury's[23] generous gift of
£1,000 towards the expenses of starting Barnett
House.

Miss Jane Addams became an Honorary Associate,
she had stayed at our house in Alfred Street in 1896,
sent to us by Canon and Mrs. Barnett, and Sidney had
stayed at Hull House, Chicago with her in 1911. The
circle was completed when she came with Mrs. Barnett in 1915 and was introduced to Barnett House by
Sidney Ball as President of the Barnett House Association. Miss Addams mentions her visit to us in her
book *Twenty Years at Hull House*, and she writes
from Hull House in May 1920 :

'Although I recall the bas-relief of Arnold Toynbee in the library of Balliol College and the window
in Christ Church to the memory of Edward Dennison
Maurice, and even more vividly the wonderful afternoon with Mr. Caird, but it was the time spent with
Mr. Sidney Ball in his old room in St. John's where
the University Settlement had been so eagerly discussed, that remained in my mind as most closely
identified with the inception of the idea.

'That there should be a group of University men
whose outlook was not limited to academic interests
but stretched beyond to the eternal problems of ignorance and poverty, has now become familiar to us,
although at the moment the number of such groups

[23] Died 1922.

was still limited. Mr. Ball's talk so graphically recalled the faith of those first young men who swam
upon the high crest of the new adventure that I was
painfully impressed with my own unworthiness for
participating in that movement which represented so
much scholarly enthusiasm.

'When I first saw Barnett House in 1915, I was
taken from the basement to the attic by Mr. Ball. It
seemed most fitting and indeed inevitable that he
should be the moving spirit in the founding and developing of this memorial to Canon Barnett as he had
been for years in spreading understanding of Toynbee
Hall among the students of Oxford. As Mr. Ball told
me of the plans for this new house erected in the midst
of the old established colleges, I was much impressed
with its vitality and sense of current service. This was
not only because large groups of working men were
utilizing its facilities as that it was the Oxford centre
of the vigorous Workers' Educational Association. I
asked Mr. Ball whether the present generation of Oxford men were at times a little uneasy as their predecessors had certainly been, in the presence of those
minds "who find their happiest exercise not along the
beaten track but in self-guided speculation and in-
quiry."

'Mr. Ball's reply was certainly reassuring as he told
of the readiness of Barnett House to help every inquiring mind, self trained though it might be, and of his
entire sympathy with Canon Barnett's belief that "the
revelation of God to our times comes by knowledge,"
although not always through the scholar.

'It was a very great pleasure to the residents of
Hull House to receive a visit from Mr. Ball when he
passed through Chicago upon his return from the
Pacific Coast in 1911. His appreciation of the difficulties inherent in the wide differences in language
and tradition found in an immigrant neighbourhood
representing all parts of Europe, and his conviction of

the peculiar value of the settlement method to such conditions, filled us with new hope and courage.

'We were always afterwards conscious that his fine mind and scholarly attainments were committed to a study of the problems confronting settlements in America as well as England.'

Miss Anne Thackeray, who had been an ardent worker at Toynbee Hall, became the first Hon. Secretary and a seat on the Council was reserved for the Warden of Toynbee Hall.

The work was initiated and carried on bravely during the weary years of war by those who remained. In 1916 Miss Mary Venables most nobly took over the office of Hon. Treasurer.

It fell to Sidney to draft the last report which he was to see and he was able to write on April 30th, 1918.

'This report might have been extended into further detail, but the above record may be sufficient to indicate that the House has made steady progress towards the fulfilment of the objects for which it was founded—the advancement of social and economic study, of the work of University Settlement and kindred organisations of working class education. It is becoming more and more a centre not only of social and economic study, but also of social service and activity, and a common meeting ground for social workers. There is no lack of work to be done, only of means to do it with. Every new associate is a source of strength, moral and material, and we venture to appeal to the Oxford and general public to help us to give the House an assured position among Oxford institutions and to add to its opportunities of useful work for the common good.'

At the beginning of 1918 the transference to Barnett House of the functions of the Oxford Social and Political Studies Association, including the work of the Social Training Committee was completed.

Miss Violet Butler is a member of this Committee of which Sidney was Chairman, and Mrs. Arthur Butler, writing to me on June 6, 1918, said of Sidney : 'In these later years he had always been most kind when we have met. My daughter Violet has been happy to work a little with him. The last time I saw him was when he called here with a message for her and told me how busy he was with the Serbians (what *can* they do without him?) and he looked to me then very tired and worn, and I feared he was pouring out his strength too much for others.'

The top floor of Barnett House is occupied by the Office and Library of the Tutorial Classes Committee. Mr. Albert Mansbridge wrote in *The Highway* for June, 1918, under the title of 'The Ideal Scholar' :

'The cause of democratic education in Oxford is closely identified with the personality of Sidney Ball. He is a great figure in the history of Ruskin College, of Barnett House and of the W.E.A. It was not that he ever sought to manage their affairs, or to arrange them to suit his own ideas, but rather that he was a kindly encouraging friend, endowed with shrewd common sense consecrated to the lofty ideal of a developed democracy. No man was ever less obtrusive or cared less about his own power.

'For myself I shall never forget the day in April, 1903, when in great trepidation, I first went to Oxford as the messenger of the newly-born W.E.A. But all fearfulness was left behind in Sidney Ball's study, and I returned to London encouraged and inspired, for he had seen at once that the idea of the W.E.A. was

sound. He and Mrs. Ball were the first hosts the
W.E.A. ever had, for, on the occasion of the conference in August, 1903, they entertained the delegates
at St. John's College. Not one of us who were present
will ever forget their gracious and kindly hospitality.
It was a new experience for us, and gave us a new
view of a wonderful place which had hitherto seemed
inaccessible.

'On the very day that Sidney Ball died, a friend
writing to me in reference to a new scheme rendered
necessary by the Education Bill, said "Sidney Ball is
keenly interested and would like to see you about it."
That was symbolical of his friendship throughout the
year. He was never absent from those splendid enthusiastic conferences we had in Oxford in the old
days. One summer his little daughter lay at death's
door. He had no sleep nor rest for days, but, the child
being better, he came to the discussion on evening
schools. It was a real and characteristic sacrifice for
him to make.

'It is well known that at the great Conference
which heralded the idea of tutorial classes he introduced the subject of "What Oxford can do for Working People," and that he was a member of the first
Oxford Joint Committee, in fact, he only resigned his
seat on his election as "A.K. Scholar," which entitled
him to a twelve months' tour of the world. It is not
our place here to try and estimate his influence upon
Oxford and upon his generation, but simply to record
that, but for his life, the W.E.A. would have been a
different and less fruitful organisation than it is, for
to its members he was the ideal scholar.'

In May, 1919, I met Mr. Reuben George in Barnett House.

'I first became acquainted with this good man,'
writes Mr. George, 'at the Summer Extension Meeting in 1907 at a Conference presided over by Bishop

Gore to consider the question of Working Men and the Universities. Mr. Sidney Ball was one of the openers of the discussion. His early remarks were these; what was wanted of Oxford was not an education as a means of livelihood but as a means of life. I think of the speech he gave, and those that others gave, and I remember his concluding remarks—"Might not be long before the working men of the country could begin to look up to Oxford as their Alma Mater." That I think, is the most important meeting I ever attended; it impresses me to-day. From that meeting I have come and have been working with its ideals before me from that day to this. But it was not in the public meeting that I best got in contact with him. He was best, I think (at least that is my experience) in taking our essays to him and reading them and talking and discussing, there we found our man. I can see him now, in his room at St. John's, that was our man, that was where we were true to ourselves, because Sidney Ball inspired us to be true to him. There it was that we realised comradeship with other classes. You couldn't start the Class War with him. You might be a Socialist and wear whatever tie you like, but you buried class feeling in his presence, the richness of his life came out. You knew he was not patronising you he was helping you, and just as I would talk to my friends on questions I should have talked with him. What has it done for me? It has told me that I belong to all classes, there are souls that beat in unison with his fellows, and that the lovely flowers inspired by God's Sunshine bloom everywhere. As long as I live I shall be indebted to him, and I shall, in thinking of him ever say, This was a man.

'Barnett House will ever be a glad and glorious memorial in the days to come, when Oxford comes to be the place of education for the miners and railwaymen, Co-operator and Socialist, Labour man and Reformer. There we shall go and sit in common with beautiful Saints that have gone on before and the thought and spirit of one, among many others, and that one bright spirit will be that of Sidney Ball.'

All the threads of memory connected with his long years of work began to twine round Barnett House. The place seemed more and more as though it might be destined to become his spiritual home. Many of the Committees on which he worked or of which he was chairman met at Barnett House. The Interdenominational Council for Social Reform, the Serbian Committee and the Citizens' Association.

His last thoughts and words were for this Citizens' Association and for the Juvenile Organisation Committee : his last messages were to them.

From Barnett House there came the proposal for a Memorial to Sidney Ball, 'it was decided that steps should be taken to make provision for a special Public Lecture to be given each year on some topic connected with the study of modern political economic and social conditions.'

It would have been exactly what he would have wished that Sir Horace Plunkett should have been asked to give the first lecture and that he should have consented.

With his great love of completeness, of perfection and of 'distinction' it had always fretted him that he could not add more to the amenities of the House in furniture and in decoration. In those last weeks he spoke to me with keen pleasure of the flowers with which Miss Margaret Deneke—then acting as Secretary—kept the rooms bright and fragrant. He came to me once asking did I not think that we could spare a table—a really nice table—for the inner library. With that meticulous care which was a part of his nature he threw himself into the choice of curtains and carpets when there was any money to be had with which to pay for them.

For the inner room of the beautiful 'King Charles' set that he had lived in at St. John's, he had made in 1889, by the then College carpenter—Mr. George Lambourne—a set of bookshelves designed for him by Mr. W. A. S. Benson. These bookshelves were adapted by Mr. Lambourne in 1892 when the dark little best back-bedroom of the small house in Alfred Street became his study, and for twenty years they had stood round the walls of his lovely sunny room at St. John's House.

In the Autumn of 1918 they were moved to Barnett House by Mr. Lambourne, who, as he worked, told me tales of former St. John's men, of their praise of Sidney. 'You can always trust Ball, he is a just man.' 'Ball's all right, he's a just man,' he had heard some of them say as he worked in their rooms so many years ago.

There in the 'Ball Library' is the revolving book-case with a lecturing desk on the top of it, which Mr. A. H. Worrall[24] had made for him as a wedding present; there is the copy of the Holbein 'Erasmus' over the mantlepiece as it used to be, and the tiny coloured print of Robert Owen benevolently watching the sports at New Lanark, which my sister discovered and gave to him. There are two lithographs of French rivers which Miss Pater left at No. 5 Alfred Street for us, when we lent it to them, after the death of Walter Pater. There is Mr. Sidney Hall's sketch of Mr. Gladstone giving the first Romanes Lecture. Mr. Hall's son, H. R. Hall, was

[24] Head Master, Victoria College, Jersey.

an old St. John's pupil. There are the caricatures of a one-time guest of ours, Sir F. Carruthers Gould, and 'Spy's' drawing of Dr. Bellamy, for forty years President of St. John's. Here, too, is a cup which he won in a race in his undergraduate days and several specimens of the Klabyle pottery, which he brought back from his first long journey and in which he took great delight. It should be possible in such a room for one with inner vision to see the former master of these treasures sitting at the table, leaning back in his chair to consult a book from the revolving book-case, or rising to pull one from the shelves.

Sidney Ball was one of those wonderful people who could feel, rather than see, what he needed.

Apparently the least methodical of men, yet he always knew just where and how to attack a heap of papers so that his hand fell on the right one. He loved his books with an intense affection. I can see him now looking at them and saying, as he said once, half to himself, 'I shall be leaving you some *very* nice books.' He lent them with the generosity which led him to give or to lend everything, but he grieved sincerely when borrowers proved faithless. One book, Pater's *Studies in the Renaissance*, which he had mourned as lost for some twenty years or more did come back to him at last. If some borrower's conscience has slumbered over any of his books—and nowhere could we find either of his two copies of Bradley's *Ethical Studies*— best-beloved of books—or some other scarcely less cherished volume, after he had gone, let them come back, to their home in Barnett House, and all shall be forgiven and forgotten.

There was a former Fellow of St. John's who left much money to the College, on condition that his heart should be buried in the chapel with this inscription on its tomb, '*Ubi Thesaurus ibi Cor.*' Sidney Ball had little treasure to leave, but some of his chief treasures are here in this room and there, one feels sure, his great heart also can find rest. 'Mr. Ball seems to be here all the time,' said Anne Thackeray to me once in that room, and to those who can see they are all there with him, Socrates and Plato, Shelley and Wordsworth, Thomas Hill Green and Arnold Toynbee, and many another. There, too, are all the generations of St. John's men, who came to him among these treasures, seeking for teaching or for counsel and who never went empty away. W.E.A. men are there, Ruskin men and the Women Students, whose battles he helped to fight and whose victory he did not live to see. It is only a very small part of what, one hopes, may prove in time to be a great whole; a rallying place and centre for the many causes to which Sidney Ball gave such devoted service and on which he spent his life.

APPENDIX II

From the *Oriel Record*, Vol. I.   February, 1909.

ARTHUR GRAY BUTLER.

By SIDNEY BALL. 1875—1880.

Certainly none of us can think of the Oriel of his day without thinking of the Dean.   And never, surely, were undergraduates under a more kindly or more beneficent rule.   It would, I think, be no exaggeration to say that he was felt to be the friend, and more particularly the friend in need, of us all. It must have fallen to the lot of few tutors to be the recipient of so many and of such intimate confidences, and he sent none empty away.   All these kindly offices he discharged with such amiable alacrity and such genial sympathy that gratitude was swallowed up in affection.   We felt that there was none of us in whom he did not take, not merely a conventional but, if I may say so, a natural interest.   There were none of us in whom he did not find more good than we could honestly lay claim to ourselves.   Not a few indeed found it difficult, at times, to live up to what he thought, or at any rate, liked to think, of us ; and his inveterate optimism made us think sometimes that he was not infrequently taken in.   But it was no small part of the secret of his influence that he was so resolutely determined to see and draw out the best side of the least amongst us. What sometimes passed for weakness was really his strength. Whenever he expressed disappointment, he did it in a way that was all the more disconcerting and even humiliating, it was not so much disapproval as disappointment.   I remember how he encouraged me to write for the *Newdigate*—the subject I think was Troy—and how, when I showed him the first draft of what, I fear, was somewhat uninspired verse, he simply indicated that it was not the way in which he would himself have treated the subject.   I burnt it up as quickly as I could.

It was only natural that there was no Don who was the centre of more stories.   At a College breakfast party when the subject of the Dons is apt to be introduced, as Socrates said of the introduction of Flute girls at Athenian entertainments, as a substitute for original and rational discourse, the Don and his ways was a veritable *pièce de resistance*.   And he was much talked about simply because he seemed to touch the life of the undergraduates at every point. He seemed to live among us in quite a literal way, to be indeed, a kind of microcososm of the varied life of the College. He ruled, as it may be truly said, by affection and, whenever he could, always by and through ourselves. This sometimes led to embarrassing situations. I remember how he once sent for some of us to help him in dealing with an ' outrage ' on College property, in the shape, if I remember right, of some tree tubs which had been placed in the College quad, only to be thrown down by some midnight marauders ! We were at once able to assure him that we ourselves were the actual offenders and indeed justified our action on æsthetic grounds. The Dean gave us to understand that he would see us again, when he had got over his surprise. As a matter of fact we never heard anything more about it—or saw any more of the offending tubs.

But the Dean was perhaps at his best and certainly in his element, at his own breakfast parties, which no undergraduate, least of all, a scholar, would have missed. His eagerness and enthusiasm as he talked out of the fullness of his spirit about poetry and literature, was contagious ; an admirable talker himself, and a still more admirable listener, he was also the cause of talk in others ; and it would be no exaggeration to say that, for many of us, the Dean's breakfast parties—they were always small and intimate—were not the least part of the ' liberal and humane ' education we received at Oriel. It was he who more than any other man quickened in us the desire for the things of the mind—for sweetness and light.

It was he who revealed to us the poetry of Arnold and Clough, and made us feel that to be too busy for poetry was to be too busy for mental health. It was partly in recognition of a lover of poetry, who was himself a poet, that the idea occurred to some of us to give a rendering of his own play, ' Charles the First,' in the College Hall, and that we boldly invited Heads of Houses and other dignitaries of the University. I do not think that anything even the presentation we made to him on the occasion of his marriage, pleased or touched him more. He represented to us, moreover, the union of μουσική and γυμναστική. There was nothing forced or unusual in his interest in sports of every kind ; it was simply a part of his nature. As has been well said of him—and they were the first words that occurred to me in writing this tribute to his memory—he had a natural affinity for whatsoever things were lovely or noble or of good report, and his passion for them was contagious.

I am only conscious that no words can bring back even the faintest image of a beautiful life and charming personality and do justice to the teacher and the friend. If I were to try to sum up in one word my impression of him as he appeared to us in those days, I should say that he represented to us the idea of chivalry. We liked to think of him as a kind of spiritual knight errant; and there was also in our lively imagination a little of the Don Quixote about him. For he was the most human man both in his strength and his weakness that I seem to have known. It was this, I think, which bound him so closely to such very different types of undergraduates; and I do not think that there were any of us who are not in some degree the better for having come into contact with a nature at once so kindly and so bracing. Of few men can it be said with so much truth that to have known Arthur Butler was, in its truest and deepest sense, a liberal education in itself.

APPENDIX III

It was always a delight to Sidney Ball to consort with ' people of importance,' with those who counted, both in Oxford and in the larger world outside, and it would give him keen pleasure if he could read what some of these felt and expressed about him and, what he cared about more than himself, his work and the effect of the work that he did both for individuals and for causes.

Earl Curzon, Chancellor of the University, wrote to the President of St. John's College :—

' I have just heard, with most sincere regret of the death of your valued Member, Fellow and Tutor, Mr. Sidney Ball. For many years he has been one of the most influential, sympathetic and far-sighted of Oxford men, identifying himself with all good works, exercising a profound and always human influence upon both the younger and the older generations, and bringing great credit both to the College to which he was so deeply attached and to the University of which he was one of the foremost sons. I was happy in being brought much into contact with Mr. Ball in the circumstances, a few years ago, that attended our efforts to bring about various important measures of University Reform ; and I recall with pleasure and gratitude his soundness of judgment and width of view, as well as his invariable desire for progress and means of conciliation.

There was no good cause in the University with which he was not identified, no reasonable and liberal aspiration which he did not labour to promote ; and the success which attended him, springing from the sincerity of his own convictions, of the absolute disinterestedness of his acts, was greatly facilitated by a personal charm that endeared him to all. I should wish to join with the College in an expression of profound sorrow with which it must be lamenting the death of one of whom it had so much reason to be proud.'

Lord Bryce wrote to Mrs. Ball :—

' My wife and I have been deeply grieved to hear of the bereavement that has come upon you, and I wish to be permitted to express to you our most sincere sympathy. Though in recent years it was but seldom that I had the opportunity of meeting him, I often heard of his public spirit and his zealous work for good causes, and he was always honoured and valued in his old College, Oriel. (He was an intimate friend there of one of my wife's brothers who died young.) He always seemed to me to be one of the most attractive and high-minded figures in Oxford life, kindly and unselfish, always seeking for means of helping others. His memory will be gratefully and affectionately cherished, not only by his University friends, but by many others in Oxford, where there is not, I think, anyone who can fill his place.'

From Mr. H. A. L. Fisher.[1]

'Will you, without troubling to answer, accept a word of deepest sympathy? So long as I can remember Oxford, your husband was the soul of St. John's and one of the great stimulating influences of the University. I greatly appreciated his kindness to me when I was a young graduate and ever afterwards, and I owe much to him in many ways. As I recall the countless pleasant occasions on which we met to discuss things worthy of discussion and his delightful hospitality, I feel how much his disappearance will mean to generations of Oxford men who held him in deep affection and regard. And his good influence was by no means confined to Oxford. Indeed, I think that when the story of Oxford's influence upon the life of England during our generation comes to be written, it will be realised that he was one of the chief of the vital forces, so hospitable was he of soul and so open to all good things.'

And Mr. William Temple.[2]

'I write both on my own behalf and also on behalf of the W.E.A., as its President, to convey to you our most sincere sympathy. The service of Mr. Ball to everything for which the W.E.A stands, as well as to the Association itself, was incalculable; and his loss is a terrific blow. For myself, I have to thank him for an abundance of help and guidance when I was beginning to concern myself with social questions, and yet more personal kindness beyond what I had any right to expect.'

The last of the pre-war guests, June 14—16, 1914, at St. John's House was Lord Charnwood,[3] and he wrote thus of his old friend in May, 1918. 'I daresay you know that he was one

[1] Vice-Chancellor of Sheffield University and Minister of Education,
[2] Bishop of Manchester.
[3] Godfrey Benson, formerly M.P. for Mid Oxon.

of the last guests in my old home, just before it broke up, and
that he came there out of sheer and unsolicited generosity
to coach me—with the result of my getting a first in Greats.
I don't recall this so much because of the benefit in which it
resulted to me as because of the kindness with which it was
done. I forget the details; I cannot distinctly say now how
much or how little we had previously known each other; but
it has always dwelt, and always will dwell, in my memory as
one of the two or three signal acts of friendship which I have
received. Looking back over the history of Oxford, so far as
I know it, from my undergraduate days till now, I feel sure
that he counts among the two or three whose work for whatsoever things are good has been at once most devoted and most
potent. And then, how greatly it enhances such a record
that, with that high aim and those untiring endeavours, he remained always so simple and delightful a companion and play-
mate.'

Sir Horace Plunkett[4] wrote :—

'I was privileged to see enough of your husband—how I now
wish I had seen him more—to realise what you have lost. Will
you allow me to send a tribute of heartfelt, if unavailing sympathy? He will leave a sad gap in Oxford's best workers,
those who serve indirectly through the rising generation, and
directly in the guidance of the most advanced social movements.
But I shall also be with the many who will remember him for
his understanding sympathy with, and willing help to, their
own altruistic works. I devoutly hope you will be able to bear
the first shock of the bereavement. The memory of his life will
soon, I trust, bring its enduring consolations.'

From our true and constant friend, Professor Dicey,[5] there
came a most moving letter :—

'Elinor, I know, has already written to you and I am sure
she will have expressed as well and sincerely as anyone can our
deep sorrow at your husband's death and our sympathy with the
sorrow you must be feeling for the loss of him. But I always
regard it as impossible that words, spoken or written, can do
anything real by way of consolation in cases of grief like yours,
and feel that condolence is, and ought to be, in the main, a
way in which friends of one who has died give expressions to
the sense of their own loss. I know you will let me write in
this spirit. I have, though in many respects my life has been
a fortunate one, begun of recent years to feel much the sense

---

[4] President I.A.O.S.; member of An Seanad, Dail Eireaun.
[5] Died 1921. Emeritus Professor of Civil Law.

of solitude which naturally comes upon a man who has passed his eighty-third birthday and has neither children nor near relations who survive. Your husband was one of the few men much younger than myself with whom I by degrees formed a really warm friendship after my settling again in 1883 at Oxford. I think perhaps at first we did not completely understand one another. But certainly I soon got to perceive your and his great kindliness and, so to speak, the moral and intellectual hospitality you both so pleasantly offered. This, among other occasions, came very strongly to my mind when, years ago now, he once asked me as an elector to do all that I could to get Caird chosen as Professor of Moral Philosophy. I did all I could to get Caird elected and am sure he was the right man for the post but in this, as on many other occasions, my efforts failed. Then, too, I came to feel more and more the charm of your husband's life and youthfulness and to perceive that agreement with a friend depended much less on identity in each others opinions than on holding even different convictions in something like the same spirit. Then Ball's splendid energy and public spirit since the War began must have impressed every one with admiration. In short, I know and feel that I have lost a dear and good friend and one quite unlike any man surviving him. This is as far as I am concerned the sum of the whole matter, and friends at my time of life are growing fewer and fewer.

I have typed because my handwriting is illegible, though I am a terribly poor typist.'

There came, also, this letter from Dr. Estlin Carpenter.[6]

'On returning from a week of meetings in London to-day I learn with deep grief of the overwhelming sorrow which has so suddenly fallen on you and your daughter. Forgive me if I intrude too rudely on such a bereavement, but in the tragic hours through which I have had to pass without warning again and again I have been silently grateful when a hand of quiet sympathy was stretched out towards me. I cannot remember how I first made your husband's acquaintance, it was soon after we came to Oxford in 1889; but he was persistently and generously kind to me ever since, and as the circle of his labours widened, I felt more and more the nobility of his nature and the privilege of his friendship. He was never daunted by difficulties or impatient of obstacles; his fine enthusiasm carried him forward from one enterprise to another, and he always seemed to have time and courage and energy for any fresh call on his goodwill. The work which he was developing so

[6] Late Principal, Manchester New College.

effectively at Barnett House has indeed lost its Master-mind; and when Ruskin College begins—like the University itself— to resume its proper work, who can counsel it like him, or bring to its administration the same wide experience and generous sympathy? And we always thought of you as a part of all this work, for you made the joy and peace of his home, which were the blessed conditions of all his labour for others. *That* life is suddenly ended, but its sweetness will still abide in your heart. All that he gave you will remain woven into undying memory, and all that you gave him is not so much lost to you as he vanishes from your sight; it is laid up in your own soul also, as a treasure which you had in common and still both possess. For I, assuredly, cannot believe that the ripe fruits of character are scattered by death. In what form they are preserved, truly, we do not know; but that ' the souls of the righteous are in the hands of God,' is one of my deepest trusts, and in the conviction that this is but the first stage of a continuously developing life I have seen one after another of those nearest to me go forward into the unseen and have committed them without fear to the care of the supporting God. May this faith be also yours. It cannot make the pain of parting less poignant, but it can bring to lonely hours thoughts of hope and love; in the new life of clearer vision and higher sevice all that you loved in him will grow in strength and beauty, and all that you unselfishly wrought for him will bear him up on to fresh levels of attainment and worth. Pardon this long letter; my wife and I both grieve for your inexpressible loss; may the Divine Comforter gradually bring healing to so sore a wound.'

Mr. Cooke-Taylor, of the Irish Literary Society, wrote:— ' I think it would be an omission if no notice were taken by any body of Irishmen (for Mr. Sidney Ball had much sympathy with and understanding of Ireland) that I must ask you to kindly accept this letter in lieu thereof.'

There was a letter from the President of the Oxford ' Majlis ' Club, recording their ' profound and heartfelt sorrow at the sad and lamentable death of Mr. Sidney Ball, for whom we, the Indian Community at Oxford, had an unbounded affection and respect for the innumerable number of ways in which he always helped us. His loss is irreparable not only in the case of a few but for everyone who came into contact with him.'

Sir Arthur Evans wrote with the condolences of the Oxford Serbian Committee and with added words of his own : ' And so I know that words are vain—though one consolation you will always have that he was able to continue his activities on be- half of others to the last, that there was no failure or decline, but he was stricken down like a brave Captain, still fighting the good fight.'

Mr. J. le B. Hammond wrote :—' I am dreadfully grieved by the news. It was not until the other day that I heard you had some anxiety about his health lately. I was at a meeting of Oxford people in London, called to consider the running of a Labour Candidate for the University, when I said that if he could be induced to stand (his name occurred to me naturally first of all) I was told that everybody would agree but there was some doubt about his health. It would have been splendid to have a real democrat in the House. But, after all, there are probably very few men who have made so many other people into democrats. One still repines at the scandalous injustice done to him over the Presidency, but his influence over genera-tion after generation of Oxford men, of every College, is a leading fact in the history of the University and the history of a larger world than the University, and his influence nobody could check or question.

' My own personal debt to him I never could hope to repay. I cannot imagine what my Oxford life would have been without him. It was an extraordinary piece of good fortune for me to come under a man whose friendship and guidance were counted as one of the chief inspirations of their lives by his pupils. It must have been some satisfaction to him and to you to know that very many men felt the wrong that was done to him and to the College more nearly than they would have felt many a disappointment of their own.'

And Captain Corbett Fisher, another old pupil :—' When I wrote a fortnight ago I was so much shocked that I failed to say anything of what I felt about Mr. Ball. And now I hesi-tate to write because my feelings hardly matter. Yet I must tell you some of it.

' You know already—but I may say it again—that there was no one whose judgment I valued as I did his. I have over and over again brought my troubles to him, and been helped out. I'm almost ashamed to remember how much I taxed his patience and generosity. I must have tried him sorely at times. But he never seemed to grudge time and trouble. It isn't surprising that I came to think of him as pre-eminently good and wise— σπουδαῖος. Is that the word I'm thinking of? And though—in the last four years I didn't see him at all, to my lasting regret, my devotion to him grew greater and greater, so that it wouldn't be exaggeration to call it worship. He had and exer-cised to the full the qualities I love ; and he seemed to me as no one else ever has, wholly without blame. And so my sense of personal loss is overwhelming.

'*The Nation* and *The New Statesman* dwell rather on the loss to the State and to Oxford, which, of course, can't be exaggerated. I wish he had been, not merely President of the College, but Vice-Chancellor after the war. It's painful to think of the posts he should have filled—the waste, I was going to say, but it wouldn't be true. For even though never President, he was the soul of the College. And I can say for certain of my own time, he left his mark on every man in it, and he *made* the best.

'I'm glad he left a daughter who was old enough to know him well. And I hope you will be a consolation to one another.'

And the last, from an old friend :—'I know that you must be almost overwhelmed by letters, and yet I must write you a word of sympathy that does truly come from my heart in this your great sorrow and desolation. That last is not quite the right word to use, I think, seeing that you can never be really desolate when such richness of life and love has been, and is, yours for ever, even though the more beautiful your time together has been the harder it is to let your man step on in front and to be courageously content to carry on *for him* with the daughter who was such a joy to him. May be, you can say with old Rutherford, "When I look over beyond the line and beyond death, to the laughing side of the world, I triumph!" Nothing of darkness or chilly shadow can ever be associated with Mr. Ball, but only life and warmth and vigour and that great genius for kindliness and fellowship that made his life and work great and full and rich with widest human sympathies and was one of the springs of his far-reaching influence. Oxford's loss is all too great, but what a glorious and gladdening record to have given to his College, his University, and the world. It surely is to a divine law his life now has yielded, "allied not to shadow and decay but to the recurrent spring, to the infinite processional." All my memories of him are of the happiest and merriest and I am grateful for them.'

INDEX

HOLYWELL PRESS, ALFRED STREET, OXFORD.